LEE CONSIDERED

LEE

CONSIDERED

General Robert E. Lee and

Civil War History

ALAN T. NOLAN

The University of North Carolina Press

Chapel Hill & London

The paper in this book meets the guidelines for permanence and durability of the Committee on Production Guidelines for Book Longevity of the Council on Library Resources.

03   02   01   00   99   8   7   6   5   4

Library of Congress Cataloging-in-Publication Data
Nolan, Alan T.
Lee considered: General Robert E. Lee and Civil War history / by Alan T. Nolan
p.   cm.
Includes bibliographical references and index.
ISBN *0-8078-1956-5 (cloth: alk. paper)*
ISBN *0-8078-4587-6 (pbk.: alk. paper)*
1. Lee, Robert E. (Robert Edward), 1807–1870.   2. United States—History—Civil War, 1861–1865—Historiography.   3. Generals—United States—Biography—History and criticism.   4. Generals—Southern States—Biography—History and criticism.   I. Title.
E467.1.L4N66   1991
973.7′3′092—dc20   90-48296
CIP

FRONTISPIECE
Robert E. Lee, 1865 (Library of Congress)

FOR JANE

Deo grátias

Contents

: : : CONTENTS : : :

Preface

It behooves me, in setting forth an unorthodox consideration of Robert E. Lee, to state precisely what I am attempting to do.

I believe that Robert E. Lee was a great man – able, intelligent, well-motivated and moral, and much beloved by his army. He did what he believed to be right. On the other hand, I have long been uncomfortable with certain aspects of the Lee tradition. I suspect that this discomfort has several sources. Without revealing too much about myself, I acknowledge that a parochial grade school education may have provoked in me a perverse skepticism of lives of the saints. Lincoln scholar Don E. Fehrenbacher characterizes the "idealized Lincoln" as "insufferably virtuous" – a characterization that I can appreciate.

In the case of Lee my discomfort has been more specific. Certain of the unqualified images presented in the Lee tradition have not fit, it seemed to me, with some of the facts of Lee's life. He was supposedly antislavery but was a Virginia aristocrat of the planter class who fought vigorously for a government expressly based on slavery. He was a lifetime soldier in the United States Army, a patriot sworn to defend his country, and he opposed secession; yet he seceded and made war on the

United States. He was a master strategist and tactician but was so committed to the offensive that he suffered grievous and irreplaceable losses that progressively limited the viability of his army. He was magnanimous toward the North but fought bitterly and aggressively against it. He was kind and protective of his soldiers but regularly risked their lives in daring offensive strokes, ordered the July 3 attack on Cemetery Ridge, and continued the war long after a Southern victory was possible. He was conciliatory after the war yet categorical in his defense of what the South had done and outspokenly critical of the North's postwar treatment of the South.

This book is an effort to rationalize these conflicting pictures of Lee. In the process of examining Lee's career, I have necessarily confronted a number of broader issues of Civil War history, and I have examined these, too. In short, while I admire Lee, I question certain aspects of the Lee tradition; and, having raised certain questions about that tradition, I cannot answer them adequately without relating the Lee tradition to Civil War history generally.

This book is not, therefore, a biography and offers no full account of Robert E. Lee's life. It is, instead, an examination of major aspects of the tradition that identifies Lee in American history. In raising questions and drawing conclusions about this tradition, I have attempted to set forth the evidence. The reader who thinks I am asking the wrong questions or disagrees with my conclusions may, in evaluating my thesis, consider the evidence on which it is based. This evidence does not include any new or sensational facts or new primary materials. On the contrary, my inquiry concerns what the familiar and long-available evidence actually establishes about Robert E. Lee. The results of my inquiry are not so much an exposé as simply an attempt to set the record straight.

Anyone who questions traditional views of Robert E. Lee must acknowledge a debt to Thomas L. Connelly and his 1977 book, *The Marble Man*. Connelly proved that one can criticize the general and live to tell the tale. I admit this debt, but my effort is quite different from Connelly's. *The Marble Man* is an intellectual history of the Lee tradition, tracing its development and describing how and why Lee became such a heroic figure. In addition, the book features a psychohistory of

: : : PREFACE : : :

Lee, an attempt to explain the man in terms of his life experiences. In making this effort, Connelly touches on several aspects of the Lee tradition with which I am concerned, but he does not systematically analyze even those aspects. My book examines the major aspects of the Lee tradition in detail. I am concerned with the merits of those major aspects, that is, I question the historicity of the tradition.

I am indebted, as a writer always is, to many persons. Unable to identify all of them, I state special thanks to Eileen Anne Gallagher of State College, Pennsylvania; Roger Hogue of North East, Pennsylvania; Carolyn Autry, Tom Krasean, Raymond L. Shoemaker, Leigh Darbee, and Peter T. Harstad of the Indiana Historical Society; Jim Trulock, Alice Rains Trulock, and Peter S. Carmichael of Indianapolis; Patrick S. Brady of Seattle; Maj. Thomas J. Romig of the Judge Advocate General's Corps; Ted Alexander of the National Park Service; A. Wilson Greene of Fredericksburg, Virginia; Marshall D. Krolick and C. Robert Douglas of Chicago; Dudley Bokoski of Mayodan, North Carolina; Professor Lloyd Hunter of Franklin College; James K. Flack and Curt and Arden Poole of Detroit; Robert B. Clemens of Indianapolis; Mark Silo of Albany, New York; David Smith of Cincinnati; Sara B. Bearss of the Virginia Historical Society; and Alan and Maureen Gaff of Fort Wayne, Indiana. My secretary, Brenda Reed, has helped all along the way, and my wife, Jane, has given valuable editorial assistance. Although Professor Gary W. Gallagher of Penn State bears no responsibility for the imperfections of this book, his wisdom, scholarship, judgment, and encouragement have been critical to its completion.

A final word. When I have had conversations with persons interested in my subject, almost invariably these persons have, upon sensing that my questions and conclusions do not square with the Lee tradition, suggested that I dislike Lee or do not believe him to have been a great man. It seems to me that there is a human tendency to deal simplistically with the figures of history, to classify them as "good guys" or "bad guys" rather than to analyze and evaluate them in detail. I reject this unhistoric approach. Lee was, after all, one of us, a human being. I do not deny Lee's greatness, but I have tried to deal with him as a human being. And I conclude as I began, believing him a great man but, indeed, a man. I offer this book as a corrective of the Lee tradition.

William Garrett Piston has remarked that "cultural roles cannot be overturned by scholarship." So be it. Nevertheless, I agree with Marshall W. Fishwick's statement regarding Lee: "To dehumanize and elevate by excessive adulation . . . does no honor to the man."[1] And, of course, excessive adulation is not the stuff of history.

Indianapolis, Indiana
July 1990

LEE CONSIDERED

Lee: "A Greek proportion – and a riddle unread."

STEPHEN VINCENT BENÉT

CHAPTER ONE

The Mythic Lee

The American Civil War, Walt Whitman's "strange sad war," is the most profoundly tragic experience of American history. Another poet, Robert Penn Warren, has gone as far as to say, "The Civil War is, for the American imagination, the great single event of our history. Without too much wrenching, it may, in fact, be said to *be* American history."[1] As a consequence, it is often difficult for Americans to think about the war with objectivity or detachment. Instead, it is defined in our consciousness by the clichés with which historians and the purveyors of popular culture have surrounded it: the troublesome abolitionists, the brothers' war, Scarlett and Tara, the faithful slave, the forlorn Confederate soldier, the brooding Lincoln, High Tide at Gettysburg, the bloody Grant, the Lost Cause, and the peerless Robert E. Lee. These images, each laden with emotion, are in our bones. Surely it is time for us to stand back, however, and look at the war free of these clichés and the traditions of the Blue and the Gray. We should at last be in a position to do so.

In 1909 Woodrow Wilson wrote, "The Civil War is something which we cannot even yet uncover in memory without stirring embers which may spring into a blaze."[2] Today, more than eighty years later, Wilson's statement is not entirely inapplicable. But despite the genuinely long shadow of the Civil War and despite Wilson's warning, things have in fact changed in the United States. Three changes in particular should permit a new consideration of the war.

In the first place, the event is now remote in time. Today's Americans are not the children or even the grandchildren of the participants; the inhabitants of the North and the South can forgive each other and forgive themselves for the war and its preliminaries and aftermath. Second, because of the passage of time and because of the explosion in communications and transportation, people North and South are well through the period of "binding up the nation's wounds." We now share a national culture, and there is no longer a social need to perpetuate the clichés. Third, racial attitudes – as one might expect in light of the role of slavery in the war – underlie many of the clichés; and although very far from ideal, racial attitudes have changed markedly in recent decades.

In his presidential address to the American Historical Association, Samuel Eliot Morison spoke to the question of the function of history and the role of the historian:

> For almost 2500 years, in the Hebraic-Hellenic-Christian civilization that we inherit, truth has been recognized as the essence of history. . . . The fundamental question is: "What actually happened, and why?" . . . After his main object of describing events "simply as they happened," [the historian's] principal task is to *understand* the motives and objects of individuals and groups . . . and to point out mistakes as well as achievements by persons and movements. (Emphasis in original.)[3]

We may, at last, be able to carry out these obligations in regard to the Civil War.

One of the central figures of the war was Gen. Robert E. Lee. Indeed, in our collective consciousness he looms almost as *the* figure of the war, rivaled only by Abraham Lincoln. There is little need to belabor the fact of Lee's heroic, almost superhuman, national stature, which has steadily enlarged since the war years. Writing in 1868, Fanny Dowling described Lee as "bathed in the white light which falls directly upon him from the smile of an approving and sustaining God."[4] The image is, of course, that of a saint. William Garrett Piston remarks accurately that during the 1870s Southern publicists "set Robert E. Lee on the road to sainthood."[5] By 1880 this process had advanced considerably. John W. Daniels of Gen. Jubal A. Early's staff could write, "The Divinity in his bosom shone translucent through the man, and his spirit rose up to the Godlike."[6]

The apotheosis of Lee is not confined to the generation that immediately followed the war. Speaking in 1909, Woodrow Wilson said that Lee was "unapproachable in the history of our country." In 1914 Douglas Southall Freeman told us that "noble he was; nobler he became."[7] In 1964 Clifford Dowdey titled a chapter in his study of the Seven Days "The Early Work of a Master." Writing in 1965 about the same campaign, Dowdey told of Lee's emergence as "a people's god."[8] According to Piston, for "Dowdey the Civil War was a passion play, with Lee as Christ."[9] Thomas L. Connelly summed up the situation when in 1977 he wrote that Lee "became a God figure for Virginians, a saint for the white Protestant South, and a hero for the nation . . . who represented all that was good and noble."[10] Other books have dealt with the development of the Lee tradition: Connelly's *The Marble Man*, Piston's *Lee's Tarnished Lieutenant*, and Gaines M. Foster's 1987 study *Ghosts of the Confederacy* all trace its evolution. This book examines the tradition. It asks whether the tradition is historical.

Born in 1807, a Virginia aristocrat of the plantation society, Lee graduated with great distinction from the United States Military Academy in 1829. He married Mary Custis, the daughter of Martha Washington's grandson, George Washington Parke Custis, who was also George Washington's adopted son. The marriage produced four daughters – Agnes, Annie, Mary, and Mildred – and three sons – George Washington Custis Lee, Robert Edward Lee, Jr., and William Henry Fitzhugh ("Rooney") Lee, all of whom were to serve in the Confederate army. General Lee's continuous and distinguished service in the United States Army included action in the Mexican War and the superintendency at West Point from September 1, 1852, to March 31, 1855. He was considered the protégé of Gen. Winfield Scott, the country's most distinguished soldier and general-in-chief of the United States Army at the outbreak of the Civil War. These facts are well known. Indeed, because so much has been written about Lee, it is tempting to believe that nothing more need be said for we already know all about him.

To be sure, professional historians and other writers have not neglected Lee. In 1950 Marshall W. Fishwick, professor of history at Washington and Lee University, wrote what was essentially a critical bibliographic essay on writings about Lee. Published in the *Virginia Magazine of History and Biography* under the telltale title "Virginians on Olympus II, Robert E. Lee: Savior of the Lost Cause," the article discussed the literature prior to 1950. Since Fishwick's catalog, additional biographical materials have appeared regularly, including eight major works: *Gray Fox* by Burke Davis (1956); *Lee after the War* by Fishwick (1963); *Lee* by Clifford Dowdey (1965); *Robert E. Lee*, a two-volume work, by Margaret Sanborn (1966 and 1967); *Lee – The Last Years* by Charles Bracelen Flood (1981); *Lee and Grant* by Gene Smith (1984); *Robert E. Lee* by Manfred Weidhorn (1988); and *The Generals* by Nancy Scott Anderson and Dwight Anderson (1988).[11]

Despite all the attention devoted to him, Lee remains a sort of historical anomaly, a major figure of history who has somehow been immune from the analyses and evaluations that are the conventional techniques of history. This immunity has two aspects. In the first place, almost all of those who have written about Lee have accepted him entirely on his own terms; whatever he has said about events or about himself, his actions and his reasons, is taken as fact. Thus Freeman tells us there was no need "to attempt an 'interpretation' of a man who was his own clear interpreter."[12] In the second place, Lee's biographers do not ask some of the conventional historians' questions about the man: were his actions rational? was he wise? what was the ethical import of his conduct? In most of the writing about Lee, there is nothing to suggest that these questions are even appropriate.

Both in being accepted on his own terms and in not being subjected to conventional historical questions Lee is unique. No other actor in the drama of Western history has enjoyed such immunity: from Caesar to Napoleon to Roosevelt, they have been questioned far more closely and judged far more strictly than Lee. In the case of Lee, history's inquiry is unaccountably curtailed. If he said something was so, it is accepted as so. Analysis of his activities stops with a determination that he did what he thought was right. Having established this motivation, ordinarily because Lee himself said it was his motivation, history stands mute.

As a consequence of Lee's immunity, there exists an orthodoxy, a dogmatism, in the writing about him. The dogmas pertain not only to the general himself. They also extend to the context of his life and to the causes, conduct, and consequences of the Civil War. Finally, they define the character of Lee's contemporaries and adversaries. Lee's biographers begin and end their accounts on the basis of a set of uniform premises, either express or implied. These premises are neither examined nor proved; they are presupposed. The result is that, although the writers tend to outdo each other in describing Lee's virtuous qualities and heroic actions, the same Lee story is told again and again. Further, with each retelling, the stated and unstated premises of that story become more deeply embedded in what purports to be the history of the Civil War.

The paradigm of the historical treatment of Lee and his times is the monumental and highly influential biography written by Douglas Southall Freeman of Virginia and published in four volumes during the 1930s. All biographies since have relied on and are plainly marked by Freeman's. Marvelously researched, the work is a wholly adulatory account of Lee's life. After setting forth every favorable fact and appealing story that could be reported and rationalizing any act that might be questioned, Freeman states this conclusion: "Robert E. Lee was one of the small company of great men in whom there is no inconsistency to be explained, no enigma to be solved. What he seemed, he was – a wholly human gentleman, the essential elements of whose positive character were two and only two, simplicity and spirituality." Freeman also says that everything related to Lee as a person "is easily understood."[13] Presumably relying on Freeman, *The Oxford Companion to American History* contains a statement that perfectly reveals the extent of Lee's historical immunity: he was "a great and simple person. His character offers historians no moral flaws to probe. Whichever choice of allegiance Lee made would have been right."[14] In other words, what he stated as a fact is a fact and there is no need to question his acts according to conventional historical criteria; whatever he did was bound to be right. This is typical of most of the writing about Lee.

People do not, as a general rule, like for their heroes or historical theories to be reexamined. In a different context, Herbert Butterfield chided the Whig historians for "still patching the new research into the old story." We are all more comfortable with the "old story." It should, therefore, be said at the outset that to examine the actions and motives of General Lee with a critical eye is to understand him rather than to diminish him. The purpose of this book is to analyze certain aspects of the Lee of tradition, to consider whether the mythic Lee is the real Lee, and to evaluate Lee and the events of his life in a larger philosophical context. This is surely appropriate. The historical process is not, after all, a neutral process. It does not permit the leader unilaterally to define the issues of his life. Nor does it simply accept the leader's answers to those issues.

Stephen Vincent Benét was correct when he called Lee "a riddle unread." To state this point more literally, Lee is a riddle *because* he has not been "read" in the same way that other historical figures have been. This book purports to read him in just that way with regard to certain major aspects of his life. It examines the mythic Lee in a conventional historical way. There is no dearth of materials to read. Lee wrote extensively about his thoughts and actions, and his writings have been mined by others many times. The period of the Civil War is well documented in primary sources. Applying the conventional techniques of the historian, free of the restrictions of the traditional Lee doctrine, what do these materials really tell us?

The conviction that underlies this study is that, because of the prevalence and strength of the Lee tradition, Lee has not in fact been considered. This book is not, therefore, a re-consideration. Its object is to look behind the dogmas to consider Lee in the light of the historical record. The reader may judge whether there is "no inconsistency to be explained, no enigma to be solved" and whether Lee is "easily understood."

CHAPTER TWO

Lee and the Peculiar Institution

"Lee had no sympathy . . . for . . . slavery," according to *The Oxford Companion to American History*. *The Illustrated Encyclopedia of the Civil War*, published in 1986, states that he was "personally opposed to slavery."[1] The 1989 edition of the *Encyclopaedia Britannica* identifies him as "a disbeliever in slavery," and the authors of a 1988 book, *The Generals*, report that one of the reasons why Mary Custis consented to marry Lee was because he shared "her anti-slavery sentiments." According to the same authors, prior to the war Lee "had supported for thirty years the liberation of black men and women," an assertion they support only by citing Lee's 1856 letter to this wife, which will be discussed later in this chapter.[2]

On February 17, 1866, General Lee appeared before a subcommittee of the Joint Congressional Committee on Reconstruction inquiring into "the condition of the states which formed the so-called Confederate States of America" so as to make recommendations to Congress regarding Reconstruction. Having been sworn, he testified at length. Along the way he stated: "I have always been in favor of emancipation – gradual emancipation." Douglas Southall Freeman, echoing Lee's statement, avows that Lee "had believed steadfastly in gradual eman-cipation."[3]

The tradition that Lee was opposed to slavery is a principal strand in the image of Lee as a tragic hero, fighting for the South in a war that was all about the abolition or the survival of slavery. Clearly, Americans would want a national hero of that war to be antislavery. But the historical record concerning Lee and slavery is complicated and seems not to support the tradition. Before reviewing the record, the issue should be refined.

Citing Lee's 1846 will in the records of Rockbridge County, Virginia, Freeman states that "he had never owned more than some half-dozen slaves, and they had probably been inherited or given him by Mrs. Custis [his wife's mother]." In another passage, Freeman reports that "the Negroes at Arlington numbered sixty-three."[4] It is therefore clear that Lee and his family did own slaves. From other sources, it is also evident that Lee was personally involved in certain of the unseemly corollaries of the slave system, including trafficking in slaves and the recapture of fugitive slaves.

On July 8, 1858, he wrote a letter from Alexandria to a Mr. Winston, presumably a dealer in slaves, which reads in part as follows:

I have made arrangements to send down the three men on Monday. . . . The man who is to carry them, is now undetermined whether he will go by the mail boat, via Fredericksburg, or by Gordonsville. . . .

He will have orders to deliver them to you at Richmond, or in the event of not meeting you, to lodge them in the jail in that City subject to your order. . . .

I may wish to send at the same time three women, one about 35 years old, one 22, and the other 17 – They have been accustomed to house work, The eldest a good washer & ironer – But I Cannot recommend them for honesty –

I wish you to hire them out, in the same manner as the men, for one or more years, to responsible persons, for what they will bring – Should you not be able to hire any or all of these people, you may dispose of them to the end of the year to the best advantage, on some farm, or set them to work at the White House, as you may judge best.

: : : LEE AND THE PECULIAR INSTITUTION : : :

Should there be an Agent in Richmond, to whom you Could turn them over, you are at liberty to do so, with specific instructions as to their disposition and security according to your suggestion.[5]

Freeman reports an incident involving a fugitive slave that took place in 1859: "A man and a young woman, ran away in the hope of reaching Pennsylvania. They were captured in Maryland and were returned to Arlington. Thereupon Lee sent them to labor in lower Virginia, where there would be less danger of absconding. That probably was the extent of the punishment imposed on them. There is no evidence, direct or indirect, that Lee ever had them or any other Negroes flogged."[6]

Although these facts are relevant to the tradition, the simple fact of Lee's owning slaves is not the appropriate issue. Like Washington and Jefferson, Lee was born into a society in which slavery was a fact and was taken for granted, and it was a society he did not create. To that extent, he is entitled to the same acceptance of his ownership of slaves that history accords to the other Virginia aristocrats. The appropriate question to consider is not whether he owned slaves but rather how he felt about the institution of slavery. For purposes of analysis, an examination of the record in regard to this question breaks down into four areas of inquiry: Lee's prewar views, his wartime relationship to slavery prior to the South's consideration of arming the slaves, his involvement in the debate over the arming of slaves, and his postwar statements concerning his earlier beliefs.

A letter written by Lee to his wife on December 27, 1856, is the first known statement of the substance of his views. Written from his station in Texas in the backwash of the 1856 presidential election, in which Democrat James Buchanan had defeated Republican John Charles Frémont, the first avowedly national free-soil candidate, and Know-Nothing–Whig Millard Fillmore, the letter suggests several attitudes. Because the letter is one of the principal sources of the tradition of Lee's opposition to slavery, it deserves to be examined in detail.[7]

Regarding slavery, as such, Lee wrote:

In this enlightened age, there are few I believe, but what will acknowledge, that slavery as an institution, is a moral & political evil in any Country. It is useless to expatiate on its disadvantages. I think it however a greater evil to the white than to the black race, & while my feelings are strongly enlisted in behalf of the latter, my sympathies are more strong for the former. The blacks are immeasurably better off here than in Africa, morally, socially & physically. The painful discipline they are undergoing, is necessary for their instruction as a race, & I hope will prepare & lead them to better things. How long their subjugation may be necessary is known & ordered by a wise Merciful Providence. Their emancipation will sooner result from the mild & melting influence of Christianity, than the storms & tempests of fiery Controversy. . . . While we see the Course of the final abolition of human Slavery is onward, & we give it all the aid of our prayers & all justifiable means in our power, we must leave the progress as well as the result in his hands who sees the end; who Chooses to work by slow influences; & with whom two thousand years are but as a Single day.

To begin with, it should be noted that the belief that black slaves were better off than they would have been in Africa was a general sentiment among white people. If presentism is to be avoided, Lee's view in this respect is not subject to exception. In regard to the religious thrust of Lee's letter, Freeman says that most religious people of Lee's class in the border states shared the view that slavery existed because God willed it and would end when God so ordained.[8] In any event, there is no basis for doubting Lee's religious sincerity; throughout his life he manifested the conviction that God intervened directly in his and all human affairs. Nevertheless, this religiosity established a laissez-faire role for Lee, and everyone else, in the controversy. It made his claim of opposition an abstraction in the midst of a national preoccupation that was anything but abstract. In this respect his statement that there were few people who did not share his abstract opinion that slavery was evil suggests either an unbelievable lack of information concerning the country's turmoil over the issue – with Southern voices demanding expansion of slavery as a positive good – or disingenuousness on Lee's part. And his express rejection of any personal opinion concerning an appropriate future time for emancipation buttressed the abstract character of his sentiment. Finally, although he was not alone in his notion that the slaves' "painful discipline" was instructional, a transitional stage to freedom, Lee's acceptance of the idea, in particular his unwillingness to suggest any means or timetable for expediting the transition, seems unreasonable in the context of his statement denouncing the evils of the institution for whites as well as blacks. Bertram Wyatt-Brown has commented on these aspects of the letter, observing that Lee's statements evince "a mixture of condescension and twinges of guilt of an indefinite sort." He also concludes that "Lee was unexceptional in maintaining such views: they were standard opinions of a class that exploited black laborers, but wished them well, that bowed to fast-gathering metropolitan opinion but did nothing to hasten the hour [of emancipation]."9

Other aspects of Lee's letter are noteworthy as well. The immediate crisis surrounding slavery at that time had arisen from the Kansas-Nebraska Act. Passed in 1854, it repealed the Missouri Compromise and provided for popular sovereignty on the issue of slavery in the territories. Democratic president Franklin Pierce, who signed the legislation, failed to win renomination in 1856 and was succeeded by Buchanan; in his December 2, 1856, message to Congress Pierce defended the Kansas-Nebraska Act and was highly critical of Northern agitation about slavery. Lee had read Pierce's message and in his 1856 letter stated his reaction:

> I was much pleased with the President's message. . . . The views of the Pres: of the Systematic & progressive efforts of certain people of the North, to interfere with & change the domestic institutions of the South, are truthfully & faithfully expressed. The Consequences of their plans & purposes are also clearly set forth, & they must also be aware, that their object is both unlawful & entirely foreign to them & their duty; for which they are irresponsible & unaccountable; & Can only be accomplished by *them* through the agency of a Civil & Servile war. (Emphasis in original.)

Referring to his belief that God should and would work out emancipation in his own good time, Lee went on:

> Although the Abolitionist must know this, & must See that he has neither the right or power of operating except by moral means &

suasion, & if he means well to the slave, he must not Create angry feelings in the Master; that although he may not approve the mode by which it pleases Providence to accomplish its purposes, the result will nevertheless be the same; that the reasons he gives for interference in what he has no Concern, holds good for every kind of interference with our neighbors when we disapprove their Conduct. . . . Is it not strange that the descendants of those pilgrim fathers who Crossed the Atlantic to preserve their own freedom of opinion, have always proved themselves intolerant of the Spiritual liberty of others?

It is apparent that Lee was not speaking simply as a Virginian about Virginia concerns. He wrote instead of Northern and Southern conflict. This sectional emphasis will be considered again in Chapter 3, but for now it will suffice to point out that Lee's views concerning the politics of Northern antislavery as revealed in his letter included the following beliefs:

1. Northerners' opposition to slavery, or to its expansion into the territories, was an "interference" with "the domestic institutions of the South," with which they had no appropriate concern.
2. In opposing slavery, Northerners were intolerant of the "Spiritual liberty" of the Southerners who supported slavery.
3. Although Northerners opposed to slavery had the right to proceed by "moral means and suasion," their opposition was somehow "unlawful," violated their duty as citizens, and predicted civil war.

Believers in a constitutional union, that is, the United States of America as one nation, accepted the notion that the domestic institutions of a state, including slavery, were beyond the scope of national power. The Republican Party acknowledged this. But the slavery issue was politically reduced to the question of its expansion into the territories. Congress had the express power to admit new states carved out of the territories. Prior to the *Dred Scott* decision of 1857 – Lee's letter was written in 1856 – Congress was deemed to have the authority to legislate concerning slavery in the territories. Believers in a constitutional union did not accept the view that using the ballot box, the press, free speech, and the political processes to advance their opposition to slavery in the territories or their views in regard to the admission of new states was "intolerant" or an infringement of the rights of others. That is what they understood as the purpose of the democratic process. It is unlikely that these believers would have understood why their "moral means and suasion," which Lee seemed on the one hand to credit, could on the other hand be, in Lee's contradictory opinion, "unlawful" and a violation of their duty as citizens. As for civil war, the opponents of slavery believed that in a democratic political system the idea of rebellion by the losing side was moot. These Northern attitudes were apparently unknown by Lee, or were at least unacknowledged in his letter.

The tradition that avers Lee's opposition to slavery also insists on separating his views from those of the disunionist Southern political leadership. As will be discussed in Chapter 3, between Lincoln's election and Virginia's secession Lee was critical of the Southern disunionists and proclaimed his belief in the Union. But in view of his 1856 letter, it is fair to say that in 1856 his views were sectional. They demonstrated a "two-nation" point of view – slavery was none of the North's business – and embraced the essential position of the disunionists that the peculiar institution was exempt from the national political process. Contrary to the traditional conclusion, and despite his rhetorical abstraction that slavery was an evil, this would seem to place Lee in 1856 in the mainstream of the attitudes of the Southern political leadership, the leadership that four years later would lead their states out of the Union to form the Confederacy and engage in civil war.

Lee's correspondence during the 1860–61 secession crisis, considered in the following chapter in more detail, is essentially free of expressions of his feelings about the institution of slavery. With the exception of a letter of January 10, 1863, to Secretary of War James A. Seddon, his wartime correspondence also tells little about his slavery views prior to his involvement in the 1864–65 Confederate debate about using slaves as soldiers. The letter to Seddon was an exhortation to the war secretary to take action to increase the size of the Confederate armies. In a concluding litany of what was at stake for the South in the war, Lee referred to saving "our social system from destruction."[10] It is commonly argued that Lee went south, and fought for the South, in spite of his opposition to slavery. Conceivably, of course, one could have sided with the Confederacy for reasons wholly unrelated to the protection of the institution of slavery. But slavery was unquestionably a preeminent aspect of the Confederacy's "social system," so that during the war Lee was aware of and embraced the preservation of slavery as a Confederate war aim.

Lee's wartime attitude toward slavery was more concretely demonstrated in three episodes. These concern his administration of his father-in-law's will, actions of his army in Pennsylvania in 1863, and the prisoner exchange controversy. Lee's father-in-law died in 1857 leaving a will that designated Lee as the executor of a complicated estate and ordered the emancipation of his slaves within five years of his demise.[11] Lee set about the estate tasks, which were to occupy his time for several years, including the early war years. A number of Lee's letters touched on the manumission charge, among them one to his son Custis written on July 2, 1859, in which, referring to the slaves, he stated that his father-in-law had left him "an unpleasant legacy."[12] In his correspondence about manumitting the Custis slaves, Lee wrote respectfully of them and showed a concern for their well-being following their emancipation.[13] Ultimately, on December 29, 1862, Lee effected the manumission pursuant to the will.[14] Biographical references to Lee's manumission of the Custis slaves sometimes suggest that Lee's action is evidence of his disapproval of the institution of slavery. Bearing in mind that as executor he was obligated to free these slaves as a matter of Virginia law, his having done so seems a neutral fact in reference to his personal feelings about the institution.

Although at times Lee bitterly criticized the behavior of Federal soldiers in Virginia and elsewhere in the South, as will be seen later, his own men did not always behave civilly when they were in the North. In Maryland in 1862 he wrote that they "wantonly destroyed" property. During the course of the Gettysburg campaign, Confederate soldiers engaged in extensive plundering in Pennsylvania. In 1864 Confederate general officers sought to extract ransom from civilians by threatening to sack Northern cities and towns.[15] Of particular interest in reference to Lee and slavery are the actions of the Confederates in 1863 in Pennsylvania involving blacks.

Jenkins's brigade, composed of Virginia cavalry regiments and accompanying Ewell's Second Corps, and other cavalry commands were with the Army of Northern Virginia throughout the move into Pennsylvania. In the course of their raiding and foraging, these units searched for blacks, seized them, and sent them south into slavery. Contemporary accounts state that some of these blacks were escaped slaves and that others were free blacks. The number of these unfortunate persons is uncertain. According to the July 8, 1863, issue of a newspaper published at Chambersburg, Pennsylvania, the *Franklin Repository*, "Quite a number of negroes, free and slave – men, women, and children – were captured by Jenkins and started South to be sold into bondage. . . . Perhaps full fifty were got off to slavery. . . . Some of the men were bound with ropes, and the children were mounted in front or behind the rebels on their horses." The authors of *When War Passed This Way*, a well-researched book based on contemporary newspaper accounts and other observations, note that "no one can estimate the numbers of Negroes who suffered this fate, for the practice continued throughout the time Lee's army was in Pennsylvania."[16] That this activity was not simply random and must have involved significant numbers of blacks is apparent from First Corps commander James Longstreet's dispatch to Maj. Gen. George E. Pickett, one of his division commanders. Written by Longstreet's adjutant on July 1, 1863, from Greenwood, Pennsylvania, the message directed the movement of Pickett's division and concluded with the statement, "The captured contrabands had better be brought along with you for further disposition." (The term "contraband" was widely used by Federals and Confederates to describe slaves who had left their owners.)[17]

It can be contended that the Confederates in Pennsylvania could not determine which of the blacks were free and which were escaped slaves, and from the Southern point of view it might have been reasonable to make a distinction between these categories of blacks. But the point is that for a Confederate army engaged in a military activity, slave-catching, let alone the enslaving of free people, was a wholly inappropriate activity. It was in no way a military activity, and there is no evidence that Confederate civilian authorities directed or authorized these acts. It can also be argued that Lee was personally unaware of the seizures, in spite of the visibility of the blacks that Longstreet and, presumably, others carried with them and in spite of Longstreet's intimacy with Lee. Finally, it may be said that if Lee did order the capture of blacks or was aware of it, his involvement was in his capacity as an army commander and the acts therefore did not necessarily reflect his personal views. All of these rationalizations may have some validity, but the incidents are nevertheless relevant to the issue of Lee's relationship to the institution of slavery.

The issue of prisoner exchange was complicated by the Confederacy's response to the Emancipation Proclamation and the Union's recruitment of regiments composed of black men, including former slaves. A detailed account of prisoner exchange negotiations can be found elsewhere,[18] but certain aspects of the controversy bear on the question of Lee and slavery and must be considered here.

On December 24, 1862, Jefferson Davis issued a proclamation setting forth his presidential reaction to several Federal actions, including the Emancipation Proclamation and the recruitment of black soldiers. Expressing the view that the Emancipation Proclamation was intended to excite "servile war," Davis's proclamation ordered that "all negro slaves captured in arms be at once delivered over to the executive authorities of the respective States . . . to be dealt with according to the laws of said State" and that all "commissioned officers . . . found serving in company with armed slaves in insurrection" be similarly delivered to the state authorities "to be dealt with in accordance with the laws of said State." In a message to the Confederate Congress on January 12, 1863, he noted that the Emancipation Proclamation meant that "several millions of human beings of an inferior race, peaceful and contented laborers . . . are doomed to extermination" and stated his opinion that Federal officers leading black soldiers who were former slaves should, if captured, be turned over to state authorities as "criminals engaged in inciting servile insurrection," a capital offense.[19]

By a series of joint resolutions, on April 30 and May 1, 1863, Congress went farther than Davis. With respect to "negroes and mulattoes who shall be engaged in war or be taken in arms" the legislators approved Davis's remedy. But the resolutions demurred to the president's plan with respect to their officers. These miscreants were not to be turned over to the states. They were, instead, to be disposed of by the Confederate government by being "put to death or . . . otherwise punished at the discretion of the court." The congressional action did not distinguish between former slaves and other black soldiers.[20]

The Federal reaction to these Confederate plans was to cancel all paroles and exchanges of captured Confederate officers.[21] Thus, the issue of the status of captured black soldiers and their officers, an issue that was to set up many communications between the antagonists, was joined.[22] At one point, the Confederates offered to authorize the exchange of free black soldiers, but the South clung to its essential position that former slaves in the Federal army were "property recaptured" and not subject to the usages of war.[23]

On October 1, 1864, Lee became personally involved in the issue of prisoner exchange, which had extended beyond the question of officers to the failure of both sides to exchange enlisted men. On that day, he directly addressed Gen. Ulysses S. Grant on the subject of prisoners, proposing "an exchange of the prisoners of war belonging to the armies operating in Virginia, man for man."[24] Grant responded the following day: "Among those lost by the armies operating against Richmond were a number of colored troops. Before further negotiations are had upon the subject I would ask if you propose delivering these men the same as white soldiers."[25] Apparently intending to distinguish between free blacks and former slaves, Lee answered that he "intended to include all captured soldiers . . . of whatever nation and color," but, he continued, "negroes belonging to our citizens are not considered subjects of exchange and were not included in my proposition." Remarking that "the Government is bound to secure to all persons received into her armies the rights due to soldiers," Grant refused the exchange proposal. On October 19, 1864, Lee accepted the role as the Confederacy's spokesman on the issue of former slaves. On that day, at the direction of his government, he wrote Grant what was in effect an extensive legalistic brief defending the Confederate policy and the right of the Confederacy to return to slavery captured black soldiers who were former slaves.[26]

Ultimately, in early 1865, a man-for-man, unconditional exchange did occur. Presumably testifying from memory, in his 1866 appearance before the congressional subcommittee concerned with Reconstruction, Lee testified with regard to prisoner exchange: "I made several efforts to exchange the prisoners. . . . I offered to General Grant, around Richmond, that we should ourselves exchange all the prisoners in our hands. . . . I offered then to send to City Point all prisoners in Virginia and North Carolina . . . provided they return an equal number of mine, man for man. . . . I heard nothing more on the subject."[27]

It may again be argued that Lee was acting as a military commander in reference to black soldiers and their exchange, and that his personal convictions regarding slavery were not involved in this issue. Contrary to what had been the case in regard to the Pennsylvania seizures of blacks, Lee's position in regard to prisoner exchange reflected the official policy of the Confederacy at the time.

Lee's personal view of slavery, unobscured by his military role, ultimately came to the fore during the great Confederate debate on making slaves into Confederate soldiers. Because this debate also involved the question of emancipation, participants were required to express their feelings about emancipation in a practical context: if the slaves were to be armed, would those who became soldiers be emancipated? This was, of course, a different kind of question from the abstract question that so many Southerners had wrestled with. In the abstract, Lee and others had it both ways; they had been able to lament slavery as an evil but to cling to it as an institution, leaving its fate in the hands of God or some other long-range force. Beginning in late 1864, the issue of emancipation, at least on a limited basis, was a real and immediate concern.

On October 24, 1864, William Porcher Miles of South Carolina, chairman of the Military Affairs Committee of the Confederate House of Representatives, wrote Lee a personal letter. He solicited Lee's views on several issues, including "the arming of a portion of our negroes and making a regular military organization of them." No letter containing Lee's response has ever been found, but Miles's follow-up letter to Lee dated November 3, 1864, suggests that Lee approved of the idea of enlisting the slaves and proposed that those who became soldiers be emancipated.[28]

The highly controversial and ironic issue of arming slaves and freeing slave soldiers moved into high public prominence during the Confederacy's dismal winter of 1864–65. President Davis and influential cabinet members supported the idea. On January 7, 1865, Andrew

Hunter, a member of the Virginia Senate, wrote to Lee requesting his view of the issue of "converting such portions of this [slave] population as may be required into soldiers, to aid in maintaining our great struggle." Hunter also raised certain specific questions: could such a plan be effective? would the plan injuriously affect the institution of slavery? would enlisting slaves permit more liberal exemption of white men, who would then be available to engage in subsistence and supply activities? and would the South's capacity for defense be enhanced? The letter did not solicit Lee's views on slavery or emancipation, as such.[29]

Lee responded to Hunter's letter on January 11, 1865.[30] By this time, Lee realistically foresaw the defeat of the South. The military circumstances were grim: since June 1864 the Army of Northern Virginia had been locked up in the Petersburg defenses, under siege by overwhelming forces; Atlanta had fallen; Lincoln had been reelected; Sherman had marched through Georgia to the sea and captured Savannah; and Hood's Army of Tennessee had been decisively defeated in the battle of Nashville.

After acknowledging the letter from Hunter, Lee began his response with these words: "Considering *the relation of master and slave*, controlled by humane laws and influenced by Christianity and an enlightened public sentiment, *as the best that can exist between the white and black races* while intermingled as at present in this country, I would deprecate any sudden disturbance of that relation unless it be necessary to avert a greater calamity to both" (emphasis added). Following this expression of his attitude about slavery, Lee stated his preference for the use of the white population as soldiers but suggested that the Confederacy's "duty to provide for continued war and not for a battle or a campaign" was likely to overtax the white population. He noted that the Federals were increasing their incursions into the South and enlisting and arming the slaves, a destruction of slavery "in a manner most pernicious to the welfare of our people." Lee's answer continued: "Whatever may be the effect of our employing negro troops, it cannot be as mischievous as this. If it end in subverting slavery it will be accomplished by ourselves, and we can devise the means of *alleviating the evil consequences to both races.* I think, therefore, we must decide whether slavery shall be extinguished by our enemies and the slaves be used against us, or use them ourselves at the risk of the effects which may be

produced upon our social institutions. My own opinion is that we
should employ them without delay" (emphasis added).

Lee then turned to the logically implicit question of why a slave
would fight for the Confederacy. As incentive he proposed "immediate
freedom to all who enlist, and freedom at the end of the war to the
families of those who discharge their duties faithfully (whether they
survive or not), together with the privilege of residing at the South. To
this might be added a bounty for faithful service." He acknowledged
that slaves could not be expected to fight for "prospective freedom"
when they could secure it at once "by going to the enemy." Addressing
this dilemma, he stated:

> The reasons that induce me to recommend the employment of
> negro troops at all render the effect . . . upon slavery immaterial,
> and in my opinion the best means of securing the efficiency and
> fidelity of this auxiliary force would be to accompany the measure
> with a well-digested plan of gradual and general emancipation. As
> that will be the result of the continuance of the war, and will
> certainly occur if the enemy succeed, it seems to me most advisable
> to adopt it at once, and thereby obtain all the benefits that will
> accrue to our cause. . . .
>
> In addition to the great political advantages that would result to
> our cause from the adoption of a system of emancipation, it would
> exercise a salutary influence upon our whole negro population, by
> rendering more secure the fidelity of those who become soldiers,
> and diminishing the inducements to the rest to abscond.

On March 13, 1865, the Confederate Congress reluctantly and nar-
rowly voted to enlist slave soldiers, but the statute contained the following provision:

> Sec. 5. That nothing in this act shall be construed to authorize a
> change in the relation which said slaves shall bear toward their
> owners, except by consent of the owners and of the States in which
> they may reside, and in pursuance of the laws thereof.[31]

Unlike Lee, the Confederate Congress was unwilling to trade emancipation for the slaves' enlistment. The war ended before the South had
a sufficient opportunity to attempt to organize slave regiments.[32] But

Lee was at last on the record with regard to slavery as an institution. His statements bear discussion.

Plainly, because of the exigencies of the war, Lee favored recruiting slaves as soldiers and emancipating those who enlisted, with later freedom for their families.[33] He therefore also favored, under the existing political and military circumstances, "a well-digested plan of gradual and general emancipation." But the question of Lee's own belief about slavery as an institution remains. Setting aside abstract qualifications concerning its evils and advantages and notwithstanding the military situation in 1865, in simplest terms was Lee at bottom for slavery or against it?

On February 17, 1866, with the war over and lost, Lee told representatives of the United States Congress that he had "*always* been in favor of emancipation – gradual emancipation" (emphasis added). But on January 11, 1865, while still at war, he had described slavery as "the best" relationship between the races and had said that emancipation involved "evil consequences" to both races. Granting that he may have seen "gradual and general emancipation" as the best means to the ends necessary for the South's survival in 1865, his letter of that year simply does not describe a genuine emancipationist, one who favored emancipation "always," "steadfastly," or otherwise. The 1865 communication makes it unreasonable for the historian to credit the 1866 statement or to rely on Lee's 1856 theoretical statement as an indication of his essential views. The latter is, of course, directly contradicted by the assertion of 1865 that slavery represented the best relationship between the races. In short, the historical record flatly contradicts the assertion of Freeman and the Lee tradition that, prior to the issue of arming the slaves, Lee was personally opposed to slavery in any practical sense. And there is no evidence to support the acceptance of Lee's self-serving characterization of himself as one who had always been in favor of gradual emancipation.

Another aspect of Lee's January 11, 1865, letter is noteworthy. Although the letter appears in the *Official Records*, Freeman's comprehensive biography affords it only a footnote reference, in which its "gradual and general emancipation" recommendation alone is mentioned. Instead of reporting Lee's words regarding slavery as the best relationship, Freeman's footnote quotes the diary of John B. Jones, the well-known Rebel War Clerk, who wrote that Lee was a "thorough emancipationist." In his biography of Lee, Clifford Dowdey refers to the letter and quotes extensively from it, but he omits that portion describing slavery as the best relationship between whites and blacks.[34] Equally suggestive is the complete omission of this letter, which so compellingly dispels the impression that Lee was philosophically an emancipationist, from *The Wartime Papers of Robert E. Lee,* a 1961 collection edited by Dowdey and Louis H. Manarin, both of whom are firmly committed to the Lee tradition.

Lee had several occasions after the war on which to disclose his prior views of the peculiar institution, that is, what he had thought of slavery before the Southern defeat. An early opportunity presented itself in November 1865 when Herbert C. Saunders, a British literary traveler, visited him in Lexington. Saunders took notes of their conversation and, requesting permission to publish, later sent a manuscript of the conversation to Lee for correction. The general corrected the document but ultimately withheld the permission requested. The manuscript was nevertheless available at Lee's death, and both his son Capt. Robert E. Lee and Freeman have relied on it. Saunders's report stated in part: "On the subject of slavery, he assured me that he had always been in favor of emancipation of the negroes, and that in Virginia the feeling had been strongly inclining in the same direction, till the ill-judged enthusiasm (amounting to rancour) of the abolitionists in the North had turned the Southern tide of feeling in the other direction."[35]

In April 1869 Lee was in Baltimore and met with, among others, the Reverend John Leyburn, a Virginia-born Presbyterian who had been a pastor in the North but was in 1869 assigned in Baltimore. According to Leyburn, Lee expressed his regret that the Northern press continued to assert that the object of the war had been the perpetuation of slavery. "On this point he seemed not only indignant, but hurt. He said it was not true." Turning to his own attitude, Lee told of manumitting "most of his slaves years before the war" and of his personal friendships with black people. Leyburn then quoted the general as saying, "So far from engaging in a war to perpetuate slavery, I am rejoiced that slavery is abolished. I believe it will be greatly for the interests of the South. So fully am I satisfied of this, as regards Virginia especially, that I would cheerfully have lost all I have lost by the war, and have suffered all I have suffered, to have this object attained."[36]

Dixie after the War, published in 1906 by Myrta L. Avary, a *New York Herald* reporter, is the source of another postwar conversation with Lee. This book appears in Freeman's critical bibliography and is said to contain "some useful anecdotes." The reporter quotes Lee as follows with reference to slavery: "The best men of the South have long desired to do away with the institution and were quite willing to see it abolished. But with them in relation to this subject the question has ever been: What will you do with the freed people?"[37]

What may be said about these postwar statements? At the outset and disregarding what Lee purported to say about his personal views of slavery, a principal thrust of all three conversations seems to be that the perpetuation of slavery was somehow unrelated to secession and the war. To Leyburn he said directly that he was hurt by the suggestion that the object of the war had been the perpetuation of slavery. To Saunders he contended that Virginia's prewar feeling had been inclining toward abolition. To Avary he alleged that the "best men" of the South had long desired abolition.

There is, of course, a difference between what Lee claimed to believe after the war about the relationship between slavery and the war and the role of slavery historically. But the Lee tradition as it concerns his views on slavery is bound up with a separate tradition, one that lingers still, that discounts slavery as the reason for secession and, therefore, as the underlying cause of the war. Indeed, Lee's postwar claims of the irrelevancy of slavery have – in an example of the way in which his claims are generally credited without examination – contributed to this separate tradition. In order to create a realistic context for a consideration of Lee's postwar statements it is necessary to consider the underlying related issue of slavery's role in reference to secession and the war.

During the long crisis that culminated with war, the participants and the political leadership made it clear that slavery was the root cause of their disagreement. Don E. Fehrenbacher has remarked that the "tendency of nearly all public controversy to fall into alignment with the slavery question bespeaks the power with which that question gripped the minds of the American people."[38] It is an astonishing anomaly that, in spite of this fact, for one hundred years historians and commentators attempted to exorcise slavery as relevant or to downplay it as incidental to the conflict. Recent scholarship has at last acknowledged that the participants, after all, knew what they were contending about. Slavery – its expansion or limitation, its abolition or perpetuation – was what the war was all about. On the one hand, there was what Wyatt-Brown describes as "the desperate commitment of Southern whites to hold black Americans forever in their power." On the other hand, the North, in the words of Fehrenbacher, insisted on "the value and sanctity of the Union," and disagreement with the South was unavoidable in light of "the hardening opinion of a Northern majority that slavery was incompatible with the destinies of the Republic." Reasons for the Northern objections were probably mixed, ranging from simple morality to material considerations such as interest in control of the territorial lands and political power, but the opposition was intense. D. W. Brogan, the Cambridge political scientist, a keen and detached observer of the American situation, has succinctly described the collision course that led to conflict: "The South was demanding of the North what it was less and less willing to give – theoretical and, as far as possible, practical equality for the 'peculiar institution.' "[39]

Southern insistence that slavery be permitted to expand, so that it could be perpetuated, and Northern resistance to these goals resulted in secession and war. Kenneth Stampp's *And the War Came* is a particularly persuasive statement of this thesis: concentrating on the political uproar before hostilities began at Fort Sumter, Stampp, like Fehrenbacher, argues convincingly that slavery was the sine qua non of all the turmoil.[40] And surely it is no coincidence that a majority of the applications for pardon filed by Southerners immediately after the war identified slavery as the paramount cause of the conflict.[41]

As described by Fehrenbacher, the years prior to secession had witnessed "the development of the Southern conviction that slavery must be protected at all costs."[42] In the interest of slavery protection, the Southern states had systematically struck down American constitutional assumptions: freedom of speech, freedom of the press, privacy of the mails.[43] Virginia, which in 1860 led the slave states in its population of slaves, had participated in this infringement on constitutional rights.

For example, its 1849 legal code made it a criminal offense to state "that owners have not right of property in their slaves."[44]

The Confederate Constitution also illuminates the question of slavery's centrality in the sectional conflict that precipitated the Civil War. As is frequently stated, it was modeled in detail on the Constitution of the United States. As is less frequently stated, it contained pointed and significant differences. Thus, for example, in Section 9 of Article I, in which bills of attainder were stated as being beyond the power of Congress, the Confederate document also proscribed any "law denying or impairing the right of property in negro slaves." In Article IV, the United States Constitution provided for the privileges and immunities of the citizens of each state. The Southern constitution added the right of citizens to travel and sojourn in any state with their slaves without impairment of "the right of property in said slaves." Section 4 of the same article of the Confederate Constitution concerned the acquisition by the Confederacy of new territory and stated, "In all such territory, the institution of negro slavery . . . shall be recognized and protected by Congress and any territorial government." No such provision was, of course, contained in the United States Constitution.[45]

As if responding to Lee's suggestion that the "best men of the South" and perhaps a majority of Virginians were antislavery, Allan Nevins has characterized the prewar status of slavery: "The South, as a whole, in 1846–61 was not moving toward emancipation, but away from it. It was not relaxing the laws which guarded the system, but reinforcing them. It was not ameliorating slavery, but making it harsher and more implacable. The South was further from a just solution of the slavery problem in 1830 than it had been in 1789. It was further from a tenable solution in 1860 than it had been in 1830."[46] Indeed, the South's "tenable solution" was made quite explicit in Vice President Alexander H. Stephens's widely noted Savannah speech, delivered March 21, 1861, prior to the firing on Fort Sumter and Virginia's secession. Referring to the United States Constitution's "assumption of the equality of races," Stephens said that "this was an error." Continuing, he stated:

Our new Government is founded upon exactly the opposite idea; its foundations are laid, its corner-stone rests upon the great truth,

that the negro is not the equal of the white man; that slavery –
subordination to the superior race – is his natural and moral condition.

This, our new Government, is the first, in the history of the
world, based upon this great physical, philosophical and moral
truth.[47]

Bertram Wyatt-Brown's conclusion is convincing: "Over the course of a
parallel and mutually sustaining existence, white man's honor and
black man's slavery became in the public mind of the South practically
indistinguishable."[48]

Today's Southern students of the prewar South share this view that
slavery occupied a central place in Southern thinking. Gaines M. Foster
states that "the decision to secede, the will to fight for four long years,
the willingness to sacrifice so many lives and so much treasure testified
to the South's desire to preserve slavery in an independent nation."[49]
Robert F. Durden's opinion appears in the preface to his book *The Gray
and the Black*: "The South had spent forty or so years convincing itself
that slavery was ordained by God as the best, indeed the only, solution to
the problem posed by the massive presence of the Negro. The debate in
the winter of 1864–1865 demonstrated anew and with sad finality that
many Southerners were unwilling or unable to consider voluntary alteration of the racial status quo, even as that status quo was crumbling
about them."[50] Referring to President Davis's efforts to encourage
emancipation of individual slaves as a reward for serving in the Confederate armies, Durden also comments that "in truth, the Confederacy
had in large part come into existence because of the larger theory . . . the
majority's belief that Negroes should, as inferior beings, be permanently kept in slavery, where they were happy and subordinate to
whites."[51]

In short, recent scholarship argues persuasively that, as causes of the
war, economic and cultural differences between the sections were not,
in fact, significant. Thus, Stampp contends that "the notion of a distinct
southern culture was largely a figment of the romantic imaginations."
The sectional difference was the controversy over slavery. Characterizing secession, Stampp observes, "Fundamentally, this movement was
not the product of genuine southern nationalism; indeed, except for the

institution of slavery, the South had little to give it a clear national identity." Slavery was "the central institution of antebellum Southern life," according to Eric Foner.[52] In order to defend it, Lee's "best men of the South" led their states out of the Union in 1860 and 1861. In 1865 many of them voted against emancipating slaves in return for the slaves' soldiering for the South.

Referring to the Southerners, Brogan has stated it plainly: "They seceded over one thing and fought over one thing, slavery." It is accurate to identify slavery as "the cause of secession and four years of military conflict."[53] In view of the breadth, intensity, and openness of the slavery controversy during Lee's lifetime, and his embracing of the Confederate Constitution, it appears that in asserting after the war that slavery was not the issue, Lee was either remarkably uninformed, had so rationalized secession that he had lost sight of the facts, or was simply not being candid.

Returning to what Lee's statements in postwar interviews reveal about his personal views of the institution of slavery, one conclusion seems clear. It is unhistoric to accept Lee as one who had "always been in favor of emancipation" in view of his January 1865 characterization of the master-slave relationship and his identification even then of the "evil consequences" of emancipation. This conclusion is reinforced by the fact that Lee's claim to Saunders was accompanied by the classic and counterfactual secessionist argument that the perpetuation of slavery was the fault of abolitionists.[54] Lee's telling Leyburn of his rejoicing at abolition and his willingness to sacrifice all that he had lost for that objective simply do not ring true.

In the final analysis, it appears that Robert E. Lee *believed* in slavery although, like many Southerners, he at the same time disliked it in the abstract and was uncomfortable with it. His attitudes and personal acts in regard to slavery, and his feelings about those who attacked the institution, were conventional. In view of his Virginia roots, none of this should be surprising. Nor does it make him censurable, even in regard to his postwar efforts to rationalize his views. What is surprising, and censurable, is that historians have not looked behind Lee's own justifications and rationalizations, have not wondered about them in light of his being a member of the Virginia planter class and a leader of the Confederacy, and thus have misrepresented him.

CHAPTER THREE

Lee Secedes

D ouglas Southall Freeman recounts Lee's decision to go south, siding with Virginia and the Confederacy after secession, in a chapter entitled "The Answer He Was Born to Make." Considering that Lee was a colonel in the United States Army and a lifetime soldier, his leaving this service to become a leader of forces making war on the United States is at first blush startling. By customary historical standards, simply to say that Lee was "born" to do what he did, to make the decision he made, is to offer no real explanation of his actions. It affords no more insight than saying that Winfield Scott and George H. Thomas, also Virginians and soldiers, were "born" to stand by the Union. In short, Lee's seceding is entitled to analysis; his actions should be explored and not just accepted.

Lee was stationed in Texas as a lieutenant colonel of the Second Cavalry in 1856 and 1857, and an examination of his recorded thoughts about the crisis of the Union begins with the letter of December 27, 1856, written from Texas to his wife. This is the same letter that was quoted extensively in the prior chapter with regard to Lee's views of the institution of slavery. In regard to the sectional conflict that would lead Southern states out of the Union – and ultimately take Lee with them – the letter commented on outgoing president Pierce's message to Congress and set forth Lee's views about slavery and the Northern agitation against the institution. Lee was in 1856 critical of "certain people of the North" who would interfere with "the domestic institutions of the South," an interference he perceived as "unlawful" and "intolerant."

Because of the death of his father-in-law, George Washington Parke Custis, Lee obtained a leave of absence from his unit in October 1857 and returned to his home in Arlington, Virginia. This leave was extended several times, resulting in his being placed in charge of state and federal forces at the time of John Brown's Harpers Ferry raid in October 1859. Inactive then until February 1860, he was on February 6 ordered again to Texas and assigned temporarily to command the Department of Texas, with headquarters at San Antonio.[1] Arriving in San Antonio on February 19, Lee assumed command on February 20. The department was troubled by Indians and Mexican bandits, but Lee was distracted by much more significant and threatening events as the irrepressible conflict between North and South intensified.

One of the climactic events in the long smoldering sectional controversy was, of course, the election of Abraham Lincoln on November 6, 1860. On November 24, 1860, in a letter to his son Custis, Lee stated his reaction to Southern newspaper discussions that followed Lincoln's election. He wrote: "The Southern States seem to be in a convulsion. . . . My little personal troubles sink into insignificance when I contemplate the condition of the country, and I feel as if I could easily lay down my life for its safety."[2] And on December 5, 1860, as secession agitation mounted, another letter went to Custis, declaring: "If the Union is dissolved, which God in his mercy forbid, I shall return to you. If not, tell my friends to give me all the promotion they can."[3] As will be discussed later in this chapter, the traditional rationale of Lee's ultimate decision is based on his Virginia loyalty. It should be noted that his December 5 letter does not speak in terms of Virginia's role; it sets up Lee's alternative courses of action depending on whether or not the Union was to be dissolved.

On December 12, 1860, Lee was relieved of the Texas command to be replaced by Gen. David E. Twiggs, a Georgian. Shortly thereafter, Lee reported to Fort Mason, Texas, the headquarters of the Second U.S. Cavalry, which he commanded. Before departing for Fort Mason, Lee was aware of President Buchanan's message to Congress of December 4, which had proposed three constitutional amendments as the basis for sectional compromise. These amendments recognized the right of property in slaves in the states where it existed or might thereafter exist; protected slavery in the territories until statehood was achieved with or without slavery, as the state constitutions prescribed; and provided for enforcement of federal fugitive slave laws and a declaration that state laws to the contrary were null and void.[4]

A letter to Custis on December 14 presented Lee's views, including his reaction to Buchanan's proposals. After expressing concern about the threat of dissolution of the Union, he stated:

> I hope, however, the wisdom and patriotism of the country will devise some way of saving it. . . . The three propositions of the President are eminently just, are in accordance with the constitution and ought to be cheerfully assented to by all the States. But I do not think the Northern and Western states will agree to them.
>
> It is, however, my only hope for the preservation of the Union, and I will cling to it to the last. Feeling the aggressions of the North, resenting their denial of the equal rights of our citizens to the common territory of the commonwealth, etc., I am not pleased with the course of the "Cotton States." . . . In addition to their selfish, dictatorial bearing, the threats they throw out against the "Border States" . . . if they will not join them, argue little for the benefit. . . . One of their plans seems to be the renewal of the slave trade. That I am opposed to on every ground.[5]

At about the time this letter was written, Lee had a conversation in San Antonio with Charles Anderson, brother of Maj. Robert Anderson who would later be in command of Fort Sumter when it was attacked by the Confederates. According to Anderson, who was staunchly pro-Union, in discussing the crisis, Lee stated that he had been taught to believe that his first obligation was to Virginia.[6]

On December 20, 1860, the talk of secession became a reality as South Carolina withdrew from the Union. During a ten-day period in January 1861, Mississippi, Florida, Alabama, and Georgia followed suit, to be joined on January 26 by Louisiana. Aware of these acts, of the seizure by the states of federal property and installations within their borders, and of the mounting symbolism of Fort Sumter, Lee continued privately to express his views in a series of letters. The first of these, written on January 22, 1861, to his wife's cousin Martha Custis Williams, stated:

God alone can save us from our folly, selfishness & short sightedness. The last accounts seem to shew that we have barely escaped anarchy to be plunged into civil war. What will be the result I cannot conjecture. I only see that a fearful calamity is upon us, & fear that the country will have to pass through for its sins a fiery ordeal. I am unable to realize that our people will destroy a government inaugerated [sic] by the blood & wisdom of our patriot fathers, that has given us peace & prosperity at home, power & security abroad, & under which we have acquired a colossal strength unequalled in the history of mankind. I wish to live under no other government, & there is no sacrifice I am not ready to make for the preservation of the Union save that of honour. If a disruption takes place, I shall go back in sorrow to my people & share the misery of my native state, & save in her defence there will be one soldier less in the world than now. I wish for no other flag than the "Star spangled banner" & no other air than "Hail Columbia." I still hope that the wisdom & patriotism of the nation will yet save it.

... I believe that the South justly complains of the aggressions of the North, & I have believed that the North would cheerfully redress the grievances complained of. I see no cause of disunion, strife & civil war & pray it may be averted.[7]

On the following day, January 23, Lee set forth reactions provoked by his reading a biography of George Washington. In a letter to his family at home he wrote:

I received Everett's life of Washington you sent me and enjoyed its perusal very much. How his spirit would be grieved could he see the wreck of his mighty labors! I will not, however, permit myself to believe till all ground of hope is gone that the work of his noble deeds will be destroyed, and that his precious advice and virtuous example will so soon be forgotten by his countrymen. As far as I can judge by the papers, we are between a state of anarchy and civil war. May God avert both of these evils from us! . . . I see that four states have declared themselves out of the Union; four more will apparently follow their example. Then, if the Border States are brought into the gulf of revolution, one-half of the country will be arrayed against the other. I must try and be patient and wait the end, for I can do nothing to hasten or retard it.[8]

Among other things, as suggested also by his 1856 letter to his wife regarding slavery, this letter expressed Lee's laissez-faire attitude. As events in April were to prove, Virginia looked to him for leadership, and he was, in fact, influential there. Margaret Sanborn, a Lee admirer, suggests that had he intervened, "it is more than a probability that he could have kept Virginia from her fateful step" of seceding.[9] But either he did not believe his opinions were significant to others, he felt his own intervention to be inappropriate, or he was otherwise inhibited. In any event, the letter predicted what was to take place: Lee let himself be carried along by the conduct of others until Sumter and its aftermath.

In another letter of January 23, written probably to Custis, he said:

The South, in my opinion, has been aggrieved by the acts of the North, as you say. I feel the aggression, and am willing to take every proper step for redress. It is the principle I contend for, not individual or private gain. As an American citizen, I take great pride in my country, her prosperity and institutions; and would defend any State if her rights were invaded. But I can anticipate no greater calamity for the country than a dissolution of the Union. It would be an accumulation of all the evils we complain of, and I am willing to sacrifice everything but honor for its preservation. I hope, therefore, that all constitutional means will be exhausted before there is a resort to force. Secession is nothing but revolution. The framers of our Constitution never exhausted so much labor, wisdom and forbearance in its formation, and surrounded it with so many guards and securities, if it was intended to be broken by every member of the Confederacy at will. It was intended for "perpetual union," so expressed in the preamble, and for the establishment of a government, not a compact, which can only be dissolved by

revolution, or the consent of all the people in convention assem-
bled. It is idle to talk of secession. Anarchy would have been
established, and not a government, by Washington, Hamilton,
Jefferson, Madison, and the other patriots of the Revolution. . . .
Still a Union that can only be maintained by swords and bayonets,
and in which strife and civil war are to take the place of brotherly
love and kindness, has no charm for me. I shall mourn for my
country and for the welfare and progress of mankind. If the Union
is dissolved, and the Government disrupted, I shall return to my
native State and share the miseries of my people, and save in
defence will draw my sword on none.[10]

Events in February 1861 placed Lee in the very midst of secession.
The Texas convention that had been called to debate the issue of secession passed its secession ordinance on February 1, and the state became
the seventh to leave the Union. Following the pattern in other seceding
states, the Texas authorities immediately raised the claim of ownership
of federal property in the state. Freeman makes an interesting observation concerning what Lee would have done in these circumstances if he
had been in command of the Department of Texas: "His own state had
not seceded; he would have had no hesitancy in obeying the orders of
the War Department; he certainly would have refused to surrender
government property."[11] This assertion seems credible in view of an
incident that took place at about the same time at Fort Mason. Concerned about the security of the fort, Lee told Capt. Richard W. Johnson, commander of Company F of the Second Cavalry, that he was
determined "to defend his post at all hazards."[12]

Lee was spared the responsibility for federal property in Texas when
on February 4 he was ordered to report to the general-in-chief in
Washington. On February 13 he left Fort Mason for San Antonio, the
first leg of the journey to Washington. According to Captain Johnson, he
asked Lee as he was leaving whether he "intended to go South or
remain North." Lee responded, "I shall never bear arms against the
United States, – but it may be necessary for me to carry a musket in
defence of my native state, Virginia, in which case I shall not prove
recreant to my duty."[13] On the road to San Antonio, he also had a
conversation with Capt. George B. Cosby of the Second Cavalry, who

reported that Lee said that if Virginia seceded, he would offer her his services because he had been taught that that was his first allegiance. Cosby also quoted Lee as having said that there was no personal sacrifice he would not make to save his beloved country from war but that under no circumstances could he ever bare his sword against Virginia's sons.[14]

Lee arrived in San Antonio on February 16, the day that Texas troops seized federal property there.[15] On the same day, he posted a letter to one of his sons in which he declared, "Our country requires now every one to put forth all his ability, regardless of self."[16] But he had further occasions in San Antonio to voice his own intent of going with Virginia if that state seceded. Charles Anderson reported that Lee told him:

> I think it but due to myself to say that I cannot be moved . . . from my own sense of duty. . . . My loyalty to Virginia ought to take precedence over that which is due to the Federal Government. . . . If Virginia stands by the old Union, so will I. But, if she secedes (though I do not believe in secession as a constitutional right, nor that there is a sufficient cause for revolution), then I will still follow my native State with my sword, and if need be with my life.[17]

To another officer he spoke with less militancy: "When I get to Virginia I think the world will have one soldier less. I shall resign and go to planting corn."[18]

While in San Antonio, Lee was confronted by Texas commissioners who advised him that if he would resign his commission and join the Confederacy, he would have every facility, but if he refused, he would not be allowed transportation for his personal property. Indignant, Lee rejected the commissioners' proposition.[19] Hurrying then from San Antonio, Lee arrived in Alexandria on March 1, 1861, by which time additional ominous events had transpired. On February 4, Virginia had elected a convention to consider the issue of secession. On February 8, six of the seceded states, meeting in convention at Montgomery, Alabama, had adopted the provisional Constitution of the Confederate States of America. The same states were raising troops in preparation for war. And on March 4, after Lee's arrival in Virginia, Lincoln was inaugurated. Although his inaugural address was essentially conciliatory and free of the bombast that had characterized political discourse in preceding years, he did declare his intent to "hold, occupy, and possess the property, and places belonging to the government."[20] On March 6, 1861, the Confederate Congress authorized the raising of 100,000 volunteers for twelve months.[21]

Shortly after returning, Lee had a long interview with Gen. Winfield Scott, the general-in-chief.[22] What these Virginia friends discussed is not known, but Freeman's reconstruction – that the conversation included the issue of Lee's role in the Federal plans to deal with the crisis – is persuasive. In the middle of March, two governments offered commissions to Lee. On March 15 Confederate Secretary of War Leroy Pope Walker forwarded a direct offer of a commission as brigadier general, the highest rank then authorized by the Confederacy, together with a proposed oath and solicitation of a letter of acceptance. There is no record of any response, and Freeman states that Lee probably ignored the offer.[23] On March 16 President Lincoln issued a commission to Lee as colonel in the United States Army. This was received on March 28. Lee accepted the advancement from lieutenant colonel on March 30.[24]

Lee's service record, now in the National Archives, does not contain an oath of allegiance in connection with the colonelcy. His 1855 oath, executed at West Point when he accepted his commission as lieutenant colonel, was already on file. Sworn to before a justice of the peace on March 15, 1855, and signed by Lee, that oath reads as follows:

I, Robert E. Lee, appointed a Lieutenant Colonel of the Second Regt. of Cavalry in the Army of the United States, do solemnly swear, or affirm, that I will bear true allegiance to the United States of America, and that I will serve them honestly and faithfully against all their enemies or opposers whatsoever; and observe and obey the orders of the President of the United States, and the orders of the Officers appointed over me, according to the Rules and Articles for the government of the Armies of the United States.[25]

On April 12, in Charleston harbor, certain "opposers" fired on Fort Sumter, and for Lee events began to move rapidly and climactically. Three days later, identifying the seven seceded states as "combinations too powerful to be suppressed by ordinary course of judicial proceedings, or by powers vested in the Marshals by law," Lincoln summoned 75,000 militia. Although Lee may not have heard the news until a day or two later,[26] on April 17 the Virginia convention voted for secession, subject to a popular referendum on May 23, 1861. Also on the seventeenth, Lee received a letter from General Scott requesting him to call at Scott's office on the following day, together with a note from his Washington cousin John Lee, advising him that Francis P. Blair, Sr., an influential Republican and Lincoln adviser, desired to meet with him at Blair's home in Washington on April 18. It seems plain that Blair disclosed to Lee, in Freeman's description, the Federal plan to raise "a large army . . . to enforce the Federal law" and, on Lincoln's authority, offered command of that army to Lee. According to Lee's later account, he stated that "though opposed to secession and deprecating war, I could take no part in an invasion of the Southern states."[27] The Blair interview was followed by the meeting with General Scott, at which the general learned of Lee's position. Freeman reports that at this meeting Scott "expressed the belief that if Lee were going to resign he ought not to delay."[28] On the night of April 18, Virginia forces seized the Federal arsenal at Harpers Ferry.[29]

By April 19, the day after his meetings with Blair and Scott, Lee was fully aware of the Virginia convention's decision to secede.[30] On the following day, April 20, 1861, a day that saw Virginia's maneuver to seize the Norfolk navy yard, Lee posted his resignation to Secretary of War Simon Cameron and wrote a letter to the same effect to General Scott, referring to their meeting on April 18 and requesting that Scott recommend acceptance of his resignation.[31] The letter to Scott reiterated the imagery of which Lee had become fond: "Save in defence of my native State, I never desire again to draw my sword." Also on April 20, he wrote his sister Mrs. Anne Marshall of Baltimore, unionist in her sympathies, and his brother Smith Lee.[32] To his sister, he stated:

> The whole south is in a state of revolution, into which Virginia, after a long struggle, has been drawn; and, though I recognize no necessity for this state of things, and would have foreborne and pleaded to the end for redress of grievances, real or supposed, yet in my own person I had to meet the question whether I should take part against my native state.

With all my devotion to the Union, and the feeling of loyalty and duty of an American citizen, I have not been able to make up my mind to raise my hand against my relatives, my children, my home. I have therefore resigned my commission in the Army, and save in defence of my native State, with the sincere hope that my poor services may never be needed, I hope I may never be called on to draw my sword.

To Smith he wrote:

After the most anxious inquiry . . . I concluded to resign, and sent in my resignation this morning. I wished to wait till the Ordinance of Secession should be acted on by the people of Virginia; but war seems to have commenced, and I am liable at any time to be ordered on duty which I could not conscientiously perform. . . . I am now a private citizen, and have no other ambition than to remain at home. Save in defence of my native state, I have no desire ever again to draw my sword.

On Monday, April 22, 1861, having received Lee's resignation, Adjutant General Lorenzo Thomas disseminated a circular to the various headquarters departments in Washington soliciting information regarding the status of Lee's financial accounts. All were in order. On April 25 Lee's resignation was accepted.[33] According to paragraph 24 of the Regulations of the United States Army, "No officer will be considered out of service on the tender of his resignation, until it shall have been duly accepted by the proper authority." Paragraph 28 states that "in time of war, or with an army in the field, resignations shall take effect within thirty days from the date of the order of acceptance."[34] But Lee disregarded these restrictions. Between the posting of his resignation on April 20 and its acceptance on April 25, Lee drew his sword with marked alacrity.

Characterizing Lee's promptitude in moving from the United States Army to the armed forces of seceded Virginia, Freeman accurately observes, "There was no questioning, no holding back, no delay." Another of Lee's biographers, Clifford Dowdey, also commented on this point: "Considering that Lee, at 54, had spent 36 years of his adult life in the service of the United States Army . . . he responded to the call of

his state with remarkably little to do."[35] Having sent his letter of resignation on the morning of April 20, Lee received a letter that same
evening from Judge John Robertson, who had for several months held
the office of commissioner for Virginia and was an agent for Virginia's
Governor John Letcher. Robertson requested a meeting with Lee the
following day. Lee arranged the meeting for 1:00 P.M. on April 21,
agreeing to meet the judge in Alexandria. Because Robertson was
unexpectedly detained in Washington, this meeting did not take place.
But on the night of the April 21 a message was received from Robertson
inviting Lee to meet in Richmond with Governor Letcher. Also on the
twenty-first, Virginia's Executive Council recommended to the governor Lee's appointment as commander of the Virginia forces.

Lee responded at once to Robertson's April 21 message, notifying
Robertson that he would accompany him on the train to Richmond the
following day. Arriving in the capital on the afternoon of April 22, Lee
was offered and accepted appointment as the commander of the military and naval forces of Virginia, with the rank of major general, which
appointment was confirmed by the Virginia convention that night.[36]

Vice President Alexander H. Stephens, whose well-known "corner-
stone speech" of March 1861 had proclaimed that the Confederacy's
foundation rested on the great truth of black slavery, had been appointed by President Davis as special commissioner to Virginia on
April 19, 1861, the day before Lee sent in his resignation from the
United States Army. Governor Letcher had previously advised Davis of
the desire of Virginia to enter into a defensive and offensive alliance
with the Confederacy. Dispatched to Richmond, Stephens was instructed by Davis to be receptive to the alliance and to negotiate with
Virginia on the premise of that state's becoming a part of the Confederacy. Stephens arrived in Richmond on April 22 and was present
during part of the activity looking toward Lee's appointment on that
day. Also on April 22 Virginia's secretary of state sent a communication
to Jefferson Davis stating, "I am directed by the Governor to inform you
that Colonel Lee is here. The Governor has sent in his nomination as
commander of the land and naval forces of Virginia, with rank of major-
general. Nomination will be confirmed."[37] Promptly after his confirmation by the convention, Lee met with Stephens and agreed that Virginia
should join the Confederacy.[38]

Once commissioned by Virginia, Lee proceeded immediately to organize the state's military establishment as events increasingly committed his sword to war on the United States. Thus, he took de facto command of troops from other Confederate states as they were forwarded to Virginia.[39] As this activity progressed, the Virginia convention perfected the relationship between Virginia and the Confederacy. On April 25 the convention ratified a pact for temporary union and accepted the Confederate Constitution, pending the May 23 vote of the people of Virginia on the issue of secession. The treaty ceded control of the military operations of Virginia to the president of the Confederacy. On May 7 the Confederate Congress, and President Jefferson Davis, accepted Virginia into the Confederate States of America. On May 10 the Confederate War Department placed Lee in charge of all Confederate forces in Virginia, and on May 14 Lee was commissioned a brigadier general in the regular army of the Confederate States.[40] On May 23 the voters of Virginia approved the secession ordinance. On June 8 a proclamation by Governor Letcher formally transferred Virginia's military forces to the Confederacy.[41]

And so the fateful cycle was completed. Col. Robert E. Lee of the United States Army had become Brigadier General Lee of the Confederate States Army. The change had taken place swiftly, and the main points in the rush of events were as follows:

March 30, 1861:
    Lee accepts the Federal colonelcy from President Lincoln.
April 20, 1861:
    Lee mails his letter of resignation from the United States Army.
April 22, 1861:
    Lee accepts Virginia's commission as major general.
April 25, 1861:
    Lee's resignation is accepted by the United States Army; Virginia accepts the Confederate Constitution.
May 14, 1861:
    Lee commissioned brigadier general in the Confederate States Army.

There passed just twenty days from acceptance of a new Federal commission to resignation, and two more days to joining the forces preparing for war against the Federal government! The intervening events had been Lincoln's call for militia on April 15 and Virginia's secession on April 17. In view of Lee's own statements, his conduct, and the timing of his move from loyalty to the United States to making war against it, what may be said about Lee's decision?

Before turning to other aspects of the matter, an interesting related question must be considered. As has been emphasized, approximately forty-eight hours passed between Lee's posting of his resignation on April 20 and his acceptance of the Virginia commission on April 22. Had Lee, in fact, been in communication with Virginia authorities before he resigned? Had he been negotiating with them before April 20? There is no direct documentary evidence in answer to these questions, but the questions are natural and fair, and an examination of such evidence as exists is suggestive of some answers.

April 20, the day that Lee wrote and dispatched his resignation, was a Saturday. On the evening of the same day, he received the initial communication from Judge Robertson, Governor Letcher's representative, requesting an interview to take place on Sunday, April 21. Lee responded at once, setting the meeting for Sunday in Alexandria. Robertson did not appear on Sunday but that night Lee received an explanation from Robertson and an invitation, in the name of the governor, to go to Richmond for a conference with the governor. Lee again responded at once, saying that he would meet Robertson the next day, April 22, in Alexandria, in time to travel with him to Richmond. The two men traveled together on April 22 to Richmond, where Lee was offered and accepted the Virginia commission and, on the same date, was confirmed by the convention. Having been posted on the twentieth, Lee's resignation was not on the twenty-second a public document. Indeed, as Lee conferred with the governor of Virginia, accepted Virginia's commission, and won confirmation from the convention, the War Department of the United States was receiving the resignation and processing it so that it could be accepted on April 25.

The key parties to the transaction were the Richmond authorities – the Executive Council and the governor – and Lee. Regarding the Richmond authorities, it may be argued that the Executive Council would not have formally recommended the appointment to the governor on April 21 or the governor have invited Lee to come to Richmond on April 21 with the intent of offering the commission had they been unaware of his willingness to accept. It seems unlikely that either the Executive Council in making its recommendation or the governor in making the offer would have risked a rejection. If they were not unaware of Lee's inclination, how and when and by whom had they been made aware of his intended response to the offer? Regarding Lee, the promptness with which he initially agreed on April 20 to see Robertson and then on the twenty-first agreed to go to Richmond with him on the following day are suggestive. It seems unlikely that he would have done these things, hastily boarding the train for Richmond on the twenty-second, without knowledge of the governor's purpose and a personal decision not to frustrate that purpose.

Do the events surrounding Lee's resignation and acceptance of the Virginia commission constitute a "program" as that term is used by modern politicians to describe an arrangement that has been made and assented to by the parties in advance? In this regard, the time frame must again be stated: resignation posted April 20 and a message from the commissioner for Virginia on the same day; Richmond's commitment April 21 and Lee's agreement to go to Richmond that same day; Adjutant General Thomas's War Department circular April 22; Lee's acceptance of the Virginia commission and confirmation on April 22. If there was a "program," it would have to have been communicated and put in place prior to the resignation.

In this respect, Lee's prompt manifestation of his awareness of and sensitivity to the narrow time frame of his activities is interesting. On May 2, 1861, in a letter to his wife, he acknowledged receipt of Washington's acceptance of his resignation. Noting that the resignation stated that it was to be effective on April 25, Lee wrote, "I resigned on the 20th & wished it to take effect on that day. I cannot consent to its running on farther & . . . must receive no pay if they tender it beyond that day."[42] In 1868 Lee gave a different date as that beyond which no pay was accepted, according to Col. William Allan's memorandum of a conversation with the general at that time. Publicly criticized in 1868 by former secretary of war Cameron because of his 1861 acts, Lee asserted that he had not drawn pay from the United States after his return from Texas. This return took place on or about March 1, 1861, a more innocent date than April 20.[43]

In 1868, in connection with a United States Senate debate about the seating of a newly elected senator from Maryland, the question of Lee's conduct associated with the Blair offer of Federal command on April 18 and his resignation on April 20 came up incidentally and negatively. For this reason, on February 25, 1868, Lee wrote to his friend, incumbent Maryland senator Reverdy Johnson, stating his version of the incidents between April 18 and 22, 1861. After noting that his resignation was proffered on April 20, he asserted: "I *then had no other intention than to pass the remainder of my life as a private citizen.* Two days afterwards, upon the invitation of the Governor of Virginia, *I repaired to Richmond; found that the Convention then in session had passed the ordinance* withdrawing the State from the Union; and accepted the commission of commander of its forces, which was tendered to me" (emphasis added).[44]

Both the accuracy and the candor of this communication are open to question. Lee had been offered high military command by the United States and the Confederacy. He had said that he would defend "any State" that was invaded, and certainly he would defend Virginia. Lincoln had called for 75,000 militia on April 15. Virginia had voted to secede on April 17. This vote was well known, a newspaper headline, by April 19 at the latest. Lee was surely aware of it on April 20 when he resigned. Bearing in mind that he agreed on the day of his resignation to see Robertson, agreed on the next day to go to Richmond to see the governor, and accepted the Virginia commission only two days after resigning, it seems unlikely that on April 20 he had "no other intention than to pass the remainder of [his] life as a private citizen." And it was simply not true that he "found that the Convention . . . had passed the ordinance" when he arrived in Richmond on April 22; he knew of the ordinance previously and accompanied the governor's representative to Richmond with that knowledge. The lack of credibility evident in this letter about the critical April days does nothing to dispel the impression that there was a preresignation arrangement with Virginia.[45]

Beyond the issue of preresignation negotiations, what else does Lee's secession say about the historic, as opposed to the mythic, Lee? In the first place, it speaks to the matter of Lee the Virginian. Appearing before the congressional subcommittee in 1866, Lee explained his view "that the act of Virginia, in withdrawing herself from the United States, carried me along as a citizen of Virginia, and that her laws and her acts were binding on me."[46] Freeman and the other biographers embrace this Virginia loyalty as the sine qua non of Lee's seceding. Lee's sense of being a Virginian was undoubtedly a factor in his decision, but unless one is to conclude that Lee would have done literally anything that Virginia asked, surely the issue of his seceding is more complicated than that. It is at the outset important to consider secession as a historical phenomenon.

Secession did not exist in a vacuum. It was an effect, not a cause, the consequence or extension of certain anterior beliefs and attitudes. In the final analysis, secession was a political technique with a specific purpose: insulating slavery from the popular-government political processes of the Union. By diluting the American constituency, the slave states intended to protect slavery from its political enemies. Secession was, therefore, analogous to gerrymandering. Dissatisfied with the prospects for slavery in the context of the democratic processes of the Union, the slave states moved to vary the boundaries of those participating in these processes so that proslavery forces would have a majority. No longer a part of the slave states' nation, the political enemies of slavery were to be disenfranchised. All of this was plain at the time. In advocating Virginia's secession, the *Richmond Dispatch* noted on March 23, 1861, that "adhering to the North . . . puts our slave system at the mercy of an abolition majority."[47] In an 1864 interview with the Northern journalist Edmund Kirke, Jefferson Davis forthrightly declared, "We seceded to rid ourselves of the rule of the majority."[48] And Robert Barnwell Rhett, who had been one of South Carolina's most adamant secessionists, explained in 1864, "We did not choose to live in political association with a people who would not leave us at peace with our institutions. . . . Therefore we cast off our political association with them."[49]

Prior to the war, as the record makes clear, Lee was distinctly opposed to secession. When he wrote on January 23, 1861, that it was "nothing but revolution," he intended to disparage it; and his other prewar communications are consistent with this letter in their expressions of disapproval of Southern efforts to dissolve the Union. But opposition to secession did not distinguish Lee. In every seceding state there were other such men who opposed secession but eventually came to lead the Confederacy. Thus, Alexander Stephens supported Stephen A. Douglas in the 1860 election and spoke against secession to the Georgia convention. Even Jefferson Davis attempted to unite the Democrats in 1860 to avoid Lincoln's election and frustrate the radical Southerners' plan to use Lincoln's election as the ground for secession.[50] But Davis and Stephens, like Lee, embraced the essential premises of the secessionists, the anterior beliefs and attitudes that led to secession. Except for the advocacy of secession before the fact, their beliefs and attitudes were indistinguishable from those of the fire-eating Southern partisans. Once secession became a fact, these beliefs and attitudes led inexorably out of the Union and into leadership of the Confederacy at war with the United States. In Lee's case, siding with the South seems to have been almost against his better judgment and surely against his commitment as a soldier. But entrapped by the beliefs and attitudes that he shared with the secessionists, he went.

What were these essential premises, the beliefs and attitudes that led Lee out of the Union in spite of his prewar objection to secession? There are four points on which he seems to have agreed with the secessionists, and each of them was profound in terms of his decision: slavery as an institution, the right of the slavers to plant slavery in the territories, Southern sectionalism, and, bound up with these, a qualified loyalty to the nation because of allegiance to one's state.

Lee's feelings about slavery were discussed at length in the preceding chapter: although he on occasion rhetorically characterized it as an evil, he assumed a laissez-faire stance, deeply resented Northern antislavery agitation, and ultimately stated late in the war that slavery was the best relationship that could exist between the races. Thus, he shared with the secessionists a commitment to slavery as an institution.

Since Lincoln and the Republicans were committed to protecting slavery in the states in which it existed, the immediate issue was slavery's expansion into the territories. The secessionists insisted that this expansion should be permitted, as did Lee. As has been noted, in his 1856 letter to his wife, Lee cheered President Pierce's message to Congress defending the Kansas-Nebraska Act and the repeal of the

Missouri Compromise. Four years later, he applauded Buchanan's proposed constitutional amendments, one of which would have paved the way for additional slave states to be carved from the territories. That proposal, Lee wrote to Custis, was "eminently just." In that letter, even his semantics were those of the secessionists; he stated his resentment of the Northerners' "denial of equal rights to the common territories of the commonwealth." Translated into practical politics, this superficially plausible concept meant that slavery was exempt from majority rule and the will of Congress. It would spread regardless of the views of a majority of the people of the United States.

Lee's embracing of the common property theory regarding the territories is significant. According to that theory, the federal government's jurisdiction over the territories was that of an agent or guardian for the states, who owned the territories in common. As such, the federal government was obligated to allow citizens from the states to move to the territories with their slaves and to require the territorial governments to protect that slave property. This theory meant that the Missouri Compromise was unconstitutional. Logically, the theory also contradicted the principle of popular sovereignty. Because the federal government could not exclude slavery from the public domain, it also could not grant the power to exclude it to a territorial legislature, a creature of the federal government. As Gerald W. Wolff has noted, the common property theory "was the most extreme position to evolve in the South regarding the rights of slaveowners in the territories."[51] It was Lee's position.

The third premise shared by Lee and the secessionists was sectionalism. In regard to sectional feelings, Freeman – bent on separating Lee from the classic secessionist position – makes one of his most gross misrepresentations of the man: "He did not admit the unity of Southern interests. . . . He had no regard at the time [prior to the secession movement] for the South as a section, much less as a confederation."[52] It is necessary to refer again to his 1856 letter to his wife. There he used a typical Southern euphemism in referring to the efforts of "certain people of the North to interfere with . . . the domestic institutions of the South," and he alluded negatively to the "descendants of [the] pilgrim fathers." It is a letter that, fairly read, suggests sectional consciousness and animosities, a letter that could have been written by any main-stream Southerner who defended slavery. Four years later, Lee's letter to Custis of December 14, 1860, acknowledged his "feeling the aggressions of the North." To Martha Custis Williams on January 22, 1861, he said that "the South justly complains of the aggressions of the North." In a letter the following day, he reiterated this theme, remarking, "The South . . . has been aggrieved by the acts of the North."

In terms of his sectional feelings, as distinguished from his feelings for Virginia in particular, the letter of January 23 is especially noteworthy in two respects. In the first place, and for the first time, he stated that he "would defend any State if her rights were invaded." In light of his expressed belief that "the North" had aggressed against "the South," and the fact that five Southern states had already seceded by January 23, it is apparent that Virginia's secession was not by itself decisive in his thoughts. In the second place, this letter makes no reference to Virginia's secession as dictating his own role. Instead, having set forth a constitutional argument against secession, he asserted, "A Union that can only be maintained by swords and bayonets . . . has no charm for me." Then, with regard to himself, he wrote that, "If the Union is dissolved, and the Government disrupted, I shall return to my native State and share the miseries of my people, and save in defence will draw my sword on none." The point is that dissolution of the Union (which in a sense had already occurred), not Virginia's secession, was to cause his leaving the United States Army. That these Southern considerations were affecting him in decisive ways is verified by his own 1868 account of his response to Francis Blair's April 18, 1861, offer of a Federal command. He told Blair, he recounted, that he "could take no part in an invasion of the Southern states." Significantly, he was unaware at the time of Virginia's vote to secede.[53] Surely it is plain that Lee was a Southerner harboring Southern sectional feelings.

Closely related to Lee's Southern sectional consciousness and sense of grievance was the final point of connection between him and the secessionists. This was the feeling of allegiance to one's state. Allan Nevins has essayed a convincing description of the prewar culture and sociology of the slave states, a description that suggests parochialism. He finds that the South was comparatively rural, fundamentalist Prot-

estant, aristocratic, socially static, and economically lagging – and intensely bound up with slavery. The differences between the sections he
summarizes as "the differences between a free labor system and a slave
labor system, between a semi-industrialized economy of high productiveness and an agrarian economy of low productiveness." And, referring to Southerners, he adds: "Clear-eyed men realized that in nearly
all material elements of civilization the North had far outstripped them;
and they knew that slavery stood indicted not merely as a moral wrong,
but as responsible for this painful lag in progress." According to Nevins,
the consequence of this was that "in the Southern mind a defensive
mechanism clicked into operation."[54]

These characteristics of the South, perhaps especially the defensive-
ness, contributed to localism, a feeling of intense state loyalty. Nevins's
description of the situation seems directly applicable to Lee:

> The Southerners loved the Union, for their forefathers helped
> build it, and the gravestones of their patriot soldiers strewed the
> land. But they wanted a Union in which they could preserve their
> peculiar institutions, ancient customs, and well-loved ways of life
> and thought. They knew that all the main forces of modern society
> were pressing to create a more closely unified nation, and to make
> institutions homogeneous even if not absolutely uniform. Against
> this they recoiled; they wanted a hegemony, a loose confederacy,
> not a unified nation and a standardized civilization. They regarded
> the Union as an association of sovereign states and an alliance of
> regions that possessed national attributes.[55]

This was the Union that Lee loved, and his feeling for it gave way when
the alliance between it and the South and Virginia gave way.

As the crisis approached, as Lee could foresee a conflict in his loyalties, he decided on his paramount loyalty. The first thing in the record
is his mid-December 1860 statement to Charles Anderson about what
he had been taught to believe. Then he spoke with Captain Johnson on
February 13, 1861, at Fort Mason, remarking that he would fight "in
defence of my native state." To Captain Cosby he said essentially the
same thing a few days later. On February 16, 1861, he spoke again to
Charles Anderson in San Antonio. And on April 18, 1861, he declared

himself to Francis Blair. Two days later he resigned from the United States Army, and in two more days he had become a Virginia major general, a capacity in which his loyalty was unqualified.

Lee's statements and his conduct during the period prior to his decision to side with the South point up several interesting characteristics of the man. Biographers and historians have not fully considered these characteristics, but it is reasonable to do so.

To begin with, it is difficult to square his patriotic statements with what he was intending to do, whether or not that intent was predicated on the fact of secession generally or Virginia's secession. On November 24, 1860, as has been said, he wrote, "I could easily lay down my life for [the country's] safety." To Captain Cosby, in February 1861, he remarked that there was no personal sacrifice he would not make to save his beloved country, but he also said that he would go with Virginia if it seceded. On February 16, 1861, he advised one of his sons, "Our country requires now every one to put forth all his ability, regardless of self." Was this simply rhetoric, or did these statements mean something? If the latter, it is plain that his country was not asking for his life but was to ask that he not make war against it. The statement regarding his willingness to sacrifice for his country, coupled with his declaration of paramount Virginia loyalty, at least candidly expressed the limits of his willingness. His country was indeed in need of "all his ability," but this did not mean his ability to make war against it.

Lee's rhetoric also suggests a gift for self-delusion. Apart from his unrealistic reiteration of the draw-my-sword-no-more theme, he characterized his situation in curious ways. In February 1861, after seven states had seceded, he spoke of leaving the army and "planting corn," a proposal that had nothing to do with the reality of his personal situation. At about the same time, he stated that he might have to "carry a musket" for Virginia, a radical understatement of what he must have known to be his likely role. On April 20, 1861, having been offered high military command by the United States and by the Confederacy, he told his sister that he sincerely hoped his "poor services may never be needed" and advised his brother that he was "now a private citizen, and have no other ambition than to remain at home." Surely at an intellectual level Lee knew that none of these statements characterized the real situation. The real issue was whether he was to become a military leader of the Confederacy at war with the United States, and he was fully aware that this was the issue.

Lee's apparent capacity to beguile himself extended to beguiling others. He told Francis Blair, on April 18, 1861, that he would not take part in an invasion of the South. He said nothing about what the March 15 offer of the Confederacy's highest commission really meant: that he might very well become a military leader of the Southern forces at war with the Union. Had his sister been aware, as he was, that the United States and the Confederacy were competing for his services, she might reasonably have questioned the sincerity of his statement that he hoped his services would not be needed. Only two days after writing this statement, he was a major general in the Virginia forces.

Of more significance in terms of deluding himself or others is his April 20, 1861, letter to General Scott. As has been indicated, on March 15, 1861, Lee had been offered a Confederate commission, a commission that he had, according to Freeman, neither accepted nor rejected. He must have known by that time that Virginia was likely to join with the Confederacy in a civil war. This was, in Freeman's words, "a manifest necessity of war."[56] He was two days away from being the major general commanding Virginia's forces. In short, he surely knew that he was likely to become a full-fledged military leader of the Confederacy. But his old friend and mentor Scott was told only that "save in defence of my native State, I never desire again to draw my sword."

When all is said and done, it appears that Lee had an unusually high tolerance for ambiguous loyalty. Thus, as has been said, he had decided as early as December 1860 that he would secede if Virginia did. On January 23, 1861, he remarked that if the Union was dissolved, he would go back to Virginia, without conditioning this on Virginia's seceding. In the same letter, he made his statement that he would defend any state whose rights were invaded. On March 15 he was offered the Confederate commission. Yet he accepted Lincoln's colonelcy on March 30 despite his several mental reservations and the qualifications to his allegiance. He met with General Scott in early March and again on April 18 and discussed the situation, still without resigning. Resigning then on April 20, he immediately accepted the Virginia commission. His prompt letter insisting that his resignation was effective on April 20, the day it was written and mailed, rather than when it was accepted, suggests his own awareness of the narrow time frame within which he was acting. Sensitive to this same time frame, referring to Lee's arrival at Arlington on March 1, Freeman attests that "there was nothing to compromise Lee's status as an officer of the United States Army."[57] This defensive assertion is open to question, especially keeping in mind the desperate circumstances of the United States at that time. Indeed, as Lee himself had written, it was a time when the country required everyone to apply his best abilities selflessly in the national interest. But Lee walked a very fine line between plainly conflicting loyalties. His allegiance at this critical time was cast along these lines: I may or may not support the United States, and I may or may not make war against the United States, depending on what other people decide to do. One may reasonably regard this as compromising his status as an officer in the United States Army.

Conflict of interest is a well-established concept. It exists when an agent attempts faithfully to represent two principals whose interests are adverse. It is presumably conceded that this may not be done because in attempting to serve adverse principals the agent must compromise the interests of one or both. But the concept goes beyond this. If, for example, an agent for one principal is considering employment by an adverse principal, and temporizes with his choice, he may while temporizing become privy to sensitive information from the incumbent principal. He receives such information because it is assumed by the incumbent principal that the agent is committed to the incumbent principal. If he then changes his agency to the competing principal, the incumbent principal may be unfairly disadvantaged because of the information that the agent carries with him to the new principal.

This seems to have been Lee's situation between the time of his return to Virginia on March 1 and his resignation on April 20. In another context, William James has written, "If we waver in our answer, that, too, is a choice." And there was nothing inevitable about Lee's being in a compromising position. He could have avoided it in at least two ways, by resigning on his return to Washington in view of his intent to go with the South in certain circumstances, or by telling Blair and Scott, up front, of his dilemma and refusing to risk their imparting to him any information that might be useful to the Confederacy. Lee did neither of these things. Instead, he met with both Blair and Scott, and it was left to Scott to recommend that the time had come, in the light of his ambivalence, for Lee to resign.

It is important to note that the Lee tradition does not argue that Lee found himself in a no-holds-barred, revolutionary context in view of secession and the incipient Civil War. This contention would, incidentally, be a reasonable one. But the tradition and Lee partisans like Freeman present the case on an entirely different footing: they insist on the strict propriety of Lee's actions in relation to the United States.

An observation on Lee and his commitment to "honor" is appropriate here. Lee had an unusual gift for self-justification. This is not to suggest that he was not conscientious; to characterize one's actions in a self-serving way is a deeply human tendency, and it is typically done conscientiously. It is what one genuinely believes. Lee invariably credited himself with honor. When alternative courses were presented to him, he did not, according to his own accounts, choose one course and reject the other because of his perception of their relative merits, or because one seemed preferable to the other. Instead, he characterized the course that he had chosen as honorable and the other course as dishonorable. Unless one would have had him act dishonorably, there had, therefore, been no choice; he simply had done the right thing rather than the wrong thing. "Honor," in short, became Lee's word for what he wanted to do and what he had in fact done.

In view of the many quotations throughout this book in which Lee uses the word "honor," two examples in which he has recourse to the notion of honor in justifying his actions will suffice. In the previously noted letter to Martha Custis Williams in January 1861, as the collision developed between the seceding states and the Union, he stated that "there is no sacrifice I am not ready to make for the preservation of the Union save that of honour." In context, this meant that if he left the Union it was because that was the only honorable thing to do. In June 1868, with "the South desolate and disfranchised, and with her sons

dead on a hundred battlefields," according to Freeman, he stated to
Wade Hampton: "I did only what my duty demanded. I could have
taken no other course without dishonor."[58] Biographers of Lee have
taken their cue from the general's use of the word "honor" to describe
his own actions. Just as he invariably credited himself with honor, his
biographers have found a sense of honor to be his most pronounced
characteristic. This calls for some inquiry into the concept of honor.

Lee's sensitivity to the concept was not unusual. It derived directly
from the social system of the Southern leadership class. In his 1982
study, *Southern Honor*, Bertram Wyatt-Brown explains that "honor"
was at the root of this system's complex taboos and imperatives. Southern honor, he states, was a combination of three related factors: the
inner conviction of self-worth, the claim of that self-assessment before
the public, and the assessment of the claim by the public based on the
behavior of the claimant, that is, reputation. Concerning the role of
honor in Southern society, Wyatt-Brown says, "Honor resides in the
individual as his understanding of who he is and where he belongs in
the ordered ranks of society. . . . It is, at least in traditional terms, both
internal to the claimant, so that it motivates him toward behavior that is
socially approved, and external to him, because only by the response of
observers can he ordinarily understand himself." As related to Lee's
decision to secede, another of Wyatt-Brown's characterizations seems
apt: "The internal man and the external realities of his existence are
united in such a way that he knows no other good or evil except that
which the collective group designates."[59]

A letter of June 10, 1863, to President Davis – a letter that we will
need to consider again in later chapters – discloses other aspects of
Lee's concept of honor. Among other subjects, this letter contained
Lee's advice concerning the Northern political situation. He wrote:

> Under these circumstances, we should neglect no *honorable* means
> of dividing and weakening our enemies. . . . It seems to me that the
> most effectual mode of accomplishing this object, now within our
> reach, is to give all the encouragement we can, *consistently with
> truth*, to the rising peace party of the North.

Nor do I think we should, in this connection, make nice distinctions between those who declare for peace unconditionally and those who advocate it as a means of restoring the Union, however much we prefer the former.

We should bear in mind that the friends of peace at the North must make concessions to the earnest desire . . . of their countrymen for a restoration of the Union, and that to hold out such a result as an inducement is essential to the success of their party.

Should the belief that peace will bring back the Union become general, the war would no longer be supported, and that, after all, is what we are interested in bringing about. When peace is proposed to us, it will be time enough to discuss its terms, and it is not the part of prudence to spurn the proposition in advance, merely because those who wish to make it believe, or affect to believe, that it will result in bringing us back to the Union. *We entertain no such apprehension*, nor doubt that the desire of our people for a distinct and independent national existence will prove as steadfast under the influence of peaceful measures as it has shown itself in the midst of war. (Emphasis added.)[60]

This, of course, is a prescription for being untruthful "consistently with truth." The point is not that the tactic of misleading the North was wrong or immoral. It was, in the context of the war, an appropriate tactic. The point is that Lee was deluding himself as he had done in his secession correspondence. He was, in fact, advocating guile but characterizing it as truthful and honorable. And Lee persisted in this contradiction. On April 29, 1865, in an interview with Thomas M. Cook of the *New York Herald*, Lee stated that the South had been putting out peace feelers for the past two years, "looking for some word or expression of compromise or conciliation from the North *upon which they might base a return to the Union*, their own political views being considered" (emphasis added).[61] This was simply not true, and Lee surely knew that it was not true.

According to Wyatt-Brown, "Honor is . . . self-regarding in character."[62] In Lee's case this was certainly true. Crediting himself with honor was therefore self-serving, a convenient label, as has been suggested, for what he wanted to do or had already done. Lee's honor was therefore on occasion simply rhetorical, a matter of saying the magic word. "Honor" was an incantation; it was self-fulfilling. Lee was honorable because he said so.

Finally, we should consider Lee's later rationale for his decision to secede. His comments during and after the war seem not to support the Lee-the-Virginian thesis. They are at best ambiguous in that regard. As early as September 9, 1861, an order exhorted his soldiers in West Virginia on the ground that they were fighting for "the right of self-government, liberty, and peace."[63] Writing to one of his daughters in December 1861, and referring to the Confederacy, he said that "all must be endured to accomplish our independence and maintain our self-government."[64] And on the eve of Appomattox, he told Gen. William N. Pendleton, "We had, I was satisfied, sacred principles to defend."[65] Independence – the right of the South to govern itself – and freedom had become his motives.

Freeman states that "as he fought for the Southern cause . . . he came to see its meaning. . . . Lee absorbed the Southern constitutional argument and was convinced by it."[66] Whether or not this was so, by November 1865 Lee had reconsidered his prewar view that secession was treasonable, a revolution. The Englishman Saunders wrote: "The great Southern general gave me, at some length, his feelings with regard to the abstract right of secession. This right, he told me, was held as a constitutional maxim at the South. As to its exercise at the time on the part of the South, he was distinctly opposed, and it was not until Lincoln issued a proclamation for 75,000 men to invade the South, which was deemed clearly unconstitutional, that Virginia withdrew from the United States."[67] Since Lincoln's decision to resist secession could only have been unconstitutional if the states had the constitutional right to secede, the implication is plain that such a right existed. A letter to C. Chauncey Burr, dated January 5, 1866 – in which Lee wrote that "all that the South ever desired was that the Union, as established by our forefathers, should be preserved, and that the government as originally organized be administered in purity and truth" – is capable of several interpretations.[68] These words may suggest that the right of secession existed, that the slaveholders had a right to slavery in the territories, or that the states had the right to reject the decisions of the federal government. The first inference, and presumably the concept of the states' paramount power, appears in a letter of July 9, 1866, to Capt. James May. "I had no other guide," Lee wrote, "nor had I any other object than the defense of those principles of American liberty upon which the constitutions of the several States were originally founded; and, unless they are strictly observed, I fear there will be an end to Republican government in this country."[69] Later in the same year, he stated to C. W. Law that the Southern cause had been "constitutional government."[70] The same view is expressed in a letter written on February 10, 1870, the year of his death, to his friend Gen. E. G. W. Butler of St. Louis:

> I am more than ever impressed with the necessity of the people of the South attending to their material prosperity, building up their individual fortunes, and taking care less of federal politics and more of their own affairs. Had this course been followed from the beginning of the government; had the resources of the states been fully developed, and the white population been increased to the extent it might; the Southern construction and the constitution and its views of federal politics would have been listened to with that attention which its weight in the councils of the nation entitled it to. It was from the want of this might and power that it failed when it attempted to maintain its views.[71]

Douglas Southall Freeman, perhaps the ultimate Virginian, remarked that Lee "had been a Virginian before he had been a soldier."[72] Like his statement that the decision for secession was one the general was born to make, this assertion somehow fails to tell us anything meaningful about Lee's course of conduct. It appears, in fact, that he was not born to secede. He did so because of certain attitudes and convictions. Although Virginia's secession was a critical element in his final resolution, and in the manner in which he was to become a military leader of the Confederacy, he was essentially committed to the Southern cause before Virginia seceded by virtue of his feelings about slavery and its expansion and by his sense of sectional loyalty. It is to be remembered that he had said he would defend any state, would draw his sword in defense if the Union was dissolved, and would "take no part in an invasion of the Southern states."

The conventional image of Lee presents him as "the Virginian," pure and simple, an abstract man somehow detached from the conflict of his fellows but born to do what Virginia asked of him, regardless of the merits, his feelings, logic, or the consequences. Tragically and nobly, he was driven into serving the South and into his Civil War role. And as the victim of tragic forces, he had no responsibility for the consequences of his acts. He is not accountable, because he was "the Virginian" and a man of "honor": there was nothing he could do except what he did. So mythmaking would have it, but the historical record suggests otherwise.

CHAPTER FOUR

General Lee

The 1989 edition of the *Encyclopedia Americana* states that Lee was "one of the truly gifted commanders of all time," "one of the greatest, if not the greatest, soldier who ever spoke the English language." The entry for Lee in the 1989 *Encyclopaedia Britannica* reflects a similar judgment. According to the 1988 revised edition of the *Civil War Dictionary*, Lee "earned rank with history's most distinguished generals." These evaluations reflect the consensus of standard reference sources. Those sources also agree that Lee's lieutenants, not Lee, were responsible for his army's failures.

The standard reference books do not stand alone. The excellence of his generalship is a Lee dogma and is widely asserted. In 1963, Marshall W. Fishwick wrote, "In his field he was a genius – probably the greatest one the American nation has produced." *Lee Takes Command*, volume 7 of the popular Time-Life Civil War series, published in 1984, reports that as of the Confederate victory at Second Bull Run, "Lee was well on his way to becoming the greatest soldier of the Civil War." In 1985 the respected popular journal *Civil War Times Illustrated* devoted an entire monthly issue to Lee under the title "Robert E. Lee: The Life and Career of the Master General." A juvenile biography of the general published in 1988 starts a new generation out with the classic, simple message: Lee was "a military genius," a "nearly invincible general." In this same biography, James Longstreet, Richard S. Ewell, and Jeb Stuart are characterized as "defective." Only Stonewall Jackson is seen as a worthy lieutenant. Indeed, the perennial question of why the South lost the war is finally disposed of: readers are told that Jackson's death at Chancellorsville "would unravel the entire Southern cause."[1] With only occasional and essentially unheeded dissent, a belief in Lee's paramount greatness as a general is the most intense and enduring aspect of the Lee tradition.[2]

Douglas Southall Freeman has stated the case for the tradition. He recounts the situation before Richmond when Lee took command of the Army of Northern Virginia on June 1, 1862, and his saving of the capital at that time. Noting the repulse of four major Federal offensives against Richmond and the delay of a fifth such effort by means of the Pennsylvania campaign, Freeman recites Lee's ten major battles – Gaines's Mill through Spotsylvania – explaining that six of these he won "but only at Gettysburg had he met with definite defeat, and even there he clouded the title of his adversary to a clear-cut victory." Freeman continues:

> During the twenty-four months when he had been free to employ open manoeuvre, a period that had ended with Cold Harbor, he had sustained approximately 103,000 casualties and had inflicted 145,000. Holding, as he usually had, to the offensive, his combat losses had been greater in proportion to his numbers than those of the Federals, but he had demonstrated how strategy may increase an opponent's casualties, for his losses included only 16,000 prisoners, whereas he had taken 38,000. Chained at length to the Richmond defenses, he had saved the capital from capture for ten months. All this he had done in the face of repeated defeats for the Southern troops in nearly every other part of the Confederacy. . . . These difficulties of the South would have been even worse had not the Army of Northern Virginia occupied so much of the thought and armed strength of the North. Lee is to be judged, in fact, not merely by what he accomplished with his own troops but by what he prevented the hosts of the Union from doing sooner elsewhere.[3]

In view of these facts – and, except for the argumentative statement suggesting that Gettysburg was not a clear-cut victory for the Union, they are facts – one questions the traditional view of Lee's generalship at his peril. At the outset, therefore, it is appropriate to define the scope of the inquiry undertaken here, to set forth what the issue is *not* as well as what the issue is.

In the first place, this book accepts the fact that Lee's campaign and battle strategy and his tactical performance were largely, although not invariably, brilliant. Granting this brilliance, there nevertheless are grounds for questioning his generalship. The questions are in reference to the grand strategy of the war from the Confederacy's standpoint. In order to evaluate Lee's performance as a general, it is imperative that we distinguish between military *tactics* and military *strategy*, including some refinements of the latter term. Definitions are therefore required.

To paraphrase Clausewitz, tactics concern the use of armed forces in battle. Gen. Henry W. Halleck's *Elements of Military Art and Science* states the same thing more elaborately: "We have defined tactics to be the art of bringing troops into action, or of moving them in the presence of the enemy." A contemporary military dictionary states that tactics are the "techniques of deploying and directing military forces . . . in coordinated combat activities . . . in order to attain the objectives designated by strategy."

In contrast, the term "strategy" is used in two ways. It has, in effect, two different definitions. On the one hand, within the context of a particular campaign or battle, it refers to the plan or idea of that campaign or battle, as distinguished from the tactical factor of employing and directing military forces in the combat activities of that campaign or battle. Thus, Halleck says that strategy in this sense "regards the theatre of war" and "forms the plan and arranges the general operations of a campaign."

But strategy has a more profound meaning in the context of war as a whole, as distinguished from the context of a campaign or battle. In this larger sense, Clausewitz defines it as "the use of engagements to attain the objects of war." An expanded modern version of this definition says that strategy is "the art and science of developing and employing in war military resources and forces for the purpose of providing maximum support for national policy."[4]

An understanding of this distinction between the two meanings of strategy is critical to this book. In order to minimize the risk of their being confused, different terms will be used. Strategy in the context of a campaign or battle will be called "operational strategy." Strategy in the more profound sense as related to the "objects of war" and the employment of military forces to carry out national policy will be identified as "grand strategy."

This book makes an additional distinction that the reader should bear in mind. It is the distinction between the *true* grand strategy of the sectional protagonists, North and South, and the *official* grand strategy of the sections. The true grand strategy is that which, in view of the circumstances of the section, would have maximized that section's chances of achieving its war objective. The official grand strategy is that which the government of the section authorized and directed its military establishment to carry out.

Much, perhaps most, of the writing about Lee's generalship never asks what seems to be the critical question in any military analysis of his generalship, that is, how his direction of military forces related to the national policy of the Confederacy and its object in the war. His campaigns and battles are typically considered almost as disembodied, abstract events, unrelated to the necessities and objectives of the war from the standpoint of the South, and without regard to whether they advanced or retarded those necessities and objectives. It is as if a surgeon were to be judged on the basis of his skillful, dexterous, and imaginative procedures, incisions, and sutures, without regard to whether the operation actually improved the patient's chances for survival. This is another way of saying that Lee is traditionally viewed as a performer, like the surgeon, or like an athlete participating in a competition or an exercise. The critical purposes and issues of warfare are not even acknowledged. Freeman and the other previously quoted sources are simply representative of this general phenomenon.

In evaluating Lee or any army commander, however, the key consideration is not the brilliance or boldness of his performance in a tactical or operationally strategic sense. These are surely matters of interest and importance, but the key consideration must be whether the general's actions helped or hurt the cause of his government in view of that government's grand strategy. In short, the appropriate inquiry is to ask whether the general's actions related positively or negatively to the war objectives and national policy of his government.

The issue addressed is not, therefore, Lee's tactics and operational strategy in any given campaign or battle. His brilliant direction of his forces during the fighting at Antietam and what happened at Gettysburg are not the point. At Gettysburg he suffered a decisive defeat, a defeat that did not alone decide the war but in which his losses, on the heels of other casualties, were so great that his army's subsequent ability to maneuver was severely restricted. The reference-book evaluations of Lee include the traditional view that this defeat was the fault of his subordinates. Contemporary students of the battle disagree on this point. Some persuasively contend that Lee's subordinates, especially Longstreet, are unfairly blamed for the Gettysburg loss. But, whatever may be said about the factors that determined the outcome of this or any battle, the issue here is more profound than explaining Lee's campaign or battle failures or successes. The issue is to understand the grand strategy of the Confederacy and to appreciate Lee's contribution to the larger success or failure of that strategy.

Lee's role as commander of the Army of Northern Virginia, a role he assumed on June 1, 1862, and retained for the duration of the war, is the critical area of inquiry in evaluating his generalship. It is true, of course, that he was military adviser to President Davis beginning on March 13, 1862, and continuing until February 6, 1865, on which date he became the Confederacy's general-in-chief.[5] But the relevant consideration of his generalship is concerned with his army command. Among other things, this statement of the issue means that the inquiry does not involve the familiar contention that Lee concentrated too much on his own army and the Virginia theater and paid insufficient attention to other parts of the country.

It is necessary to acknowledge an underlying factor that is bound up with any consideration of Lee's generalship. For almost one hundred years after the war, the conventional view was that the defeat of the South was inevitable. Part of the romance of the Lost Cause was the assumption that it literally could not have been a successful cause. It was, in short, the impossible dream. One of the premises of this inevitable-loss tradition was that the South was fatally handicapped from the beginning because of the relative manpower and material resources of the two sections. The North, and historians generally, seemed to accept an oft-quoted and probably apocryphal statement by a former Confederate: "They never whipped us, Sir, unless they were four to one. If we had anything like a fair chance, or less disparity of numbers, we should have won our cause."

More recent scholarship concedes the North's advantage in population and the capacity to make war but rejects the inevitable-loss tradition and its premise in regard to men and material wealth. It is generally believed today that the South could indeed have won the Civil War. In 1956 Southern historian Bell I. Wiley suggested:

> In the years since Appomattox millions of Southerners have attributed Confederate defeat to the North's overpowering strength. This is a comforting conclusion and it is not without a substantial basis of fact. For the North unquestionably had an immense superiority of material and human resources. But the North also faced a greater task. In order to win the war the North had to subdue a vast country of nine million inhabitants, while the South could prevail by maintaining a successful resistance. To put it another way, the North had to conquer the South while the South could win by outlasting its adversary, by convincing the North that coercion was impossible or not worth the effort. The South had reason to believe that it could achieve independence. That it did not was due as much, if not more, to its own failings as to the superior strength of the foe.[6]

In a 1960 volume edited by David Donald, a number of distinguished professional historians also argued that the defeat of the South was not a foregone conclusion; the South could have won.[7] More recently, in 1986, historians Richard E. Beringer, Herman Hattaway, Archer Jones, and William N. Still, Jr., expressed the same view. Noting that "no Confederate army lost a major engagement because of the lack of arms, munitions, or other essential supplies," these authors summarized the case as follows:

> By remarkable and effective efforts the agrarian South did exploit and create an industrial base that proved adequate, with the aid of

imports, to maintain suitably equipped forces in the field. Since the Confederate armies suffered no crippling deficiencies in weapons or supply, their principal handicap would be their numerical inferiority. But to offset this lack, Confederates, fighting the first major war in which both sides armed themselves with rifles, had the advantage of a temporary but very significant surge in the power of the tactical defensive. In addition, the difficulties of supply in a very large and relatively thinly settled region proved a powerful aid to strengthening the strategic defensive. Other things being equal, if Confederate military leadership were competent and the Union did not display Napoleonic genius, the tactical and strategic power of the defense could offset northern numerical superiority and presumably give the Confederacy a measure of military victory adequate to maintain its independence.[8]

In his book *Ordeal By Fire*, James M. McPherson lays out the facts that set up the grand strategic situation, including the necessity on the part of the North "to invade, conquer, and destroy the South's capacity and will to resist." McPherson also observes that "invasion and conquest are logistically far more difficult than defense of one's territory." He notes that, at the beginning of the war, British military experts, recalling their nation's experience in America one hundred years before, believed that a country as large as the Confederacy could not be conquered. It was expected that the North would ultimately have to give up the effort.[9]

The task of the North was to conquer and occupy an area as large as the Northern states themselves, if faraway California and Oregon are disregarded. This area was crossed by rivers and streams, mountains and valleys, and wooded, unimproved roads. These natural circumstances impeded an invader who sought to penetrate or hold the area. The South could work on interior lines, in friendly country, and with maximum terrain advantages. The North, with the constant necessity to advance, had to fight on extended lines of communication in hostile country. This required the availability of large numbers of men stationed in the rear to protect these extended lines. And the North could have been defeated in any one of three ways, each inextricably mixed with the other two. It could have been defeated militarily, by actual combat in the field, although given its resources in men and material this was unlikely. It could have been defeated politically, by discouragement of the Northern people, who had the power simply to vote a defeat for the North. And it could have been defeated diplomatically, that is, by European intervention.

Much has been casually written about the risk of British or French recognition of the Confederacy. Such a diplomatic act, not an unlikely prospect – at least until the issuance of the Emancipation Proclamation – would surely have changed the nature of the war in terms of international law and custom. Whether this change of status would have led to European military intervention is quite another question. Although those who discuss recognition seem sometimes to assume military intervention as a consequence of recognition, this is simply an assumption and is speculative at best. Naval activity at the expense of the North might have occurred. But given the distances and their logistical implications, and in view of the always fractious state of relations among the European powers, it is far from certain that either Great Britain or France would have committed naval forces, let alone ground forces, to the contest. As pointed out in Chapter 6, Lee himself did not expect European assistance to the Confederacy, and he was a realist in this respect. The unlikelihood of such assistance should be borne in mind in considering the appropriate Confederate grand strategy and the discussion later in this chapter of the reasons offered to justify Lee's aggressive military leadership.

In any event, the point is that the task of the North was literally gigantic. It was the task of organizing and harnessing its superior resources and committing them to warfare on a geographic and financial scale that was historically unprecedented. The South, too, had a similar organizing job to do, but inertia was on its side and would have been fatal to the North. In short, disregarding for the moment the concepts of military science and drawing instead on a legal metaphor, one side, the North, was the plaintiff. It had the burden of proof, the necessity to conquer. The South was the defendant; it could win the war simply by not being conquered. It did not have to seize or occupy a foot of ground outside its borders.

It seems plain that the traditional premise – that the South simply could not have won the war – has had much to do with establishing Lee's reputation as an almost perfect general. Indeed, the entire direction of one's inquiry into Lee's generalship depends on whether one accepts the tradition of the inevitable loss of the Lost Cause or alternatively sees the success of that cause as a possibility. If the cause was from the beginning simply a forlorn hope, the criteria in the evaluation of its military leadership are immediately lowered because advancing the objective of victory is read out of the case. As in the situation of the hypothetical surgeon or the athlete, the war is reduced to a forum in which the performance of the general is considered outside of the context of his government's war objective. The criteria of evaluation then pose such questions as, did the general put up a good fight? did he inflict significant losses on the enemy? did he win battles? On the other hand, if the evaluator believes that the war could have been won, a sterner test arises: did the general maximize the chance for victory?

Lee's task as commander of the Army of Northern Virginia was not to put on a martial show, a performance; it was to make the maximum contribution toward the South's chances of winning the war. Meaningful consideration of his generalship must refer to this task. Evaluating Lee's generalship in this context is not to say that the South would necessarily have won the war had Lee conducted himself differently. Had Lee been fully effective in the Virginia theater, the Union's military victories and inexorable advance in the West, and then from the West to the East, might ultimately have caused the collapse of the Confederacy. It is nevertheless fair to examine Lee's generalship with reference to his contribution to the South's chances of winning the war.

Before proceeding, it is necessary to say a quick word about the problem of counting casualties during the Civil War. As any student of the war knows, this is a difficult task because strength and casualty returns were frequently not made and when made were frequently carelessly done. In citing strength and casualty data in this chapter, no attempt is made to question or rationalize the numbers used by the authorities cited even when they are in disagreement, because a choice of numbers does not affect the analysis. Disagreements concerning numbers and losses are not material in terms of the issues with which this chapter is concerned.

What has been said about the physical situation and the tasks of the North and South suggests an identification of their respective military circumstances and true grand strategy in a military sense. Kenneth P. Williams, in a work entitled *Lincoln Finds a General* (the general being, of course, U. S. Grant), credits Grant with having recognized and executed as general-in-chief what had from the beginning of the war been the true Federal grand strategy. Essentially, as distinguished from the piecemeal and episodic engagements followed by withdrawal that had marked the war in the East before Grant, this true Federal grand strategy was to destroy the South's capacity to carry on the war. As characterized by the English general J. F. C. Fuller, Grant's "central idea was concentration of force from which he intended to develop a ceaseless offensive against the enemy's armies, and the resources and *moral* [*sic*] of the Confederacy" (emphasis added). Grant's plan for dealing with the Confederate field armies called for the Army of the Potomac to operate against Lee's Army of Northern Virginia, while William Tecumseh Sherman's Army of the Tennessee engaged Gen. Joseph E. Johnston's army in the West. Gen. Franz Sigel was to occupy the Confederates' attention in western Virginia and the Shenandoah Valley, and Gen. Benjamin F. Butler's Army of the James was to move south of Richmond. As stated by Fuller, "All four armies were to attack simultaneously. . . . This continued movement Grant hoped would prevent any one Confederate army reinforcing the other."[10] In addition, Gen. Nathaniel P. Banks, commanding the Department of the Gulf, was to be active. At the time of Grant's appointment as general-in-chief, Banks was embarked on the Red River expedition. Under Grant's plan, Banks was promptly to complete that mission and then lead an assault against Mobile, a fifth front on which simultaneously to challenge the Confederacy.[11]

Grant's intention for each army was very plain. It was to destroy the opposing Confederate military force. In a communication dated March 15, 1864, to General Banks, Grant wrote: "I look upon the conquering of the organized armies of the enemy as being of vastly more importance than the mere acquisition of territory." A similar message went to Gen. George Meade: "Lee's army will be your objective point. Wherever Lee goes, there you will go also."[12] And, as noted by Fuller, "Meade's attack . . . was to be an attack in such overwhelming force that

Lee would suffer so heavily that the Confederate Government would be unable to reinforce any other army. . . .It was also to be a continuous attack, in order to prevent Lee's army recuperating." As further interpreted by Fuller: "Grant's grand tactics were . . . to lead to such an attenuation of [Lee's] strength that he would be compelled to use his entire force on the defensive."[13]

It is widely conceded that Grant's grand strategy was the true grand strategy of the Union. Grant was the general-in-chief; Lincoln had literally turned the military aspect of the war over to him. As of the advent of Grant, the true grand strategy and the official grand strategy of the Union coincided. General Fuller explains the logic of this grand strategy: "Grant was right in deciding that both his tactics and strategy must be offensive; for it was obvious to him that the longer the war lasted the less likely would the North hold out." And this, of course, was the risk for the Union – that the human, emotional, and financial cost of subduing the South would become so burdensome that the Northern people would abandon their support of the war. This was a genuine risk. In the 1862 elections, the Republicans had suffered losses as a result of Northern discouragement. According to Massachusetts senator Charles Sumner, in 1863 Lincoln feared " 'the fire in the rear' – meaning the Democracy, especially in the Northwest – more than our military chances." And in August 1864, before the fall of Atlanta, Lincoln had written his private prediction: "It seems exceedingly probable that this Administration will not be re-elected."[14] A politician of unusual insight, Lincoln was personally aware of the mounting sense of frustration in the North and was in close touch with party leaders in the Northern states. War-weariness was growing, as was the belief that the conquest of the South was an impossibility. From the beginning, the true grand strategy of the North was to destroy the South's capacity to resist, and this required the destruction of its armies, before the Northern people gave up the contest.

If the true grand strategy of the North was offensive, as indeed it was, what grand strategy was most likely to contribute to the South's chances of winning the war? The South's goal was to be released from the Union. It neither desired to conquer the North nor had the need or resources to do so. Accordingly, the true grand strategy for the Confederacy, the only grand strategy that afforded a chance to win the war, was defensive. Edward Porter Alexander, chief of ordnance of the Army of Northern Virginia and later chief of artillery of Longstreet's corps, identified the premises of this policy:

> When the South entered upon war with a power so immensely her superior in men & money, & all the wealth of modern resources in machinery and transportation appliances by land & sea, she could entertain but one single hope of final success. That was, that the desperation of her resistance would finally exact from her adversary such a price in blood & treasure as to exhaust the enthusiasm of its population for the objects of the war. We could not hope to *conquer* her. Our one chance was to wear her out. (Emphasis in original.)[15]

McPherson is correct in stating that "to 'win,' the Confederates did not need to invade the North or to destroy its armies; they needed only to stand on the defensive and to prevent the North from destroying Southern armies."[16] As stated earlier, the South as well as the North had the rifled gun, and that ordnance created the relative power of the strategic, as well as the tactical, defensive. William Garrett Piston confirms the power of the defense for the same reason.[17]

The feasibility of the grand strategy of the defensive was sensed by British observers as the war began. As has been said, harking back to their own experience in America, they did not see how the South could be conquered. The War of Independence analogy is not perfect, but it is illustrative of the circumstances. Military historian Col. George A. Bruce made the point. Washington, he writes, "had a correct insight into the minds of his own people and that of the enemy, *the strength of resolution of each to endure heavy burdens*, looking forward with certainty to the time when the public sentiment of England, led by Chatham and Burke, would be ready to acknowledge the Colonies as an independent nation. With these views he carried on the war for seven years, all the way from Boston to Yorktown, on a generally defensive plan, the only one pointing to the final goal of independence" (emphasis added).[18] The Americans, on the grand strategic defensive, lost many battles and retreated many times, but they kept forces in the field so as not to be ultimately defeated, and they won because the British decided that the struggle was either hopeless or too burdensome to pursue. General Fuller describes this grand strategy with another historical reference: "In truth, Lee's one and only chance was to imitate the great Fabius, and plot to win the war, even if in the winning of it he lost every battle fought."[19]

In short, as suggested by its status as the defendant, the South's true grand strategy of the defensive could have kept its armies in the field long enough to wear down the North's willingness to carry on the war. And despite the Southern armies' manpower disadvantages, this grand strategy was at the outset feasible because of the North's logistical task and the relative power that the rifled gun afforded the defense.

The grand strategy of defense would not have required Southern armies always to be on the strategic operational or tactical defense. As Fuller points out, "It is possible to develop an offensive tactics from a defensive strategy."[20] Thus, if Lee's grand strategic sense of the war had been defensive, he could nevertheless on appropriate occasions have pursued offensive campaigns and offensive tactics in the context of that defensive grand strategy. The Revolutionary War again provides an illustration. Although pursuing a grand strategy of defense, the Americans were sometimes aggressive and offensive, as exemplified in their conduct of the battles of Trenton, Saratoga, and Yorktown.

This is not to say that the South should have adopted a perimeter or frontier defense. The Confederacy did not have the manpower or other resources to engage exclusively in a war of position. It is also conceded that Southern home front morale and political pressure would, on occasion, have dictated offensive thrusts. Because General Johnston was removed, history does not tell us at what point he would have been the aggressor in a battle for Atlanta, how successful he would have been, or whether he could have protected Atlanta against a siege. But there are significant degrees between Johnston's backward movement toward Atlanta and Lee's direction of his army. Identifying the South's true grand strategy as defensive, is not, therefore, the same as embracing Johnston's apparently exclusively defensive operational strategy and tactics in Georgia. Nor is it contended that offensive thrusts would have been wholly proscribed by the grand strategy of defense.

Identifying the Confederacy's official grand strategy, that is, the grand strategy that the Confederate government ordained, is a complex task about which much has been written. McPherson observes that "no one ever defined this strategy in a systematic, comprehensive fashion."[21] Commentators have therefore fashioned interpretations from selected official correspondence and reports and from particular military actions. These interpretations contain significant variations and disagreements. General Fuller writes that "President Davis . . . had no grand strategy beyond a rigid defensive."[22] Louis H. Manarin agrees, maintaining that the South adopted "a strictly defensive policy."[23] A second school of thought – to which Russell F. Weigley, Emory M. Thomas, and Frank E. Vandiver all belong – holds that Davis and the Confederate government emphasized a grand strategy of defense, but with a significant modification that contemplated attacking invading armies on appropriate occasions. These authors accordingly deny that the official grand strategy was entirely defensive. In their analyses, Thomas and Vandiver acknowledge Davis's concept of the "offensive defensive." Vandiver interprets this "offensive defensive" as premised on the Confederacy's maintaining its armies but also undertaking counterthrusts when the chance of victory and the availability of supply existed. In this way, according to Vandiver, the South was to prolong the war until the North desisted.[24] A third view of the South's official grand strategy is that, in effect, there was none. Thus, in evaluating Davis as a commander-in-chief, Wiley asserts that "a basic shortcoming . . . was his failure to map an overall strategy." And in *The Politics of Command*, Thomas L. Connelly and Archer Jones trace in detail the erratic and makeshift course of the government's grand strategy, suggesting that a meaningful Confederate grand strategy may never have existed.[25]

In the absence of a systematic official statement from the Confederate authorities, and in view of the conflicts in the evidence and among the writers who have studied the matter, McPherson's conclusion must be accepted. The South's grand strategy was never really defined. In any event, it is unnecessary to pursue the point here. The correctness of the government's policy is not at issue, and it is not contended that Lee was responsible for the Confederacy's grand strategy in the war as a whole. At issue here is the correctness of Lee's sense of grand strategy in regard to his own army.

As will be discussed in Chapter 6, Lee fully accepted civilian control, reported regularly to Richmond, and did not act without the authority of President Davis and his administration. But he was unquestionably the

author of his own sense of the grand strategy pursued by the Army of
Northern Virginia. Connelly and Jones correctly state that although
President Davis asserted "unity of control over the Confederate war
effort," there was "a large measure of autonomy for department commanders." The notion that "Lee had little power" they describe as "one
of the great myths of the Civil War."[26] In point of fact, it was Lee, not
Davis, who proposed and initiated the movements of Lee's army, movements that brought on its battles, including the Maryland campaign and
Gettysburg, and he had complete tactical control of that army.[27] Davis
and the administration were drawn into the grand strategy that Lee pursued with his army, and therefore share responsibility for Lee's generalship, but the grand strategy was Lee's. He was not acting out a grand
strategy formulated or directed by his civilian superiors.

What, then, was Lee's grand strategic sense of the war? How did he
understand "the use of engagements to attain the objects of war"
as it related to his and the Confederacy's situation? It is not surprising
that Lee at no time sat down and made a detailed and comprehensive
statement of his view of the grand strategy for securing Southern independence. And since there were no War Department, Security Council,
or staff minutes in which his views were recorded, one must resort to
indirect sources to identify Lee's grand strategic thinking. Three such
sources are available: his occasional communications indicating how he
thought the war was to be won, the military movements and actions that
he planned and advocated, and the campaigns and battles of the Army
of Northern Virginia.

The first of Lee's occasional communications setting forth his sense
of the appropriate grand strategy for the Confederacy appears in a letter
dated June 25, 1863, to President Davis, from Williamsport, Maryland.
This letter states: "It seems to me that we cannot afford to keep our
troops awaiting possible movements of the enemy, but that our true
policy is, as far as we can, so to employ our own forces as to give
occupation to his at points of our selection." The letter argues that "our
concentration at any point compels that of the enemy."[28] It is important
to note that this letter was concerned with Confederate military forces
on a wide range of fronts, including Virginia, North Carolina, and

Kentucky. Since it contemplates the drawing of Federal armies to Confederate points of concentration to "give occupation" to the Federals, the letter is a prescription for military confrontation. It is therefore a statement of an offensive grand strategy, whether the confrontation at the "point of concentration" was to take the form of the offensive or defensive on the part of the South. A later letter to Davis on July 6, 1864, shortly after the siege of Petersburg began, was quite plain in its statement of Lee's grand strategic sense. Lee wrote: "If we can defeat or drive the armies of the enemy from the field, we shall have peace. All our efforts and energies should be devoted to that object."[29] Such was Lee's view of the way in which the South could achieve its war aims.

How did this grand strategic view translate into the specific movements that Lee planned and advocated? On May 30, 1863, shortly before starting for Pennsylvania, Lee wrote Davis from Fredericksburg, Virginia, lamenting his inability to take the offensive: "I have for nearly a month been endeavoring to get this army in a condition to move, to anticipate an expected blow from the enemy. I fear I shall have to receive it here at a disadvantage, or to retreat. . . . If I was stronger, I think I could . . . force him back . . . There may be nothing left for me to do but fall back."[30] A curious letter went to Secretary Seddon on June 8, 1863. Although Lee had actually begun the movement that would end at Gettysburg, he seemed both to be anxious to begin offensive action and to want to shame Seddon into agreeing with him:

> As far as I can judge, there is nothing to be gained by this army remaining quietly on the defensive, which it must do unless it is reenforced. I am aware that there is difficulty and hazard in taking the aggressive with so large an army in its front, entrenched behind a river, where it cannot be advantageously attacked. Unless it can be drawn out in a position to be assailed, it will take its own time to prepare and strengthen itself to renew its advance upon Richmond. . . . Still, if the Department thinks it better to remain on the defensive, and guard as far as possible all the avenues of approach, and await the time of the enemy, I am ready to adopt this course.[31]

As is well known, Lee initiated and carried forward the Gettysburg campaign and did, indeed, "assail" the Army of the Potomac on that ground. After Gettysburg, on August 31, 1863, from Richmond where he was meeting with Davis, Lee posted a dispatch to Longstreet who was at army headquarters in the field. He instructed Longstreet to "use every exertion to prepare the army for offensive operations. . . . I can see nothing better to be done than to endeavor to bring General Meade out and use our efforts to crush his army while in its present condition."[32] Later, in September, he filed his report of the Chancellorsville campaign and spoke in these approving terms of the Army of Northern Virginia: "Attacking largely superior numbers in strongly entrenched positions their heroic courage overcame every obstacle of nature and art, and achieved a triumph most honorable to our arms." This, of course, was the good news. The bad news was candidly reported: "The returns of the Medical Director will show the extent of our loss, which from the nature of the circumstances attending the engagements could not be otherwise than severe. Many valuable officers and men were killed or wounded in the faithful discharge of duty."[33]

The Chancellorsville report of September was followed on October 11, 1863, by a report to Seddon from near Madison Court House, Virginia, in which Lee announced, "Yesterday I moved the army to this position with the hope of getting an opportunity to strike a blow at the enemy."[34] Less than a week later, he informed Davis from Bristoe Station:

> I have the honor to inform you that with the view of bringing on an engagement with the army of Gen. Meade, which lay around Culpeper Court House, extending thence to the Rapidan, this army marched on the 9th instant by way of Madison Court House and arrived near Culpeper on the 11th. The enemy retired toward the Rappahannock at the railroad bridge declining battle, and removing all his stores. I determined to make another effort to reach him, and moved through Warrenton towards the railroad north of the Rappahannock.

Lee then described Meade's continued retreat, skirmishing with his rear guard, and the ultimate decision not to pursue the Federals further. Toward the end of the communication he reported, "Our own loss was slight, except in the action at this place, where it was quite severe."[35] Later in 1863, the Army of the Potomac moved south to Mine Run but Meade decided against an attack when he found Lee in what seemed a strong position. On December 3, 1863, Lee reported to Adjutant and Inspector General Samuel Cooper: "This movement of General Meade, and all reports received as to his intention, led me to believe that he would attack, and I desired to have the advantage that such an attempt on his part would afford. After waiting his advance until Tuesday evening, preparations were made to attack him on Wednesday morning. This was prevented by his retreat. The dense forest which covers the scene of operations prevented our discovering his withdrawal until he was beyond pursuit."[36] Frustrated in his hope for a battle at Mine Run, Lee turned in February, 1864, to thoughts of a spring offensive, writing to Davis: "I can do nothing for want of proper supplies. With these & effective horses I think I could disturb the quiet of the enemy & drive him to the Potomac."[37] On April 15, 1864, he wrote again to Davis: "If Richmond could be held secure against the attack from the east, I would propose that I draw Longstreet to me & move right against the enemy on the Rappahannock."[38] Even after Grant's campaign had begun – after the Wilderness and Spotsylvania – Lee proposed to Davis on May 23, 1864, "It seems to me our best policy to unite upon it [Grant's army] and endeavor to crush it."[39]

Lee's sense of the offensive was not confined to his own army. Having dispatched Longstreet and certain divisions of the Army of Northern Virginia to Gen. Braxton Bragg's Army of Tennessee, Lee wrote Davis from Orange Court House, Virginia, on September 9, 1863, regarding the Chattanooga situation. "I think," he stated, "Rosecrans is maneuvering to cause the evacuation of Chattanooga, & for Burnside to form a junction with him. He ought to be attacked as soon as possible."[40] And writing to General Early in the Shenandoah Valley on July 11, 1864, he declared, "None of the forces . . . will be able in my opinion to resist you, provided that you can strike them before they are strengthened by others."[41]

It may be argued that these examples of Lee's military thinking concern his concepts of operational strategy or his tactical views, having in mind, as stated earlier, that a defensive grand strategy can involve offensive operational strategy or the tactical offensive. However, it is impossible to read the documents in *The Wartime Papers of R. E. Lee*, the dispatches from Lee to Davis and the War Department, and Lee's communications in the *Official Records* without being struck by the fact that they bristle with offensive rhetoric and planning: striking a blow, driving the enemy, crushing the enemy. In short, they are consistent with Lee's expressed theory that peace would come when the Confederates "defeat or drive the armies of the enemy from the field." This was an idée fixe with Lee. Porter Alexander was witness to the ultimate flash of Lee's predilection for the attack. He writes of April 5, 1865, and the Army of Northern Virginia's "last mile" en route to Appomattox. Elements of the army had stopped at Amelia Court House that morning. As reported by Alexander:

> About 1 P.M. . . . we took the road for Jetersville, where it was understood that Sheridan with his cavalry was across our path, & Gen. Lee intended to attack him. I rode with him & his staff & Gen. Longstreet, & we were not long in coming to where our skirmish line was already engaged. I never saw Gen. Lee seem so anxious to bring on a battle in my life as he seemed that afternoon, but a conference with Gen. W. H. F. Lee in command of the cavalry in our front seemed to disappoint him greatly.
>
> [W. H. F.] Lee reported that Sheridan had been reinforced by two infantry corps who were entrenching, & that force was more than we could venture to attack.[42]

Any doubt that Lee was committed to the offensive as the South's appropriate grand strategy is presumably eliminated when one considers the third source for identifying his grand strategic thinking, the campaigns and battles of the Army of Northern Virginia. Consistent with the grand strategy that he said he believed in and repeatedly planned and advocated, Lee from the beginning embraced the offensive. Appointed to command the Army of Northern Virginia on June 1, 1862, he turned at once to the offensive, beginning with major engagements on the Peninsula – Mechanicsville, Gaines's Mill, Frayser's Farm, and Malvern Hill.[43] Following on the heels of the Seven Days, the Second Bull Run campaign was strategically offensive in an operational sense, although except for Longstreet's August 30 counterattack it may be classified as defensive from a tactical standpoint. At Antietam Lee stood on the defensive, but the Maryland campaign was strategically offensive. His moving into Maryland assured a major battle in that state. At Chancellorsville, he chose not to retreat when confronted by the Federals' pincer movement. Instead, he repeatedly attacked, and the Federals retreated back across the river.[44]

Gettysburg was, of course, the most daring of Lee's operationally strategic offensives, and he attacked repeatedly there all along the admirable Federal defensive line. As indicated by his communications set forth above, he maneuvered so as to attack after Gettysburg and failed to attack only because Meade would not accept battle. And in the Wilderness, although Grant was initiating the final Federal offensive, Lee again attacked. Even during the final days of the war, Lee attempted the offensive. On March 25, 1865, he ordered an attack on Fort Stedman, a Federal stronghold in the Richmond-Petersburg line. Having described the overwhelming odds that faced the attackers, Alexander rationalizes the effort as "worth all it cost merely as an illustration of the sublime audacity of our commander." It was, he writes, "very characteristic of Gen. Lee . . . one of the greatest instances of audacity which the war produced." He comments further, however, that "the few who got back, of all those sent forward to execute the plan, had to run a gauntlet of terrible fire."[45]

The point is not that each of these campaigns and battles represented an error by Lee. As has been said, the grand strategic defensive may at times translate into the operational or tactical offensive. Thus, driving the Federals away from Richmond in 1862 may have been required in view of Southern morale and the practical consequences of the loss of the capital. Going on the offensive in the Wilderness may have been strategically or tactically justified. The point is that the offensive *pattern* is plain. Lee believed that the South's grand strategic role was offensive. He had consistently planned and advocated the offensive. He had told President Davis that the way to peace was to drive the opposing army from the field, and this is what he sought to accomplish. Thus, Manarin asserts that "Lee never seems to have forgotten that although on the defensive the only way to win was by attacking and driving the enemy."[46] And Connelly and Jones conclude that "Lee's frequent offensive thrusts and his almost invariable assumption of the offensive in battle" suggest that he believed the war was to be won by "annihilation of the enemy army."[47]

There was a profound problem with Lee's grand strategy of the offensive: it was not feasible to defeat the North militarily as distinguished from prolonging the contest until the North gave it up. And indeed to attempt an outright defeat of the Federal army was counterproductive in terms of the Confederacy's "objects of war." Curiously, that Lee's attack grand strategy was misplaced is suggested by his own awareness of factors that argued against it.

The primary factor that made the attack grand strategy counterproductive was numbers, and Lee was sensitive to the South's manpower disadvantage and the implications of that disadvantage. A letter of January 10, 1863, to Secretary of War Seddon, written between Lee's victory at Fredericksburg and Burnsides's abortive Mud March, reflects this. He wrote:

> I have the honor to represent to you the absolute necessity that exists . . . to increase our armies, if we desire to oppose effectual resistance to the vast numbers that the enemy is now precipitating upon us. . . .
>
> The success with which our efforts have been crowned . . . should not betray our people into the dangerous delusion that the armies now in the field are sufficient to bring the war to a successful and speedy termination.
>
> . . . The great increase in the enemy's forces will augment the disparity of numbers to such a degree that victory, if attained, can only be achieved by a terrible expenditure of the most precious blood of the country. . . .
>
> The country has yet to learn how often advantages, secured at the expense of many valuable lives, have failed to produce their legitimate results by reason of our inability to prosecute them against the reinforcements which the superior numbers of the enemy enabled him to interpose between the defeat of an army and its ruin.
>
> More than once have most promising opportunities been lost for want of men to take advantage of them, and victory itself has been made to put on the appearance of defeat, because our diminished and exhausted troops have been unable to renew a successful struggle against fresh numbers of the enemy.[48]

Further awareness of the numbers problem appears in Lee's letter of June 10, 1863, to Davis, after Chancellorsville and at the outset of the Gettysburg campaign:

While making the most we can of the means of resistance we possess . . . it is nevertheless the part of wisdom to carefully measure and husband our strength, and not to expect from it more than in the ordinary course of affairs it is capable of accomplishing. We should not therefore conceal from ourselves that our resources in men are constantly diminishing, and the disproportion in this respect between us and our enemies, if they continue united in their effort to subjugate us, is steadily augmenting. The decrease of the aggregate of this army as disclosed by returns affords an illustration of this fact. Its effective strength varies from time to time, but the falling off in its aggregate shows that its ranks are growing weaker and that its losses are not supplied by recruits.[49]

On July 8, 1863, immediately after the defeat at Gettysburg, Lee again discussed the strength issue in a letter to Davis, remarking that "though conscious that the enemy has been much shattered in the recent battle, I am aware that he can be easily reinforced, while no addition can be made to our numbers."[50]

Again in regard to his army's strength problem, Lee wrote to Seddon on August 23, 1864, after the siege of Petersburg had begun. He observed, "Unless some measures can be devised to replace our losses, the consequences may be disastrous. . . . Without some increase of our strength, I cannot see how we are to escape the natural military consequences of the enemy's numerical superiority." On September 2, 1864, he wrote in a similar vein to the president, remarking, "As matters now stand, we have no troops disposable to meet movements of the enemy or strike where opportunity presents, without taking them from the trenches and exposing some important point. . . . Our ranks are constantly diminishing by battle and disease, and few recruits are received. The consequences are inevitable."[51]

Consciousness of his numerical disadvantage, of the ever-increasing Federal disproportion, did not mute Lee's commitment to the grand strategic offensive. Nor did that grand strategy permit his army to husband its strength. During the Seven Days battles on the Peninsula, George McClellan lost approximately 9,796 soldiers killed and wounded, 10.7 percent of his forces; Lee's casualties were 19,739 men, 20.7 percent of his army. Although Federal casualties in killed and wounded at Second Bull Run exceeded Lee's by approximately 1,000, the Army of Northern Virginia lost more than 9,000 men, which represented almost 19 percent of the army, as compared to the Federals' 13.3 percent. In spite of McClellan's ineptitude, Lee lost 10,000 men, 31 percent of his force, at Antietam, including missing, immediately following losses in excess of 2,500 at South Mountain on September 14. At Chancellorsville, a victory, Lee lost 13,000 of 61,000 effectives, more than 21 percent, a much higher percentage loss than that suffered by the Federals. Lee's admirer Clifford Dowdey has remarked that "this was the high cost of performing miracles with an undermanned army, to which no significant replacements were coming." In the defeat at Gettysburg, according to a conservative estimate, 21,000 men, one-third of Lee's army, went down, again a higher percentage than the Federal losses. In 1914, before he had decided that Gettysburg was not a "clear-cut victory" for the Federals, Freeman wrote that Lee's "army . . . had been wrecked at Gettysburg." As is well-known, Grant lost heavily in the Wilderness, but Lee's casualties, again by a conservative count, exceeded 7,000 men.[52]

Battle casualties were not, however, the only source of attrition for Lee's army. On September 21, 1862, Lee reported to President Davis, describing his first three and a half months of command – a period of aggressive warfare that included the Seven Days, Second Bull Run, and the Antietam campaign – and acknowledged that the army "has had hard work to perform, long and laborious marches, and large odds to encounter in every conflict." Porter Alexander's comment about September 17, 1862, at Antietam is consistent with this description: "When at last night put a welcome end to the bloody day the Confederate army was worn & fought to a perfect frazzle."[53] As one would expect, a price was paid for this kind of service. In regard to Antietam, Piston states, "Desertions reached nightmare proportions during and after the Campaign. Perhaps as many as 20,000 men left the army either before it crossed the Potomac, or prior to the fight at Antietam. Significantly, desertions *increased* after the Confederates returned to Virginia" (emphasis added).[54]

Lee's communications confirm these morale problems. Writing to Davis from Hagerstown, Maryland, on September 13, before the battle at Sharpsburg, Lee stated: "One great embarrassment is the reduction of our ranks by straggling, which it seems impossible to prevent with our present regimental officers. Our ranks are very much diminished – I fear from a third to one-half of the original numbers." In the above-quoted letter of September 21, after the battle, he described the state of the army:

> Its present efficiency is greatly paralyzed by the loss to its ranks of the numerous stragglers. I have taken every means in my power from the beginning to correct this evil, which has increased instead of diminished. A great many men belonging to the army never entered Maryland at all; many returned after getting there, while others who crossed the river kept aloof. The stream has not lessened since crossing the Potomac, though the cavalry has been constantly employed in endeavoring to arrest it. . . . Some immediate legislation, in my opinion, is required, and the most summary punishment should be authorized. It ought to be construed into desertion in face of the enemy, and thus brought under the Rules and Articles of War. To give you an idea of its extent in some brigades, I will mention that, on the morning of the battle of the 17th, General Evans reported to me on the field, where he was holding the front position, that he had but 120 of his brigade present, and that the next brigade to his, that of General Garnett, consisted of but 100 men.

On September 22, 1862, Lee again addressed Davis on the subject: "In connection with the subject of straggling, about which I had the honor to write to you again yesterday, the destruction of private property by the army has occupied much of my attention. A great deal of damage to citizens is done by stragglers, who consume all they can get from the charitable and all they can take from the defenseless, in many cases wantonly destroying stock and other property." With this letter of September 22 Lee enclosed an earlier letter dated September 7, 1862, in which he stated that the "greater number" of stragglers were "the cowards of the army, [who] desert their comrades in times of danger" and recommended that a military commission accompany the army to provide punishment for these offenders. On September 25 he advised Davis that after withdrawing from Sharpsburg into Virginia, he had intended to cross the Potomac again "to advance on Hagerstown and endeavor to defeat the enemy at that point," but he changed his mind, deciding this would be too hazardous because the army did not "exhibit its former temper and condition."[55]

Lee apparently appraised his army correctly, according to a letter of September 27, 1862, from Brig. Gen. J. R. Jones. In charge of one of the cavalry commands trying to "arrest" the "stream" of stragglers referred to in Lee's letter of September 21, Jones reported from Winchester, Virginia, that he had sent 5,000 or 6,000 men back to the army. Significantly, he stated that "The number of officers back here was most astonishing. . . . There are about 1,200 barefooted men here. I am satisfied that a large number throw away their shoes in order to remain. If barefooted men are permitted to remain here, the number will continue to increase."[56]

In view of the casualties from death and wounds and the Confederate morale problems after Antietam, Piston comments that "Lee's offensive tactics were bleeding the army white, and many of those who remained with him during the Maryland excursion took 'French leave' as soon as they returned."[57] Piston's judgment is supported by the conclusions of Manarin, a staunch champion of Lee's generalship: Antietam, he states, "momentarily paralyzed" the army. In another passage he revises this characterization and states that "Lee's army never fully recovered" from that battle.[58]

What Freeman calls "mass desertion" was a source of losses to Lee's army after Gettysburg as well.[59] Reporting to President Davis on July 27, 1863, Lee stated, "There are many thousand men improperly absent from this army." On the same day, he advised Davis that on July 4, before his army had quit the battlefield, "on sending back the train with the wounded, it was reported that about 5,000 well men started back at night to overtake it. I fear most of these were captured by the enemy's cavalry and armed citizens, who beset their route." Desertion after Gettysburg extended to distinguished fighting regiments, such as the Twenty-second and Thirty-eighth North Carolina, from which fifty men deserted on July 29, 1863.[60]

Immediately prior to the North Carolina incident Lee had requested Davis to issue a general amnesty for deserters who would return to duty. On August 11, 1863, Adjutant and Inspector General Cooper issued General Orders No. 109 to this effect.[61] Desertions nevertheless continued. Lee advised Davis on August 17, 1863, that "immediately on the publication of the amnesty . . . many presumed on it, and absented themselves from their commands. . . . In one corps, the desertions of North Carolinians, and, to some extent, Virginians, has grown to be a very serious matter. . . . General [John Daniel] Imboden writes that there are great numbers of deserters in the valley, who conceal themselves successfully from the small squads sent to arrest them." On the same day, Imboden was ordered to collect and send back deserters from the Valley and northwest Virginia. Lee was further troubled by reports from North Carolina of an "organization of deserters . . . a formidable and growing evil" there. These men, according to Secretary of War Seddon, were engaged in "dangerous combinations and violent proceedings."[62]

Colonel Bruce, basing his observations on a particular interval of time – apparently Gaines's Mill through Gettysburg – and entirely disregarding desertions, sums up the attrition problem. He cites Lee's "principle of aggressive warfare which was congenial to his impulsive nature" and states:

> In the short period of one year and seven days he fought six of the greatest battles of the war. In history there is no record that equals it. In this short time there had fallen, killed and wounded, of his men 82,208, not counting losses in skirmishes, minor engagements, and the hardships of forced marches and exposure, which would probably swell these figures to a full hundred thousand; the Union loss, figured in the same way, during the same period, was 74,720.[63]

The Confederacy faced a constant dilemma concerning the deployment of its limited manpower between its eastern and western armies. Connelly and Jones provide casualty statistics that graphically address this tension: "Lee's losses in the Seven Days' exceeded the number of effectives in the Army of Tennessee the previous autumn. In the Gettysburg campaign, Lee lost more men . . . than Braxton Bragg had in his Army of Tennessee in October of 1862. At Chancellorsville, Lee's casualties almost equaled those of the combined Confederate surrenders of Forts Henry and Donelson. In fact, during his first four months as commander of the Army of Northern Virginia, . . . Lee lost almost fifty thousand troops. Such a number far exceeded the total troop strength of the Army of Tennessee . . . during the same time span."[64]

Because Lee's biographers seem to overlook the point, it is necessary to emphasize that there was a profound difference between Federal casualties and Lee's casualties. Federal casualties could be, and were in fact, made up with additional manpower. Lee's were irreplaceable, including the severe losses, even prior to Gettysburg, in field-grade officers and other mid-level commanders. As Robert K. Krick has noted, these leadership casualties were especially crippling for the Army of Northern Virginia.[65] Writers like Freeman would impress us with statements of Federal losses that on occasion exceeded Lee's in absolute numbers. They miss the point that the losses were of very different significance for the two antagonists because of the replacement factor. As his own correspondence indicates, Lee realized this difference and said so. His advocates disregard it.

Lee was conscious of another problem related to numbers as well, namely, the consequences to his army of a siege. He consistently expressed the view that his army's being besieged in the Richmond defenses was bound to result in its defeat. Writing in the Southern Historical Society Papers, General Henry Heth quoted Lee as having said this regarding his 1863 situation: "I considered the problem in every possible phase, and to my mind it resolved itself into a choice of one of two things – either to retire on Richmond and stand a siege, which must ultimately have ended in surrender, or to invade Pennsylvania." On June 8, 1863, he wrote to Secretary of War Seddon that the siege eventuality would be a "catastrophe." In June 1864, in a letter to A. P. Hill, he said that if he was "obliged to take refuge behind the works of Richmond and stand a siege, [his defeat] would be but a work of time." General Jubal A. Early reported that Lee had said to him in 1864, "We must destroy this army of Grant's before he gets to the James River. If he gets there, it will become a siege, and then it will be a mere question of time."[66]

There are two possible defenses to a siege: the availability of sufficient military power to break the siege, or protection of the supply routes of the besieged site, so that the siege fails. Both require numbers, that is, sufficient personnel to attack the enemy and drive it away by force or to protect lines of communication and supply, which in Lee's case meant such avenues as the Weldon and Petersburg Railroad and the Southside Railroad at Petersburg. Lee knew this. Knowing also that the ratio of his manpower relative to the Federals' was constantly decreasing, he accurately foresaw the catastrophic character of a siege. Accordingly, he hoped to avoid being caught in a siege in the first place. But in order for an army to avoid being fixed, to avoid a siege, that army must be mobile. And mobility, the ability of an army to maneuver, also requires numbers in some reasonable proportion to the enemy's. In Lee's phraseology, the risk of being besieged was a "natural military consequence" of the increasing disproportion of the size of his army.

According to Dowdey, referring to the day the siege of Petersburg began, "June 18th [1864] marked the end of Grant's campaign against Richmond, and it also marked the end of Lee's capacity to maintain maneuver. In achieving a stalemate against Grant's hosts, Lee had been forced into static fortifications, the one eventuality he most dreaded."[67] Freeman addresses the same issue of mobility in a part of the statement quoted at the outset of this chapter and concludes that mobility was lost at Cold Harbor. He entirely disregards Lee's concern about disproportionate numbers. And in boasting of Lee's prowess, he unwittingly makes the same case concerning the relationship between Lee's casualties and his loss of mobility that is presented here. As previously noted, Freeman states: "During the twenty-four months when he had been free to employ open manoeuvre, a period that had ended with Cold Harbor, he had sustained approximately 103,000 casualties and had inflicted 145,000. Holding, as he usually had, to the offensive, his combat losses had been greater in proportion to his numbers than those of the Federals."[68] Referring to the final Virginia campaign, McPherson remarks that "Lee could no longer risk his limited manpower outside his trenches,"[69] another way of expressing the loss of mobility. In short, it is apparent that Lee's heavy and disproportionate losses had contributed to the disparity in manpower that led to the siege. Contrary to Dowdey's implication, these losses long preceded Grant's Virginia campaign. They had in fact occurred throughout the period of Lee's command and were a consequence of his attack grand strategy. His grim anticipation of a siege did not, however, moderate that grand strategy.

A third consideration that might have suggested to Lee that his grand strategy of the attack was mistaken was his understanding that it was critical for the South to maintain the existence of its armies. As has been noted, on the eve of Gettysburg, which suggests an irony, he had written to Davis that "it is the part of wisdom to carefully measure and husband our strength." In a letter to General Samuel Jones, the commander of the Department of Western Virginia, Lee on January 21, 1864, addressed the supply aspect of his situation. After thanking Jones for cattle and beef that had been forwarded to the Army of Northern Virginia, Lee pointed out, "It is necessary to make every exertion to procure supplies in order to keep our armies in the field." Lee's appreciation of the necessity that the armies be maintained was later expressed in a letter of March 14, 1865, to Davis, in which he discouraged a "general engagement" in North Carolina by Gen. Joseph E. Johnston. "The greatest calamity that can befall us," he wrote, "is the destruction of our armies. If they can be maintained, we may recover from our reverses, but if lost we have no resource."[70] The extent of the casualties that were inherent in his offensive approach risked Lee's capacity to maintain his own army as a viable force.

Finally, Lee also seems to have had intimations that the outcome of the war depended on the North's political reaction and will rather than on military defeat of the North. A letter to his son Custis on February 28, 1863, expresses the view that a "revolution" among the Northern people was the only check on the intent of the "present administration" vigorously to prosecute the war against the South.[71] A more comprehensive statement of this thinking appears in a letter to Mrs. Lee written on April 19, 1863:

> I do not think our enemies are so confident of success as they used to be. If we can baffle them in their various designs this year & our people are true to our cause & not so devoted to themselves & their own aggrandisement, I think our success will be certain. We will have to suffer & must suffer to the end. But it will all come right. This year I hope will establish our supplies on a firm basis. On every other point we are strong. If successful this year, next fall there will be a great change in public opinion at the North. The Republicans

will be destroyed & I think the friends of peace will become so strong as that the next administration will go in on that basis. We have only therefore to resist manfully.[72]

On June 10, 1863, after Chancellorsville but before Gettysburg, Lee raised the same point in a letter to President Davis that was quoted in the preceding chapter. In that letter he said, "We should neglect no honorable means of dividing and weakening our enemies . . . the most effectual mode of accomplishing this object, now within our reach, is to give all the encouragement we can, consistently with truth, to the rising peace party of the North." In this letter, Lee also discussed specific political and diplomatic strategies that he believed would divide and weaken the Northerners who were interested in prosecuting the war. Among these was permitting the North to believe that the South would accept peace on the basis of returning to the Union. In this regard he wrote, "Should the belief that peace will bring back the Union become general, the war would no longer be supported, and that, after all, is what we are interested in bringing about."[73]

In the above-quoted letter to his wife, Lee shows that he relied especially on the defeat of the Lincoln administration in the 1864 election. That letter was written before Chancellorsville and Gettysburg. In the former battle, Lee engaged in a brilliant series of slashing attacks and took heavy losses accordingly. The entire thrust of the Pennsylvania campaign was offensive, strategically and tactically. He punished the Federals heavily in both battles but lost 34,000 of his own men. As has been said, these losses, combined with losses previously suffered, limited his mobility and increased the risk of a siege. And, in fact, by the time of the 1864 election, he was locked in the defenses of Richmond and was in the process of being surrounded by an overwhelming force.

In sum, there were at least four aspects of Lee's own assessment of his army's situation that ran counter to the logic of his grand strategy of the offensive. He was aware of his numerical disadvantage, believed a siege would assure his defeat, and thought it critical for the South to keep its armies in the field. Yet his offensives consistently produced high casualty rates, and these casualties exacerbated the manpower differential, made a siege more likely, and reduced the Confederacy's ability to maintain an effective fighting force. In addition, he saw the loss of Northern support for the war as "what we are interested in bringing about." He nevertheless did not abandon his offensive campaigns until 1864, by which time they were practically impossible. Lee pursued the war with what Colonel Bruce calls "that spirit of aggression, which remained permanently his most prominent characteristic as a soldier."[74]

Rationalizations of Lee's offensives and the resultant prohibitive casualties abound. In the first place, we are told that Lee did not intend for his most daring offensive thrusts to result in major battles. A few examples of this rationalization will suffice. Freeman writes that Lee did not intend to give battle at Manassas in 1862. Manarin and Col. Charles Marshall, an aide-de-camp of Lee, argue that it was Jackson's attack on the Iron Brigade on August 28, 1862, at the Brawner Farm on the Warrenton Turnpike that committed Lee to the battle there. And in a letter to Davis dated August 30, 1862, in the midst of the battle of Second Bull Run, Lee himself stated, "My desire has been to avoid a general engagement."[75] But having destroyed Gen. John Pope's depot at Manassas Junction and interdicted his communications, and having moved his own army a scant twenty-five miles from Washington, it was inevitable that the Federals would have to try to find him. Lee did not like to avoid a fight; thus battle was inherent in Lee's Manassas maneuver.

In September 1862, Lee entered Maryland with the intention of proceeding on to Pennsylvania, a plan that ended at Antietam on September 17. Dowdey contends that "Lee definitely did not cross the Potomac to seek battles."[76] In his justification of this campaign, Freeman draws a picture that would be more at home in a novel by Sir Walter Scott: "Secure in western Maryland or in Pennsylvania, the Army of Northern Virginia would be able to harass if it might not destroy the Federals, and while the farmers of Virginia harvested their crops, untroubled by the enemy, Lee could wait with equanimity the arrival of cold weather."[77] An analysis of Lee's communications with Richmond, which has been ably set forth by Stephen W. Sears, persuasively contradicts the assertion that Lee did not intend a battle.[78] After the war, as Sears notes, Lee himself said that he went into Maryland to give battle. Indeed, he told William Allan that he "intended then to attack McClellan."[79] But whatever his intent, it is apparent that, contrary to Freeman's idyllic anticipation, the Union could not let Lee invade a loyal state and move north of the capital with impunity. In short, when Lee crossed the Potomac in September, he was pursuing the grand strategic offensive. He was on his way to a battle that Sir Frederick Maurice, one of his admirers, says "must be numbered among the unnecessary battles."[80]

And there is also Gettysburg, Lee's most dramatic offensive move and the most costly in its result. Recent military writers have substituted the word "raid" for the word "invasion" in reference to the Pennsylvania campaign. It is frequently suggested that Lee intended simply to forage in Pennsylvania, not to become involved in a battle. This is the argument, for example, of Hattaway and Jones in *How the North Won*. On the other hand, Maurice justifies the campaign on the ground that "Lee was still convinced that the one way for the Confederacy to obtain the peace which it sought was to convince the public opinion of the North that the attempt to keep the South within the Union was not worth its cost, and that the surest way to bring that about was to win a victory on Northern territory." Alternatively, Krick, also conscious of Lee's foraging intent, states that Pennsylvania "offered Lee wider chances to maneuver" whether or not a battle was intended.[81] But in his letter to Seddon on June 8, 1863, Lee referred to his move as "taking the aggressive" and adverted to the possibility of drawing out the enemy into "a position to be assailed." In addition, in his outline report of the campaign, dated July 31, 1863, Lee at first refers to the "valuable results [that] might be attained by military success." Later in the same communication he asserts, "It had not been intended to fight a general battle at such a distance from our base, unless attacked by the enemy," but recites the circumstances that in his view meant that "a battle thus became, in a measure, unavoidable." These comments by Lee mesh with another of Hattaway and Jones's conclusions: "Lee could have been under no illusion that he could bring off such a protracted campaign without a battle. . . . If he raided enemy territory, it would be politically if not strategically imperative for the Union army to take the offensive." As had been true for McClellan in Maryland in 1862, they remark, "Meade would have been under irresistible political pressure to attack any Confederate army in Pennsylvania."[82]

Another explanation of Lee's pursuit of the offensive in the North is the contention that "there was no alternative." This argument is most pronounced with respect to the Maryland campaign. We are to believe that the only thing Lee could do after Second Bull Run was move into Maryland and perhaps Pennsylvania. Colonel Marshall argues this point, as follows:

> It follows therefore that as General Lee could not remain in Virginia near enough to Washington to detain the enemy's army there, and could not retire without the loss of the moral effect of a successful campaign, and without encouraging the enemy to return to his former position near Richmond, or at least without affording him such an opportunity to return as it cannot be supposed that the enemy would have neglected, General Lee had nothing left to do after the battle except to enter Maryland.[83]

Accepting this conclusion, Freeman states the thesis in detail. He attempts to foreclose all other options: Lee could not have moved eastward because that would have placed his army "under the very shadow of the Washington defenses"; not southward because that would have taken his army into the "ravaged land" of Virginia and "bring the war back toward Richmond"; not westward because that would have put the army in the Shenandoah Valley, from which a retreat would have moved the army "steadily back toward the line of the Virginia Central Railroad." Freeman also refers ambiguously to the possibility of Lee's moving the army a "slight distance southward" from Manassas, "to Warrenton, for instance. . . . That would put the Army of Northern Virginia on the flank of any force advancing to Richmond, and would give it the advantage of direct rail communication with the capital." He does not say why this "slight distance southward" move was not feasible, but the thrust of his argument is plain: crossing the Potomac was the only practical thing for Lee to do.[84]

In regard to Marshall's statement, it appears that the "moral effect" argument cuts the other way. Having won a victory at Manassas, having driven the Federals into the defenses of Washington, Lee was from a standpoint of morale in an ideal position to desist from a prompt offensive move. Marshall's other contentions are presented more elaborately by Freeman and may be dealt with by considering Freeman's thesis.

Disregarding his failure to foreclose the "slight distance southward" option, which was surely an available alternative, it seems on analysis that Freeman has constructed a series of straw men. As noted later in this chapter, after the retreat from Maryland, Lee supplied his army in the "ravaged land" until the Gettysburg campaign. Avoiding moving the war back "toward Richmond" surely did not mean that Lee *had* to go into Maryland. His army's being in the Shenandoah Valley would not have led necessarily to a retreat, let alone a steady retreat, for any distance. And as for the move toward Washington, Kent Masterson Brown has argued that advancing to the defenses of Washington, a feint to confront the defeated and disorganized Federal armies in their own capital, even for a time, was action most likely to move the British politicians toward recognition. Lee could have demonstrated the military and political viability of the Confederacy by even a brief "strategic checkmate" at the gates of Washington, and avoided Antietam and its losses.[85]

The rationale that there was no alternative also overlooks the time between Lee's crossing into Maryland, September 4 through September 7, 1862, and the onset of the battle of Antietam on September 16 and 17. Alexander makes the point that whether or not Lee should have entered Maryland, he should not have accepted battle on September 17 along Antietam Creek. He writes: "News of the surrender at Harpers Ferry reached Gen. Lee that night [September 15]. That was the time for him to have . . . recrossed into Va. & saved the blood shed for no possible good on the 17th." Alexander went further with this point. Remarking that the Confederates "could have been easily retired across the river," he states that "we would, indeed, have left Maryland without a great battle, but we would nevertheless have come off with good prestige & a very fair lot of prisoners & guns, & lucky on the whole to do this, considering the accident of the 'lost order.' "[86] There was, in short, an alternative to a battle at Antietam. Even Manarin seems to concede that accepting battle there was a mistake. Having recited the disadvantages that Lee faced, Manarin tries to find a reason for his having "invited attack." His analysis contains a conventional, Lee-as-a-performer conclusion: "To stand and fight was a gamble and Lee gambled."[87]

The no-alternative rationale for the Gettysburg campaign is not as vigorous as it is for Antietam, but it has been elaborately presented by

Colonel Marshall.[88] His analysis is worthy of close examination because it is typical of much of the argumentative advocacy in Lee's behalf.

During the period following Chancellorsville, Lee's army remained near Fredericksburg on the Rappahannock, facing Gen. Joseph Hooker's Army of the Potomac situated on the north side of that river. Marshall begins his argument by reasoning that "after the battle of Chancellorsville, . . . the questions presented to General Lee were not only how to avert the manifest danger to which his army was always exposed but also how to use his army so as to bring the enemy's plans to naught." He then posits three options available to Lee: attacking Hooker in his position opposite Fredericksburg, remaining where he was awaiting the enemy's advance, or crossing the Potomac and marching into Pennsylvania. Persuasively disposing of the option of attacking across the river, Marshall turns to the option of waiting for the enemy's advance, which he evaluates in relation to the remaining option, the Pennsylvania move.

Marshall begins his discussion of the option of waiting for the Federals' move by declaring that Lee "was bound to *assume* . . . the enemy would abandon his effort to dislodge him from his position at Fredericksburg, and would move his army to Richmond by water" (emphasis added). This, he says, would have required Lee to withdraw to defend Richmond and:

> During the retreat . . . accident *might* bring on an engagement on ground unfavourable to the Confederates, . . . but even if that eventually [sic] were avoided nothing could justify the *deliberate adoption* of a policy the *immediate* and *unavoidable result* of which would be to impose upon the Confederate army the burden of such a defense. Better far to risk the battlefield which chance might bring us during a movement northward than *deliberately* to accept *what we knew* to be altogether favourable to the enemy, and altogether unfavourable to us. (Emphasis added.)

This argument is too clever by far. It depends in the first place on the assertion that there were only three available options. This was not necessarily so. Lee could have fallen back to favorable defensive ground in northern Virginia with the reasonable expectation that Hooker would have followed him. In the second place, the argument rests on the assumption, for which no proof is offered, that instead of moving against Lee by land the Federals would necessarily have proceeded directly to Richmond by water. In fact, the evidence since the 1862 withdrawal from the Peninsula pointed to the fact that the North was committed to the overland route.[89] In any event, having set forth his assumption, Marshall then treats it as an established fact, which effectively eliminates the option of Lee's defending at the Rappahannock: he would have to rush toward Richmond.

After converting his hypotheses of the water route and the necessity for Lee's retiring to Richmond into categorical facts, Marshall proceeds to set up the possibility of catastrophic events during that retreat. Lee "might" have had to fight on unfavorable ground, which speculation is also immediately converted into a certainty: "the immediate and unavoidable result of which . . . we knew to be altogether favourable to the enemy, and altogether unfavourable to us." Thus Marshall destroys the option of Lee's waiting to defend against a Federal move at Fredericksburg by the argumentative device of disparaging it with gratuitous assumptions and unfounded factual assertions.

Marshall's ultimate comparison of the relative merits of Lee's defending in northern Virginia or moving into Pennsylvania is classic. Having characterized these options in his own freewheeling way, he is able to conclude as he wants to: "Better far to *risk* the battlefield which *chance* might bring us during a movement northward than deliberately to accept *what we knew* to be altogether favourable to the enemy, and altogether unfavourable to us" (emphasis added). This conclusion is entirely logical, but it rests on Marshall's tendentious analysis, including the assumptions that Lee would have had to fight on unfavorable terms during a retreat to Richmond, which he treats as objective facts. Having set up only three options for Lee and eliminated two of them, the third – marching into Pennsylvania – is all that is left.

A more convincing scenario than Marshall's would anticipate the Federals' again undertaking an overland offensive and Lee's having an opportunity to defend against it, as he had done at Fredericksburg and was to do again in 1864, by which time his numbers were much reduced as a result of Gettysburg. There may have been a theoretical risk of the Union's resorting again to the water route, but this was unlikely in view of the Federal requirement that the task of Northern forces in the theater was to remain between Lee and Washington. Further, the mounting of the armada would have taken time and would have been open for all to see. If the Federals had undertaken to organize the fleet and move the army to a staging area, Lee would at that time have had options other than simply retreating to Richmond. These would have included crossing the Potomac so as to deter the Federal embarkation. In any event, to convert the theoretical risk of the water route into a certainty as the premise for justifying the objective risk of Lee's extending his communications in a move into Pennsylvania is casuistry.

Lee himself was quoted after the war on the issue of his options after Chancellorsville. In what seems a shorthand version of Marshall's argument, Lee, as has been previously noted, is alleged to have said that his alternatives were to "retire on Richmond and stand a siege . . . or to invade Pennsylvania." Although there are those who accept this statement as justification for Gettysburg, it is unsupported with any data and seems on its face unreasonable. There were many miles and many places between these alternatives.

As noted above, Lee's outline report argues that having stumbled onto the Federals at Gettysburg, "A battle thus became, in a measure, unavoidable." Although not presented as a rationale for the campaign as a whole, this statement does raise the question of alternatives in regard to the Confederate offensive thrusts of July 2 and 3. In other words, whether or not there was an alternative to the campaign, were there alternatives to Lee's actions on the latter two days of the battle? Alexander has also addressed this point:

Now when it is remembered that we stayed for three days longer on that very ground, two of them days of desperate battle, ending in the discouragement of a bloody repulse, & then successfully withdrew all our trains & most of the wounded through the mountains; and, finding the Potomac too high to ford, protected them all & foraged successfully for over a week in a very restricted territory along the river, until we could build a bridge, it does not seem improbable that we could have faced Meade safely on the 2nd at Gettysburg without assaulting him in his wonderfully strong position. We had the prestige of victory with us, having chased him off the field & through the town. We had a fine defensive position on Seminary Ridge ready at our hand to occupy. It was not such a really *wonderful* position as the enemy happened to fall into, but it was no bad one, & it could never have been successfully assaulted. . . . The onus of attack was upon Meade anyhow. We could even have fallen back to Cashtown & held the mountain passes with all the prestige of victory, & popular sentiment would have forced Meade to take the aggressive.

I cannot believe that military critics will find any real difficulties in our abstaining from further assault on the following day, or in pointing out more than one alternative far more prudent than an assault upon a position of such evident & peculiar strength. (Emphasis in original.)

According to Alexander, "I think it must be frankly admitted that there was no real difficulty, whatever, in our taking the defensive the next day [July 2]; & in our so manouvring afterward as to have finally forced Meade to attack us . . . 60 per cent of our chances for a great victory were lost by our continuing the aggressive." Concluding, he remarks:

Now the gods had flung to Meade . . . a position unique among all the battlefields of the war, certainly adding fifty percent to his already superior force, and an adversary stimulated by success to an utter disregard of all physical disadvantages & ready to face for nearly three quarters of a mile the very worst that all his artillery & infantry could do. For I am impressed by the fact that the strength of the enemy's position seems to have cut no figure in the consideration [of] the question of the aggressive.[90]

Historians have also rationalized Lee's Antietam and Gettysburg campaigns on other grounds. In the case of Antietam, the political advantage of a victory on Northern soil, which might have carried with it British recognition of the Confederacy, is said to justify the obvious risk of the campaign. The potential effect of the campaign on the Northern election later in 1862 is also seen as justification. These are credible contentions, although, as has been said, the recognition prospect was not the panacea that some writers suggest. Even so, there is still the problem of the irreplaceable losses that would result from a victory as well as from a defeat. In addition, although such a victory would have had great value, to try for it was to risk the negative consequences of falling short of victory, consequences which Lee's army, of course, came to realize. Porter Alexander is again worth consulting. Regarding Antietam, he writes:

> And this, I think will be pronounced by military critics to be the greatest military blunder that Gen. Lee ever made. . . .
>
> In the first place Lee's inferiority of force was too great to hope to do more than to fight a sort of drawn battle. Hard & incessant marching, & camp diseases aggravated by irregular diet, had greatly reduced his ranks, & I don't think he mustered much if any over 40,000 men. McClellan had over 87,000, with more & better guns & ammunition, &, besides that, fresh troops were coming to Washington & being organized & sent him almost every day. A drawn battle, such as we did actually fight, was the best *possible* outcome one could hope for. Even that we only accomplished by the Good Lord's putting it into McClellan's heart to keep Fitz John Porter's corps entirely out of the battle, & Franklin's nearly all out. (Emphasis in original.)

Alexander states flatly that Lee "gave battle unnecessarily at Sharpsburg Sept. 17th, 1862. . . . He fought where he could have avoided it, & where he had nothing to make & everything to lose – which a general should not do."[91]

Antietam is further justified by some of Lee's admirers because of the general's need for food supplies and forage, expected to be available north of the Potomac and scarce in northern Virginia. There are at least two logical flaws in this justification. In the first place, Lee recrossed the Potomac on the night of September 18, and his army subsisted in Virginia until the Gettysburg campaign. Accordingly, it was not in fact necessary for him to go to Maryland for commissary supplies. Indeed, as Hattaway and Jones note, "Having left Maryland . . . [Lee] adhered to his original military objective by remaining close to the south side of the Potomac. Here he found abundant forage and subsistence."[92] The rationale is further flawed because it was surely unnecessary to send an entire army to obtain these supplies. On the eve of Chancellorsville,

Longstreet and two of his divisions engaged in what Freeman calls a "commissary campaign" in southern Virginia in which they collected provisions.[93] This could have been done in Maryland in 1862, and such a raid would not have drawn the entire Federal army into pursuit and thereby set up a battle.

The Gettysburg justifications include the necessity to upset Federal offensive plans, avoidance of a siege, alleviation of supply problems in unforaged country, encouragement of the peace movement in the North, drawing the Federal army north of the Potomac, and even the relief of Vicksburg. Again, these were worthwhile goals, but the risks were plain to Lee – and, win or lose, significant casualties inhered in the campaign. Citing Gettysburg as an occasion on which Lee's celebrated audacity was "overdone," Alexander makes this comment: "Then perhaps in taking the aggressive at all at Gettysburg in 1863 & certainly in the place & dispositions for the assault on the 3rd day, I think, it will undoubtedly be held that he unnecessarily took the most desperate chances & the bloodiest road." Indeed, referring to the third day, Alexander states, "I thought it madness to send a storming column out in the face of [the Federal artillery], for so long a charge under a mid-day July sun."[94]

When all is said and done, the commentators' rationalizations of Lee's most daring offensive thrusts seem contrived. Although these commentators are aware that Lee's efforts were unsuccessful, costly, and destructive to the South's chances of victory in the war, they are committed to the Lee tradition and seem to strain to absolve him. If simple logic rather than complicated and contradictory rationalization prevails, these offensives can be seen to fall readily into the pattern of Lee's mistaken grand strategy, the grand strategy of attack.

Still other arguments have been put forward in behalf of Lee's leadership. Some who admire his performance argue that he in fact pursued a defensive grand strategy but did so in the form of the previously noted "offensive defensive," at a distance from Richmond. Freeman, among others, presents this argument. As has been emphasized, a defensive grand strategy may involve reasonable offensive operational strategy and tactics. But regardless of the general validity of this strategic concept, as applied to Lee the "offensive defensive" is a sham. The facts at hand reveal a general who specifically stated that military defeat of the Federals to "drive the armies of the enemy from the field" was what the South had to achieve in order to win the war, who consistently advocated the attack and undertook movements that were designed for giving battle or foreseeably led to battle, and who until his army was decimated and penned up in the Richmond defenses persisted in using his forces offensively. The contention that Lee's strategy entailed an "offensive defensive" is not credible in the face of the facts: the facts identify a general who believed that the offense was the appropriate grand strategy.

Perhaps the most thoughtful rationalization of Lee's generalship was that presented after the war by aide-de-camp Col. Charles Marshall. Marshall underscored the critical importance of the safety of Richmond and then summarized what he called "Lee's military policy":

> In these circumstances there was but one course left for General Lee to pursue, if he would save Richmond from the peril which he knew would attend its investment by the large army of the enemy. He must give occupation to that army, and such occupation as would compel the largest concentration of its forces. By this means he might even induce the enemy to withdraw troops from other parts of the Confederacy, and thus obtain additional reinforcements for himself.

Marshall argued that, consistent with this course, Lee sought "to employ the enemy at a distance and prevent his near approach to the city." The Maryland and Pennsylvania campaigns and the entire war in Virginia had this purpose, according to Marshall.

Marshall's rationale is plausible, but it fails because it is built on false premises. Thus Marshall states that Lee was "unwilling to incur the risks and losses of an aggressive war having for its object the destruction of the enemy." According to Marshall, mindful of his strength problem,

> General Lee thought that to expose our armies to the sacrifices of great battles the object of which was only to disperse or destroy those of the enemy would soon bring the Confederacy to the verge of exhaustion. Even victory in such engagements might prove di-

sastrous. The North could readily raise new armies, while the means of the South were so limited that a few bloody victories might leave it powerless to continue the struggle.[95]

But Lee did in fact incur the risks and losses that Marshall abjured. He advised President Davis that military victory was the way to peace. In his efforts to defeat or drive the Federal armies from the field he did expose the Army of Northern Virginia to the "sacrifices of great battles," some of which were "bloody victories" that did bring the Confederacy to the "verge of exhaustion." In short, the policy that Marshall described is not the policy that Lee carried out.

The no-alternative thesis regarding Antietam and Gettysburg has been previously discussed above. In more general terms, the same contention underlies much of the traditional Lee literature: especially in view of the constant necessity of protecting Richmond, there was no practical alternative to the entire conduct of Lee's army command, conduct that was dominated for two years by the grand strategy of the offensive. Lee's admirers do not ask whether he could reasonably have carried out his leadership in a different way. Indeed, many of them do not acknowledge that the question of alternatives exists. This traditional assumption leads to anomalous conclusions. A recent fervently admiring commentary is marked by unusually graphic, unintended irony. The author notes that Lee went "from one victory that led nowhere to another" and refers to Lee's "glorious . . . campaign filled with victories that resulted in total defeat."[96]

Was there an alternative to Lee's glorious campaign leading to total defeat? A perimeter defense or war of position was not feasible. Johnston's apparently entirely defensive policy in Georgia did not have promise. But there was another option: a defensive grand strategy, within the context of which Lee could on occasion have undertaken offensive thrusts, appropriate operationally strategic and tactical offensives, while avoiding the costly pattern of offensive warfare that he pursued in 1862 and 1863.

Of course, there is no guarantee that a defensive grand strategy would necessarily have succeeded. In terms of negatives, it could have involved the loss of Confederate territory, but so did the offensive grand strategy that Lee adopted. It could have risked dampening home front morale among a civilian population that craved victorious offensives, but so did Lee's offensive grand strategy. When he was ultimately forced to resort to the defensive in 1864, that strategy was effective even though his army and its leadership by that time had been grievously reduced by the casualties that resulted from his prior offensives. Had Lee adopted this defensive approach during the two years that he spent on the offensive, he could have had available a fair proportion of the more than 100,000 of his soldiers and officers who went down during the offensive years. With these additional numbers, he could have maintained mobility and avoided a siege. Maneuvers like Early's 1864 movement down the Valley could have been undertaken with sufficient numbers. The Union, on the offensive, could have suffered for an earlier or longer period the ceaseless Federal casualties that began in May 1864. The war could have been prolonged and the Northern people could have abandoned their political support of the war.[97] All of these things are conjectural, but they arise reasonably from the fact that there was an alternative. The truth is that in 1864 Lee himself demonstrated the alternative to his earlier offensive strategy and tactics. In the process he demonstrated the feasibility of the grand strategy of the defense.

When compared to the defensive, Lee's offensive grand strategy, because of the losses entailed, led inexorably, to use his words, to the "natural military consequences of the enemy's numerical superiority," that is, surrender. That superiority was enhanced by Federal reinforcements, but it was also heightened by Lee's heavy and irreplaceable losses. The grand strategy of defense would have muted these "natural military consequences" because it would have slowed the increase in the enemy's numerical superiority insofar as that numerical superiority arose from Lee's heavy and disproportionate losses. Further, because of the strategic and tactical advantages of the defense, that numerical superiority would have been less significant had Lee assumed the defensive in 1862–63. Lee proved this when massively outnumbered on the defensive in 1864–65. In 1864, Lee's defense, in Porter Alexander's words, exacted "a price in blood" that significantly threatened "the enthusiasm of [the North's] population." Adopted earlier, this defensive policy might have worn the North out. The grand strategy of the defense was therefore not only a feasible alternative; it was also more likely to have led to victory.

The views of historians who have recently examined Lee's general-ship are worth consulting. In 1984, Hill Junior College at Hills-boro, Texas, presented a Confederate history symposium. The subject was Lee. Five professional historians appeared on the program. One of the Hillsboro participants, Grady McWhiney, discussed Lee's preoc-cupation with the offensive: "From the outset of the South's struggle for independence," he said, "Lee suggested offensives to President Jeffer-son Davis and urged other generals to be aggressive." McWhiney also stated that "though Lee was at his best on defense, he adopted defen-sive tactics only after attrition had deprived him of the power to attack." Ending his remarks, McWhiney concluded: "The aggressiveness of Robert E. Lee, the greatest Yankee killer of all time, cost the Con-federacy dearly. His average losses in his first six big battles were six percent greater than his opponents' losses; his total casualties exceeded 120,000."[98]

Another distinguished military historian, Frank E. Vandiver, pro-vided a survey account of Lee's leadership at the Hillsboro symposium that is worth describing at length. Beginning with Lee's assumption of command in 1862 on the Peninsula, Vandiver remarked that "the plan for the Seven Days showed that Lee had a sound grasp of what I call 'grand tactics' – tactics elevated almost to the level of strategy. But the casualty ratio was extremely high. In this kind of attack, the attackers are at risk; the Confederates coming up against strongly fortified Fed-eral positions paid heavily for an advance." Turning to Antietam, Van-diver stated,

> One of the most uncomfortable concerns for Jackson and Long-street and the other Confederate commanders is that Lee, his army weakened and wearied after the second day of Antietam, . . . wants to stay another day, is even thinking of attacking. With what? He has put into action every man he can get on the field, even A. P. Hill's Division coming up from Harpers Ferry. McClellan has a whole Federal Corps he has not committed. Lee's generals know this and they don't want to stay around much longer. But it is clearly in Lee's mind; he does not want to relinquish the offensive. He does not want to cease to be audacious. He won't retreat if he can help it.

At Gettysburg, according to Vandiver, Lee "failed to accept reality. . . . He simply wanted to go on and attack because he wanted to attack." Referring to the situation later in 1863, mindful of Lee's correspondence with subordinates and Krick's thesis in regard to the loss of officers, Vandiver asserted that Lee could not undertake a particular maneuver because "attrition was cutting away the high command. Lee was unable to find division and corps commanders, even brigade commanders with the kind of ability that he had come to expect during the past two years." Proceeding into 1864 and referring to the Wilderness, Vandiver noted that "attrition is affecting [Lee's] thinking and limiting his options. For the first time he is forced seriously to consider yielding the strategic offensive." Finally, with Lee besieged at Petersburg, according to Vandiver, "The strategic and tactical and permanent defensive he cannot accept and keeps looking for a way to break through the lines and get back to audacity."

In an ambiguous characterization of his prior comments, Vandiver also remarked: "I would emphasize though, that again by pushing audacity, always audacity, Lee practiced the high art of grand tactics. He also lost a lot of men by attacking and attacking and attacking." Ultimately, conceding "some trepidation" in doing so, Vandiver ventured this conclusion: "Lee may have been too addicted to the offensive, even against outstanding firepower. Now, I'm not sure about that assertion. I think you have to balance the fact that he lost a lot of men and stuck to the offensive against *what he considered to be the strategic necessities of attack*. So I would level the charge that he might have been too addicted to the offensive" (emphasis added).

In the statement just quoted, Vandiver abandons an objective analysis of the casualty problem in midstream and begins to speak in terms of what *Lee* considered his necessities to be. Vandiver's analysis is provocative in another way as well. In charging that Lee was "too addicted to the offensive," Vandiver was clearly stating a criticism. It is also plain that Vandiver believed that the problem with Lee's addiction to the offensive was the losses it entailed. But addiction to the offensive and the taking of losses are not in and of themselves negative. They become negative with reference to some strategic criterion. It seems that Vandiver had in mind but did not express such a criterion, the same one that has formed the basis for criticism of Lee's attack grand strategy in this chapter, namely, that Lee's addiction and his losses limited the South's chances of winning the war. But having implicitly acknowledged this criticism, and in spite of it, Vandiver returned to the Lee tradition: "I think he will forever stand among the world's great captains."[99]

Vandiver missed the point in his admiration of Lee's audacity. However much one admires audacity, Lee was not engaged in a theatrical event. He was an army commander charged with using his army so as to maximize the South's chances of achieving independence. The aggressiveness that Vandiver and McWhiney point out was not an incidental flaw; it reflected a fundamental misconception of the proper Southern grand strategy.

Believing that Lee's job was to fight the war so as to make a maximum contribution to victory, General Fuller states that Lee "never seems to have realized the uselessness of squandering strength in offensive actions as long as the policy of the Richmond government remained a defensive one." And he pronounces this judgment: "[Lee] did not create a strategy in spite of his government; in place, by his restless audacity, he ruined such strategy as his government created." Indeed, he "rushed forth to find a battlefield, to challenge a contest between himself and the North." This characteristic is also proclaimed in substance by Lee admirers. Fishwick notes that Lee "never defended when he could attack." Dowdey, referring to Antietam, states that for Lee "it went against the grain to quit the field without battle."[100] To insist on the offensive, regardless of a defensive opportunity, is simply not strategically sound. Whether or not to commit an army to battle is not appropriately a question of the commander's "grain."

As acknowledged by General Fuller in describing the Virginia campaign of 1864–65,

> The fight [Lee] put up exceeded in courage and grandeur anything he had yet accomplished. . . . Hitherto his strategy and tactics had been offensive, now they were defensive; and by combining rapidity of movement with earthworks he blocked Grant's advance at every turn, holding Richmond and Petersburg for nine months against every attack. . . . With his back against the wall, he parried every thrust, until Sherman's advancing columns and Grant's unceasing pressure brought the Confederacy to collapse.

No one would deny that this defense, characterized by Fuller as "skilful, masterful and heroic," was a remarkable one.[101]

But the point is that it was too late for this masterful defense. During the two years prior to the Virginia campaign of 1864, lacking a real understanding of the practical circumstances of the antagonists, or lacking the capacity to relate his grand strategy to those circumstances, Lee had pursued the counterproductive grand strategy of the offensive. Although the Federal military establishment prior to Grant's advent as general-in-chief had not recognized or carried out the true Federal grand strategy of relentless offensive, Lee's direction of his army had unilaterally accomplished the destruction of his force that was the objective of the true Federal grand strategy. Although he had recognized in June 1863 that being besieged in the Richmond defenses would predict the surrender of his army, Lee thereafter initiated the risky and costly Gettysburg offensive and then went on the offensive again, also at great cost, in the Wilderness. These losses helped to seal him up in the trenches around Richmond. Maurice states that "Lee's great weapon was manoeuvre, and Grant had taken it from him," but Lee's attack grand strategy, prior to Grant's Virginia campaign, was also a large factor in Lee's loss of this great weapon.[102]

Writing in 1913, Colonel Bruce offered this characterization of Lee's grand strategy:

> The population of the Confederate States was little less than half that of the Northern States. If the resolution of one was equal to that of the other, it would be easy to calculate the end of a war where the losses on each side in every contest were equal. To illustrate, if a manufacturer or merchant worth a million dollars should enter into a trade warfare with a competitor worth two millions, and so aggressively carry it on as to entail a loss to each of $250,000 a year, the result would be that at the end of four years one would be bankrupt and the other still rich. This was the kind of war inaugurated by General Lee.[103]

In sum, Lee's "kind of war," the grand strategy of the offensive, contradicted the South's true grand strategy. It therefore contributed to the loss of the Lost Cause.

Douglas Southall Freeman, Lee's unquestioning and devoted biographer, sets forth the qualities that he believes to have been responsible for Lee's strategic eminence: "his interpretation of military intelligence, his wise devotion to the offensive, his careful choice of position, the exactness of his logistics, and his well-considered daring." Later, after characterizing Lee's repeated offensives, he describes the circumstances of the army, without relating the offensives to that condition: "The army's hard-won battles left its ranks depleted, its command shattered by death or wounds, its personnel exhausted, its horses scarcely able to walk, its transportation broken down, its ammunition and its commissary low."[104] The loss of mid-level officers as described by Krick is presumably included in the shattering of command that Freeman notes. According to Krick, "The heart of the Confederate army was starting to feel this difficulty . . . just *before Gettysburg*" (emphasis added).[105] These conditions were not inevitable. They did not fall from the sky. They were in significant part the consequences of Lee's "devotion to the offensive" and his "daring."

Porter Alexander writes of Lee: "He had the combative instinct in him as strongly developed as any man living." Admiration for this attribute underlies a 1984 characterization of the general, a classic statement of Lee's greatness, appearing in volume 7 of the above-noted Time-Life Civil War series: "Perhaps his greatest asset was pure audacity – his willingness to run risks, his eagerness to attack, his instinct of taking the initiative at just the right moment."[106]

These, then, are the martial qualities of the Lee of tradition: devotion to the offensive, daring, combativeness, audacity, eagerness to attack, taking the initiative. Whether these qualities were wise or unwise, well considered or ill considered, assets or liabilities, would seem to depend on one's criterion. If one covets the haunting romance of the Lost Cause, then the inflicting of casualties on the enemy, tactical victory in great battles, and audacity are enough. On the other hand, in the words of Colonel Bruce, "If the art of war consists in using the forces of a nation in a way to secure the end for which it is waged, and not in a succession of great battles that tend to defeat it," a very different assessment of Lee's martial qualities is required.[107]

CHAPTER FIVE

Those People –
The Magnanimous Adversary

Douglas Southall Freeman, who accepts the traditional view of Lee as a promoter of postwar reconciliation between North and South, recites a conversation that took place after the war at White Sulphur, Virginia, between Lee and a young Southern woman, Christiana Bond. In the course of the conversation, according to Bond, who purported to quote directly, she asked, "But, General Lee, did you never feel resentment toward the North?" In response, "He stopped and in a low voice answered: 'I believe I may say, looking into my own heart, and speaking as in the presence of God, that I have never known one moment of bitterness or resentment.'"

Bond first reported this conversation some sixty years after the fact in her *Memories of General Robert E. Lee.*[1] Whatever the extremely belated nature of the report may say about its reliability, Freeman used the story as the premise for recounting another of the Lee traditions: that he was a man of remarkable charity, the man who could not hate, who loved his enemies and turned the other cheek. The imagery is, of course, obvious.

The tradition of Lee's magnanimity is an invariable aspect of the writing about him. A major and typical theme in this writing concerns the manner in which the general identified his adversaries. It has long been reported that Lee never spoke negatively of the Federals and referred to them simply as "those people." The Reverend J. William Jones, a prominent postwar Lee traditionalist, who published his first book in 1875 by authority of the Lee family and the faculty of Washington and Lee University, stated that "those people" was the "severest" term Lee "was accustomed to employ." According to Jones, Lee rebuked others who spoke negatively of the Yankees. Jones is also the source for an account of a postwar incident similar to that described by Bond. This concerned a clergyman preaching at Washington College during Lee's presidency of that institution. The minister spoke indignantly about the North in connection with Lee's 1865 indictment for treason. Lee reminded the speaker of "a good old book which I read" and then stated that "I have never cherished toward [the people of the North] bitter or vindictive feelings, and have never seen the day when I did not pray for them."[2] Gamaliel Bradford, Sir Frederick Maurice, Marshall W. Fishwick, Clifford Dowdey, and others have passed this image on. More recently, in 1984, author Gene Smith wrote that Lee never voiced "a word of bitterness for those everyone around him called 'the enemy' or 'the Yankees.' . . . It was always 'those people.' " An avowal of the generous forgiveness with which the general regarded his erstwhile foes is now a part of the Lee hagiography.[3] The question is whether the tradition of Lee's remarkable magnanimity is historical.

That tradition notwithstanding, the reader of *The Wartime Papers of R. E. Lee* is at once struck by Lee's habitual use of the term "the enemy" (not "those people") to describe the Federals. The term first appears on April 29, 1861, in a letter to Col. Andrew Talcott about river fortifications, and continues on to the very end in both his official and personal correspondence.[4] Lee's usage was, of course, appropriate and correct. After Lee accepted his Virginia commission on April 22, the soldiers and other representatives of the Union, and the Union itself, were indeed "the enemy." His use of that designation is therefore noteworthy only because the Lee tradition naively tells us that he somehow fought vigorously for the Confederacy without a sense that the Federals were his enemies.

But the tradition is contradicted by evidence more material than

Lee's terminology in reference to the Federals. In a letter to his wife on May 2, 1861, one can see the first hint of what was to become his preferred description of the Northerners. He wrote, "Our opponents . . . feel their power & they seem to have the desire to oppress and distress us."[5] By December 1861, with warfare having begun in earnest and Federal troops on Virginia soil, Lee's anger and bitterness were fully aroused. He wrote to his daughter Annie on December 8, referring to "the ruin & pillage . . . at the hands of our enemies." But he went further: describing the Federal soldiers as "vandals" and expressing his fear for the residences of his friends who were within reach of the enemy's forces, he wrote, "I fear too the yankees will bear off their pretty daughters."[6] Shortly thereafter, he dispatched a letter to Secretary of War Judah P. Benjamin. The communication is confusing in its wording but clear in its message concerning Lee's feelings toward the North. Regarding the Federal effort to block the Charleston harbor by sinking vessels in the channel, he declared, "This achievement, so unworthy of any nation, is the abortive expression of the malice & revenge of a people which they wish to perpetuate by rendering more memorable a day hateful in their calendar."[7]

The same black mood marked his Christmas letter in 1861 to one of his daughters. Referring to Arlington, he told her, "Your old home, if not destroyed by our enemies, has been so desecrated that I cannot bear to think of it." Continuing, he stated, "I should have preferred it to have been wiped from the earth, its beautiful hill sunk, and its sacred trees buried, rather than to have been degraded by the presence of those who revel in the ill they do for their own selfish purposes."[8] A letter from South Carolina to his son Custis a few days later reported that the Federals were "pillaging," "burning," "robbing," "marauding," and "alarming women & children."[9]

The letter to Benjamin reveals aspects of Lee's state of mind other than his bitterness and resentment, aspects that were also to mark much of his correspondence throughout the war. He seemed somehow shocked that warfare involved killing and property destruction by the Federals, a curious reaction for a lifelong soldier. And his attitude suggested a double standard. It was apparently all right for the Confederacy to bombard Fort Sumter and force its surrender, but the North's effort to block Charleston harbor in order to limit the Confederates' use of that port was malicious and vengeful. On January 19, 1862, in a letter to Custis, he protested the Federal raids on the Carolina coast with this outburst: "No civilized nation within my knowledge has ever carried on war as the United States government has against us."[10]

In keeping with his view of the Federals as a hateful enemy, Lee warned his wife about them on April 4, 1862, as McClellan's army gathered on the Peninsula. In urging her to leave White House, Virginia, so as not to find herself within the Federal lines, he wrote that "to be enveloped in it would be extremely annoying & embarrassing, as I believe hundreds would delight in persecuting you all for my & F[itzhugh]'s sake."[11] As a matter of fact, when Mrs. Lee did become trapped within enemy lines, Federal general Fitz John Porter offered her a protective guard on one occasion, and, on another, General McClellan himself met her at his headquarters and sent her in a carriage, with a Confederate escort, to meet General Lee. Even Dowdey made this acknowledgement: "During the Peninsula Campaign, Mrs. Lee was twice caught within Federal lines, and each time ceremoniously escorted to safety; the second time, she was delivered from McClellan's headquarters to a Confederate officer."[12]

Reacting to especially harsh orders by Federal general R. H. Milroy regarding the treatment of alleged Confederate guerrillas in Tucker County, Virginia, Lee denounced Milroy's "savage and brutal policy" in a letter of January 10, 1863, to Secretary of War James A. Seddon. The principal concern of this letter was the necessity of the South's increasing its armies because there was "no alternative but success or degradation worse than death, if we would save the honor of our families from pollution, our social system from destruction." On the same day, in his rage at Milroy's conduct, Lee suggested to Seddon "that prisoners from his command captured by our forces be not exchanged, but that they be held as hostages for the protection of our people against the outrages which he is reported to be committing."[13]

En route to Gettysburg, in the Confederates' second eastern excursion into Federal territory, Lee reported on the state of northern Virginia in a dispatch to Seddon on June 13, 1863. He advised the secretary, "I grieve over the desolation of the country and the distress to innocent women and children, occasioned by spiteful excursions of the enemy, unworthy of a civilized nation."[14] Returning to Virginia after

Gettysburg, on July 26, 1863, he wrote his wife from Culpeper and discussed the fact that their second son, Brig. Gen. "Rooney" Lee, had been captured and was a prisoner of war. "I hope his exchange may soon be effected," he wrote, "But nothing can be done to hasten it. The more anxiety shewn on our part, the more it will be procrastinated by our enemies, whose pleasure seems to be to injure, harass & annoy us as much as their extensive means enable them." Lee's grief and concern for his prisoner son were soon intensely compounded when Rooney's wife died. On December 29, 1863, Lee wrote to his wife, "I now long to see him more & more & wish I could communicate with him without affording to his jailers the opportunity of rejoicing in his misery."[15]

There was more of the same in Lee's other correspondence. The Federals had engaged in "entire disregard of civilized warfare and the dictates of humanity"; they were "cowardly persecutors"; their acts were "unchristian & atrocious."[16] The historical record shows that Lee constructed a demonic image of the Federals. From the beginning, he did not see them as honorable military opponents engaged in a good-faith effort to sustain their view of the Union. He perceived, and disseminated to others, a picture of the Federals as barbaric invaders in the mold of the Germanic tribes that had brought Rome down.

The point here is not, of course, that Lee was without provocation. Nor is it that the Federals behaved well or lawfully, or that Southern troops behaved no less badly on Northern soil.[17] As any student of war knows, hating the enemy, perceiving the enemy as malicious and evil, and indulging in hateful rhetoric about the enemy are characteristic of warfare. Lee is not to be judged negatively for acting as so many soldiers and leaders have in this respect. The point is that the tradition of the general who referred to his enemies only as "those people," the tradition of Lee as a man of great magnanimity toward his adversaries, is manufactured and unhistorical.

CHAPTER SIX

The Price of Honor

The meaning and significance of the doggedness with which Lee pursued the Southern cause all the way to Appomattox have never been seriously analyzed by historians, who seem to assume that his persistence was wholly admirable. The general's place in history has been established without questions about the consequences of his persistence and without inquiry into his motives. Such an inquiry is, however, appropriate. Whether the South could have won the war and, if so, why it lost, are not at issue in the inquiry; rather, the relevant questions concern what Lee himself believed at various times about the risk of losing the war, how he carried out his leadership in view of what he believed, his motivation, and the consequences of his acts.

Lee's biographers have candidly reported Lee's view of the Confederacy's chances of winning the war. They have credited two 1865 statements attributed to Lee concerning his beliefs at the outset of the contest. The first of these was reported by John S. Wise, son of a former Virginia governor. According to Wise, Lee spoke to him in April 1865, near Farmville, as the Army of Northern Virginia moved toward Appomattox. Referring to the Confederate disaster at Sayler's Creek, Lee said, "A few more Sailors' Creeks and it will all be over – ended – just I have expected it would end from the first." The second statement was reported by Gen. William N. Pendleton, at one time chief of artillery of the Army of Northern Virginia and a confidant of Lee's. According to Pendleton, immediately prior to the surrender Lee said to him: "I have never believed we could, against the gigantic combination for our sub-jugation, make good in the long run our independence unless foreign powers should, directly or indirectly, assist us."[1]

Because the Pendleton report contained the proviso regarding for-eign assistance, it is necessary to inquire of Lee's expectations in this respect. Freeman states that Lee did not believe that foreign assistance would be forthcoming, but there is more direct evidence. Lee wrote to his wife on December 25, 1861, at the time when the *Trent* affair threatened war with England; rejecting her suggestion of the possibility of British intervention in the war, he asserted: "We must make up our minds to fight our battles & win our independence alone. No one will help us." And in November 1865 he told the Englishman Herbert C. Saunders that "taking . . . the well-known antipathy of the mass of the English to the institution [of slavery] into consideration, . . . he had never expected help from England."[2]

Taken at face value, these statements indicate that Lee believed from the beginning that the war was in vain. But the statements were made after the reality of defeat. Perhaps Lee did not feel as hopeless in April 1861 as he suggested in April 1865. Setting these reports of his 1861 feelings aside, it is instructive to trace his beliefs about the South's chances of winning as the war progressed – and for purposes of analysis, it is useful to examine those beliefs at three particular periods of time: in 1863, after the defeats at Gettysburg and Vicksburg; in 1864, as of the early weeks of the siege of Petersburg; and during the period following Lincoln's reelection in November 1864.

On June 10, 1863, prior to Gettysburg, in a previously mentioned letter to President Davis, Lee commented on the mounting odds against a Southern victory. In portions of the letter Lee entrusted the South's cause to heaven and to prayer; additionally, he wrote:

Conceding to our enemies the superiority claimed by them in numbers, resources, and all the means and appliances for carrying on the war, we have no right to look for exemptions from the military consequences of a vigorous use of these advantages.... We should not, therefore, conceal from ourselves that our resources in men are constantly diminishing, and the disproportion in this respect between us and our enemies, if they continue united in their efforts to subjugate us, is steadily augmenting.[3]

The letter went on to discuss the importance of encouraging the Northern peace movement. According to Freeman's interpretation, the letter reveals that "twenty-two months before Appomattox" Lee "could see no other outcome of the struggle than the ultimate defeat of the Confederacy by the more powerful Union," unless the Northern people became so discouraged that the North would no longer support the war.[4]

Although Lee's letter does not constitute a statement of hopelessness, it is at least a statement of grave doubt. Significantly, the statement was made after the victory at Chancellorsville but before the Gettysburg and Vicksburg defeats. The reality of Lee's pessimism at this time has been described by Coddington. Referring to Chancellorsville, he says: "Although the Northern army had suffered heavy losses, it was still intact and could renew the offensive if given a breathing spell.... Even as they celebrated the glorious triumph at Chancellorsville they saw ominous developments unfolding in the Mississippi Valley. General U. S. Grant had ... gotten his army on the same side of the river as the defenders of Vicksburg."[5] As noted in Chapter 4, these facts were among those that, however imperfectly, led to the Pennsylvania campaign, on which the Army of Northern Virginia embarked on June 3, 1863.

Whether or not Gettysburg and the chronologically coincidental surrender at Vicksburg were the decisive events of the war, they were of great significance in the final analysis. The loss of John C. Pemberton's army of 29,491 men[6] and the casualties suffered by Lee at Gettysburg were plainly heavy blows, and they were recognized as such by thoughtful Confederate leaders. Thus, on July 28, 1863, Gen. Josiah Gorgas, chief of ordnance, wrote in his diary: "One brief month ago we were apparently at the point of success. Lee was in Pennsylvania threatening

Harrisburg, and even Philadelphia. Vicksburg seemed to laugh all Grant's efforts to scorn. . . . Now the picture is just as sombre as it was bright. . . . Yesterday we rode on the pinnacle of success – today absolute ruin seems to be our portion. The Confederacy totters to its destruction."[7]

The Confederate military disasters of July 1863 were followed by other disasters. British domestic politics, bungled diplomacy between the British and French governments, and the setbacks at Gettysburg and Vicksburg put to rest any serious possibility of European recognition of the Confederacy. On July 23, 1863, Henry Adams reported from London that "all idea of intervention is at an end."[8] The British, responding to American pressure and their perception of the South's waning hopes, on September 6, 1863, detained the Laird rams that were being built in England for the Confederacy. At home, Bragg's Army of Tennessee, after a September victory at Chickamauga, was routed at Chattanooga and Missionary Ridge in November. And on December 4, 1863, the Confederates abandoned their costly effort to seize Knoxville.

Lee did not at the time record his views of the impact of these events on the war's outlook; but given that he had in June adverted to the fact that "our resources in men are constantly diminishing, and the disproportion . . . between us and our enemies . . . is steadily augmenting," Lee's sense of defeat must have been intensified by this series of misfortunes. It is reasonable to conclude that at some point between mid-July and mid-December 1863, from twenty to fifteen months before Appomattox, Lee was aware that the cause was lost.

The whirlwind of 1863 raged into 1864. Sherman struck for Atlanta in May, and in the same month the Army of the Potomac crossed the Rapidan to enter the Wilderness in Virginia. After grievous losses on both sides, in mid-June the Federals invested the Richmond defenses at Petersburg. The siege of Petersburg began.

As was noted in Chapter 4, Lee believed that being besieged in the Richmond defenses signaled the surrender of his army. Porter Alexander is quite specific about the meaning of what transpired. Referring to Grant's eluding Lee and his successful move from Cold Harbor to the

James River and Petersburg in mid-June 1864, Alexander comments that Grant "gained a strategic position of such controlling value that the fall of Richmond, and with it of the Confederacy, was, after that, only a question of a few moves more or less." With this event, according to Alexander, "the last hope of the Confederacy died down and flickered out." Amplifying his conclusion, Alexander states, "The position which [Grant] had now secured, & the character of the military operations he now contemplated, removed all risk of any serious future catastrophe, however bold we might be, or however desperately we might fight. We were sure to be soon worn out."[9] Insight into Lee's personal sense of ultimate defeat during the Petersburg siege can be gained from his correspondence. According to Freeman, Lee's letters from Petersburg "give more than a hint that he believed the Southern cause was becoming hopeless."[10] On August 23, 1864, in a letter previously quoted, he told the secretary of war, "Without some increase of strength, I cannot see how we are to escape the natural military consequences of the enemy's numerical superiority." On September 2, 1864, Lee warned President Davis, "As matters now stand we have no troops disposable to meet movements of the enemy or strike when opportunity presents, without taking them from the trenches and exposing some important point."

A note of desperation also marked Lee's communications as the siege progressed. On September 26, 1864, in a letter to Braxton Bragg about his failure to receive enough men to replenish his immediate losses, he wrote, "If things thus continue, the most serious consequences must result." Pleading to Bragg for slaves to replace army teamsters, cooks, and hospital attendants, he said that if the slaves did not arrive promptly, "it may be too late." And on October 10, 1864, he told Adjutant and Inspector General Samuel Cooper that, "I fear it will be impossible to keep him [Grant] out of Richmond."[11]

In his foreword to *R. E. Lee*, Freeman discusses the summer of 1864 and Lee's sense of the risk of defeat at that time. He writes: "Looking backwards, it is obvious, of course, that the reduction of the food supply, the death of Jackson, the defeat at Gettysburg, the virtual starvation of the horses in the winter of 1863–64, the inability of Lee to force Grant back across the Rappahannock after the battle of the Wilderness, and the failure of conscription in the summer of 1864 marked definite stages in the approach of defeat. . . . *Lee saw clearly and without illusion"* (emphasis added).[12]

It appears, therefore, that, leaving aside his conclusions in 1863 about the likelihood of defeat, by the time of the siege of Petersburg in June 1864, ten months before Appomattox, Lee believed that his surrender was inevitable. It was simply a question of *when* he would surrender. Alexander's analysis of the situation in June 1864 is informative:

> Of this period the future historian will doubtless write that by all the rules of war & of statecraft the time had now fully arrived for President Davis to open negotiations for peace. Now was the time to save his people the most of blood, of treasure, & of political rights. The last chance of winning independence, if it ever existed, *had* now expired, and all rules must condemn the hopeless shedding of blood.
>
> . . . And, perhaps, by a peace he might have saved the South five hundred, or even a thousand million dollars, & doubtless also some thousands of lives. (Emphasis in original.)[13]

It is fair to suggest, however, that there may have been an unstated proviso to Lee's belief that the war was lost. This proviso concerned Northern war-weariness, a factor to which Lee was sensitive. As seen earlier, his letter of June 10, 1863, to President Davis, after describing the growing manpower disadvantage of the South, addressed the issue of the North's will. He wrote that "under these circumstances, we should neglect no honorable means of dividing and weakening our enemies, that they may feel some of the difficulties experienced by ourselves. It seems to me that the most effectual mode of accomplishing this object, now within our reach, is to give all the encouragement we can, consistently with truth, to the rising peace party of the North."[14]

In practical terms, Northern war-weariness was to be at issue in the presidential election in November 1864. If Lincoln and the Republicans and Union Democrats were defeated, it was at least possible that there would be some sort of effort to end the war on terms acceptable to the Confederacy. This proviso was eliminated when Atlanta fell and Lincoln and his party were overwhelmingly reelected. It was plain then that a military decision was to be made, not a political one, and that the

North would carry on the war to victory. Clifford Dowdey remarks that "With the passing of the possibility of a political change bringing peace, no rational hope remained for the Confederacy to gain its independence." As characterized by Alexander, "The re-election of Mr. Lincoln . . . might well have been generally recognised as the very funeral of our last chances."[15] Surely by November 1864, with this election result, Lee knew unconditionally that the war had been lost. Appomattox was five months away.

The question at hand is, when did Lee come to believe that defeat was inevitable? At the very latest, it must, of course, have been when he in fact decided to surrender his army in April 1865. But was there was an earlier time – between April 1861 and April 1865 – when this was his conviction? In view of his own statements, it is plain that Lee was at no time optimistic of a Southern victory. Indeed, he at all times seemed to feel that defeat was likely. If he is to be judged on his 1865 statements to Wise and Pendleton, it appears that he believed from the beginning, as he left the United States Army and traveled to Richmond, that the war was bound to be lost. But disregarding these expressions after the fact, the evidence composed of his own wartime statements points to at least three periods of time when he seems to have believed, perhaps with varying degrees of certainty, in the inevitability of the loss of the war. The first of these, presumably when his conviction of defeat was most tentative, was in 1863 following Gettysburg and Vicksburg. The second was in June 1864 at the onset of the Petersburg siege, approximately ten months prior to Appomattox. At that time he characterized his conviction as categorical and unqualified, but in fact he may have harbored some hope that the South would be aided by the results of the November election in the North. The third was in November 1864, five months from the end, when Lincoln was reelected.

At each of these times, Lee persisted in the fight despite what he believed about ultimate defeat. The implications of his persistence went far beyond the Army of Northern Virginia; they affected the continuation of the war as a whole. Freeman has accurately portrayed the effect of Lee's resolve in fighting on:

The final major reason for Lee's successes . . . was his ability to maintain the hope and fighting spirit of the South. . . . As months passed with no hopeful news from France or from England, while the Union forces tightened their noose on the Confederacy, the Southern people looked to their own armies, and to them alone, to win independence. Vicksburg fell; the Confederacy was cut in twain. The expectations raised by the victory at Chickamauga were not realized. The Army of Tennessee failed to halt the slow partition of the seceded states. Gradually the South came to fix its faith on the Army of Northern Virginia and its commander. . . . On the Rapidan and the Rappahannock there was still defiance in the flapping of each battle flag. The Southern people remembered that Washington had lost New York and New England, Georgia and South Carolina, and still had triumphed. Lee, they believed, would do no less than the great American he most resembled. As long as he could keep the field, the South could keep its heart. . . . Morale behind the line, not less than on the front of action, was sustained by Lee.[16]

Dowdey has echoed Freeman's conclusion. Referring to the autumn of 1864 and the relatively high morale in Petersburg, he writes: "It was not that the spirit in Petersburg promoted an illusion in Lee. The issue remained for him 'a question of time.' . . . He, a solitary mortal . . . had become the primary factor in prolonging a war with the United States." Frank Vandiver has commented on another aspect of this phenomenon, Lee's awareness that the Southern people pinned their hopes on him and the Army of Northern Virginia. Lee, he writes, "understood the special position that his army came to have in relation to Congress and to the Confederate people. . . . He knew he and his men embodied Southern hopes in the public mind. He, and by extension his army, were more symbols than realities."[17]

The consequences of Lee's persistence are plain. They included civilian hardship, North and South; heavy casualties in the several armies of the Confederacy and Federal casualties, East and West; and severe economic losses. Given the vantage point from which Lee himself viewed the situation, it is unnecessary to quantify all of these factors; it is enough to measure the price of persistence simply in terms of casualties in the Army of Northern Virginia.

As is well known, Lee's casualties frequently were not officially reported. Without attempting to rationalize the always-conflicting data about casualties, we can let Thomas L. Livermore's estimates of Confederate losses in several of the battles after Lee came to sense defeat serve to make the point:[18]

Wilderness (May 5–7, 1864)	7,750
Spotsylvania (May 12, 1864)	9,000–10,000
Petersburg (June 15–18, 1864)	2,970
(Hill's corps and the divisions of Field and Kershaw)	
Weldon Railroad (August 18–21, 1864)	1,619
Winchester (September 19, 1864)	3,921
Cedar Creek (October 19, 1864)	2,910

This list omits other 1864 engagements such as Cold Harbor, the Petersburg Mine, Deep Bottom, and Boydton Plank Road. It also excludes casualties suffered after Lincoln's reelection. In addition to the casualties resulting from the almost-constant deadly sniping in the Petersburg-Richmond siege lines,[19] the Army of Northern Virginia suffered unascertainable but severe losses at Hatcher's Run in February 1865. Col. Walter H. Taylor, adjutant general of the army, reported that during the last thirty days of the siege of Petersburg "the loss to the army by desertion . . . was . . . an average of one hundred per day";[20] nevertheless, as previously described, on March 25, 1865, Lee ordered the unsuccessful attack on Fort Stedman. Freeman concedes that Federal estimates of 4,800 to 5,000 casualties incurred by the Confederates at Fort Stedman are not "greatly exaggerated."[21]

And finally, Lee moved west with Richmond burning behind him as a result of Confederate efforts to prevent Federal use of its manufacturing and stores. On April 20, 1865, Lee himself characterized the state of his army before Richmond. To Davis he reported:

The operations which occurred while the troops were in the entrenchments in front of Richmond and Petersburg were not marked by the boldness and decision which formerly characterized them. Except in particular instances, they were feeble; and a want of confidence seemed to possess officers and men. . . . On the morning of the 2d of April, when our lines between the Appomattox and Hatcher's Run were assaulted, the resistance was not effectual: several points were penetrated and large captures made. At the commencement of the withdrawal of the army from the lines on the night of the 2d, it began to disintegrate, and straggling from the ranks increased up to the surrender on the 9th.[22]

But Lee led this army on to Appomattox, fighting all along the way. The "still defiant Lee," according to Marshall W. Fishwick, "still held out," as his army "lurched westward" and "staggered" toward Appomattox. In the process of this hopeless effort, from March 29 to April 9, the Confederates lost 6,266 men, *killed and wounded*, according to Livermore.[23]

Lee's belief in the inevitability of his final defeat, and the contrast between that belief and his combative persistence, raises the question of his motivation. There are several worthwhile lines of inquiry regarding his motives, but before examining them it is necessary to consider briefly the question of his authority to surrender: did he have the authority to surrender his army and, if so, what circumstances permitted him to exercise that authority?[24]

It is plain that Lee did have the right to surrender and was aware that he did. Between April 7 and April 9, 1865, as his correspondence with Grant proceeded, Lee consulted certain trusted aides and debated with himself the issue of surrender. But he insisted that, "if it is right, then *I* will take *all* the responsibility" (emphasis in original).[25] On April 9, the deed was done at Appomattox. On April 12, Lee reported the surrender to Jefferson Davis, explaining that maintaining the battle "one day longer . . . would have been at a great sacrifice of life, and at its end I did not see how a surrender could have been avoided."[26] In short, on April 9, 1865, believing that ultimate surrender was inevitable, he could not justify the sacrifice of life that further prolonging the combat would entail.

The situation at Appomattox was surely grim, but as has been noted, Lee had viewed the South's situation in the same grim terms for anywhere from twenty to five months prior to April 9, 1865. He had the same authority then to surrender as he had on April 9. As the casualties and other losses – physical, financial, and emotional – mounted, what interest did Lee believe he was serving in continuing the hopeless struggle? His own statements suggest four possible answers to this question: he believed that the North was such a monstrous tyrant that defeat and death were the only moral responses; God willed his continuing to fight in spite of the inevitability of defeat; he was bound to persist because he was subject to Confederate civilian control, which did not want him to surrender; or his personal sense of duty demanded it.

The first answer suggests the philosophical proposition that there are worse fates than defeat and death. Americans in Lee's day, as well as today, were the heirs of a liberty-or-death tradition. Lee identified with this tradition. Despite his personal opposition to secession, he is quoted as having said, "We had, I was satisfied, sacred principles to maintain and rights to defend, for which we were in duty bound to do our best, even if we perished in the endeavor."[27] On April 7 or April 8, sometime within two days of the surrender, General Pendleton, representing a group of officers, suggested surrender to Lee. Lee rejected the idea, stating that rather than surrender "we must all determine to die at our posts."[28] But the liberty-or-death motive does not adequately explain Lee's prolonging the war after his belief in its futility, bearing in mind that he did in fact surrender, despite his prior rhetorical flourishes. Furthermore, he flatly rejected Gen. Porter Alexander's suggestion of guerrilla warfare as an alternative means of continuing the war because of its deleterious effect on the country as a whole.[29] The April 20, 1865, letter to President Davis, quoted above, also discouraged Alexander's guerrilla warfare suggestion and urged Davis to seek a general peace.[30] And on June 13, 1865, Lee applied for amnesty and the "benefits and full restoration of all rights and privileges" as a citizen of the United States.[31] Each of these facts contradicts the notion that Lee was motivated by the belief that ultimate resistance to the Federals was the appropriate moral position.

Untroubled by any questions concerning the correctness of Lee's conduct, Freeman comes close to suggesting that Lee persisted in the war because he believed that, regardless of the odds and the inevitability of defeat, God wanted him to keep fighting. Thus, Freeman states that "nothing of his serenity during the war or of his silent labor in defeat can be understood unless one realizes that he submitted himself in all things faithfully to the will of a Divinity which, in his simple faith, was directing wisely the fate of nations and the daily life of His children."[32] It is certainly true that Lee had a strong personal sense of the presence of God and God's responsibility for human events. But given the general's Herculean efforts, and his reliance on God to give him victories, it seems unreasonable to suggest that he persisted in futile combat because of some sense that God intended him to do so. Had this been his conviction, he presumably would not have surrendered on April 9, 1865.

Freeman is at pains to point out that Lee accepted wholeheartedly the American constitutional premise of military subordination to the civil government: "Lee . . . applied literally and loyally his conviction that the President was the commander-in-chief." This constitutional principle was consistent with one of the general's life principles, described by Freeman as "respect for constituted authority" and "his creed of obedience to constituted authority."[33] Dowdey's description of certain events in February and March 1865 provides an interesting insight into the question of Lee's deference to authority. Referring to the period following the Hampton Roads meeting of February 3, 1865, between Confederate representatives and Lincoln and his aides, Dowdey writes:

> Lee had held a private conversation with Virginia's Senator R. M. T. Hunter. . . . Lee urged him to offer a resolution in the Senate that would obtain better terms than, as Hunter reported Lee as saying, "we're likely to be given after a surrender." Hunter claimed that Davis had already impugned his motives for seeking peace terms, and told Lee, "if he thought the chances of success desperate, I thought he ought to say so to the President." Though Lee held frequent conversations with Davis during February, it is unlikely that he ever brought himself to introduce a subject which would be so distasteful to the president.

Dowdey then recounts the views of Secretary of War Seddon, his successor in that office, Gen. John C. Breckinridge, and Longstreet, all of whom shared Lee's recognition of the fact that the war was lost and peace was needed. Dowdey concludes by observing, "The crux of the matter was that men in a position to know recognized that the South was defeated, *but no one was willing to assume the responsibility of trying to convince Davis of this!*" (emphasis added). Lee had by this time become general-in-chief of the Confederate armies. Considering Dowdey's unflinching admiration for Lee, his attributing Lee's position and that of the others mentioned to an unwillingness to take responsibility is surely an unintended indictment. In any event, although it is evident that Lee accepted subordination to civilian authority, he ultimately took responsibility for the surrender and simply announced it to Davis.[34] It cannot, therefore, be said that civilian control was the reason for Lee's persistence.

Finally, can Lee's resolve to fight on in the face of certain defeat be explained by his sense of duty and honor? Gaines M. Foster has described the South as "a culture based on honor,"[35] and, as noted previously, Bertram Wyatt-Brown has detailed the entire complex white culture of the South in terms of a code called "Honor." The authors of *Why the South Lost the Civil War* have attempted to give a short definition of the concept: "When Confederates talked of honor they did not mean pride so much as moral integrity, personal bravery, Christian graciousness, deference to and respect for others, and self-worth, recognized by their peers."[36]

In Lee, honor and its companion, duty, were, to be sure, highly and self-consciously developed; so too was their consequence, the self-regard that Wyatt-Brown describes. All biographies of Lee quote at length his many aphorisms about these values. As previously noted, he said that the Confederates were "duty bound to do our best, even if we perished." On February 22, 1865, in a letter to his wife, he stated, "I shall . . . endeavor to do my duty & fight to the last." In a March 1865 interview with Gen. John B. Gordon, he spoke of "what duty to the army and our people required of us." Preparing to evacuate the Petersburg-Richmond line and move west toward Appomattox, "he acted," Colonel Taylor notes, "as one who was conscious of having accomplished all that was possible in the line of duty, and who was undisturbed by the adverse conditions in which he found himself."[37]

In regard to the effort to escape the pursuing Federals between Richmond and Appomattox, Freeman observes: "So long as this chance was open to him, his sense of duty did not permit him to consider any alternative" and "As long as there was a prospect of escape Lee felt it was his duty to fight on. He would not yield one hour before he must."[38] Freeman also notes approvingly Lee's memorandum to himself: "There is a true glory and a true honor: the glory of duty done – the honor of the integrity of principle."[39] Commenting on "the dominance of a sense of duty in [Lee's] actions," Dowdey states that "this is not so much a sense of duty in the abstract as a duty to do the best he could. The point can clearly be seen when duty, *as a sense of the pride of a professional in his craft*, caused him to practice meticulously the techniques of command *long after any military purpose could be achieved*" (emphasis added).[40]

Such a narrow definition of Lee's sense of honor and duty seems to be another unintended indictment by Dowdey. However defined, this sense of honor appears, after all, to have been an essentially personal emotional commitment that compelled Lee to fight on, regardless of the cost and long after he believed that it was futile to continue the contest. Referring to the Confederacy's hopeless situation during the winter of 1864–65 and sympathetic to this personal commitment, Dowdey recognizes "the moral obligation that required [Lee] to act as though defeat could be held off."[41]

In a chapter entitled "The Sword of Robert E. Lee," Freeman sets forth "an accounting of his service to the state," part of which has already been presented in Chapter 4. Having noted Lee's mobilization of Virginia, the Seven Days, the repulse of Federal offensives against Richmond, and his victories in six of ten major battles from Gaines's Mill through Spotsylvania, Freeman proceeds, as quoted previously:

> During the twenty-four months when he had been free to employ open manoeuvre, a period that had ended with Cold Harbor, he had sustained approximately 103,000 casualties and had inflicted 145,000. Holding, as he usually had, to the offensive, his combat losses had been greater in proportion to his numbers than those of the Federals, but he had demonstrated how strategy may increase an opponent's casualties, for his losses included only 16,000 prisoners, whereas he had taken 38,000. Chained at length to the

Richmond defenses, he had saved the capital from capture for ten months. All this he had done in the face of repeated defeats for the Southern troops in nearly every other part of the Confederacy. . . . These difficulties of the South would have been even worse had not the Army of Northern Virginia occupied so much of the thought and armed strength of the North. Lee is to be judged, in fact, not merely by what he accomplished with his own troops but by what he prevented the hosts of the Union from doing sooner elsewhere.[42]

In reciting what Lee accomplished, Freeman does not allude to the fact that for perhaps the last twenty months of these efforts, and surely for a substantial lesser period, Lee was proceeding in a cause that he personally believed was lost.

James M. McPherson has summarized the ultimate consequences of the prolonging of the war, to which Lee's accomplishments made a significant contribution:

the South was not only invaded and conquered, it was utterly destroyed. By 1865 the Union forces had . . . destroyed two-thirds of the assessed value of Southern wealth, two-fifths of the South's livestock, and one-quarter of her white men between the ages of twenty and forty. More than half the farm machinery was ruined, and the damage to railroads and industries was incalculable. . . . Southern wealth decreased by 60 percent (or 30 percent if the slaves are not counted as wealth). These figures provide eloquent testimony to the tragic irony of the South's counterrevolution of 1861 to preserve its way of life.[43]

In conjunction, the statements of Freeman and McPherson raise reasonable questions regarding Lee and history and Lee's role as an American idol. On the one hand, the Lee tradition projects a tragic hero, a man who courageously pursued a cause that he believed to be doomed. On the other hand, this heroic tradition must be balanced against the consequences of Lee's heroism. There is, of course, a nobility and poignancy, a romance, in the tragic and relentless pursuit of a hopeless cause. But in practical terms such pursuit is subject to a very different interpretation.

In reality, military leadership is not just a private or personal activity. Nor is a military leader's sense of honor and duty simply a private and personal impulse. Military leadership and the leader's sense of duty are of concern not only to the leader but also to the followers and to the enemy, ordinary people, many of whom die, are maimed, or otherwise suffer. In short, military leadership involves responsibility for what happens to other persons. There is, therefore, no matter how sincerely a leader may believe in the justice of a cause, a difference between undertaking or continuing military leadership in a cause that the leader feels can succeed and undertaking or continuing such leadership in a cause that the leader feels is hopeless. In the latter circumstance, the leader knows that his order "once more into the breach" will kill and injure many of his soldiers as well as the enemy's and also realizes that his order and these deaths and injuries are without, in Dowdey's phrase, "any military purpose." Lacking a military purpose, they also have no political purpose. Thus they are without any rational purpose.

The absence of any rational purpose behind Lee's persistence is suggested by his sense of the meaning of the deaths of his men as revealed by his early advocate, the Reverend J. William Jones. Among the general's wartime papers that Jones found after his death were "maxims, proverbs, quotations from the Psalms, selections from standard authors and reflections of his own." One of these, in Lee's own hand, read, "The warmest instincts of every man's soul declare the glory of the soldier's death. It is more appropriate to the Christian than to the Greek to sing: 'Glorious his fate, and envied his lot, who for his country fights and for it dies.' "44

As suggested earlier by McPherson's description of the war's impact on the South, the conflict involved catastrophic consequences for the people of the United States, both North and South. During the war as a whole more than half a million soldiers died. Untold thousands were maimed. The families of all of these men also suffered grievously. Whatever portion of the catastrophe occurred after the time when Lee had become convinced that the war was lost — whether Lee came to believe this twenty, fifteen, ten, or only five months before the end — significant harm took place, in the West as well as the East, before Lee finally called a halt to the fighting. For the plain people who suffered, Lincoln's "him who shall have borne the battle, and . . . his widow, and his orphan," the consequences of the prolonging of the war were dire in the extreme.[45]

Freeman writes bitterly about Southerners who were fearful or doubtful or who wished for peace, comparing them unfavorably to the dauntless Lee and to President Davis. But the authors of *Why the South Lost the Civil War* make a different observation: "By late 1864, very likely earlier, those Confederates who argued for an end of war, even if that meant returning to the Union, did not include only the war-weary defeatists. Many among those who took that statesmanlike position may have lost their will, but they weigh more on the scales of humanity than those who would have fought to the last man."[46]

The Lee orthodoxy insists that the Confederate officers and soldiers at Appomattox were tearful and heartbroken at their surrender – they wanted to keep fighting. But even purveyors of the orthodoxy occasionally, perhaps unwittingly, contradict the tradition. Thus, quoting Col. Charles Venable, Dowdey writes that soldiers who learned of Lee's intent to surrender were "convulsed with passionate grief." But Dowdey also reports that "Lee was aware that many of his soldiers, officers and men, were ready to end 'the long agony.' . . . He could sense the attitude." He also describes enlisted men who, en route to Appomattox, "overcome by exhaustion . . . were lying stretched out flat or sitting with their heads on their knees, waiting to be gathered up by the enemy." A suggestive Federal account by an eyewitness agrees with Dowdey's report. "Billy," an enlisted man in the First Michigan Volunteers, wrote to his family from Appomattox on the day of the surrender. He described the pursuit to Appomattox and then added, "The best of it is the Rebs are as pleased over the surrender as we are, and when the surrender was made known to them cheer after cheer went up along their whole line."[47]

If one steps back from the romantic tradition, the intensity of Lee's resolve seems startling. By the early weeks of 1865, the Confederacy was an empty shell. Its ports and, except for Richmond, its major cities were in Federal hands. Its Western army had been effectively dispersed in the December battle at Nashville. Having marched across Georgia at will, Sherman was poised to start from Savannah into the Carolinas, and no significant force was prepared to oppose him. Lee was trapped in the Richmond defenses. Much of the civilian population was suffering serious hardship and civil order was at the breaking point. In these circumstances, Lee on January 11, 1865, sent to Senator Hunter the letter discussed in Chapter 2 regarding the enlisting of slaves as soldiers. He wrote of "our duty to provide for continued war and not for a battle or a campaign." He sounded the same note in discussing the same issue in his letter of February 18, 1865, to Congressman Ethelbert Barksdale: "I believe that we should provide for a protracted struggle, not merely for a battle or a campaign."[48] On February 19, 1865, he advised the secretary of war, "I fear it may be necessary to abandon all our cities, & preparation should be made for this contingency."[49] On March 14, 1865, with Appomattox less than a month away, he wrote to Davis, as noted in Chapter 4, concerning the necessity to avoid the "destruction of our armies. If they can be maintained, we may recover from our reverses." Ten days later, he requested from Virginia all "negroes, slave and free, between the ages of eighteen and forty-five, for services as soldiers . . . to enable us to oppose the enemy."[50] Lee's army was shrinking daily as a result of desertion. His above-quoted letter to Davis of April 20, 1865, acknowledges that his army had been demoralized "in the entrenchments in front of Richmond and Petersburg." After Sayler's Creek on April 6, 1865, where approximately 8,000 of the harried Confederates fleeing westward from Petersburg were overpowered and surrendered, Lee spoke to Gen. William Mahone of his remaining soldiers as "true men." In Lee's mind the captured men were by implication untrue; a "true man" was one who could somehow stay in the fight as long as Lee's personal sense of honor demanded it.[51] So Lee fought on regardless of the consequences to the Southern people and in spite of the absence of any rational purpose.

As the evidence presented in this chapter indicates, there is every reason to question the aspect of the Lee tradition that has glorified and does not question his pursuit of the war even after he believed it was lost. The analysis here has not addressed the implicit question of whether, prior to Appomattox, Lee had an alternative to continuing the fight as of the time he knew that such continuation had no rational purpose. As has been said, in terms of military law and custom he had the technical authority to surrender his army when he believed its situation was hopeless. General Order No. 9 and the April 12 letter to President Davis were drafted on the premise of this authority: defeat was inevitable and postponing surrender would uselessly bring additional deaths to the soldiers for whom he was responsible. But in practical terms, although the same premise had existed for some months, the exercise of that authority prior to Appomattox would doubtless have presented serious problems because of the views of President Davis and at least some of the Confederate political leadership and the opinions and expectations of the army and the Southern people. Granting that Lee had to take these factors into account, what were his practical alternatives to carrying on the war until Appomattox? This question is essentially philosophical. Perceiving that useless death and destruction are the consequences of an army commander's continuing to fight, but that his government or the army or the people expect him to continue, the issue concerns the commander's personal responsibility.

In stating that the war was effectively lost in June 1864 at Petersburg and that President Davis should have sought peace at that time, Alexander says that "both the army and the people at that time would have been loth to recognize that the cause was hopeless. In the army, I am sure, such an idea was undreamed of." But he then writes, "Gen. Lee's influence could doubtless have secured acquiescence in it, for his influence had no bounds, but nothing short of that would."[52] This, then, is the first answer to the question of Lee's practical alternatives to continuing the fight: he could have surrendered and persuaded the government and the people to accept the fact of the loss of the war. But assuming that his sense of personal responsibility did not extend to this exercise of his technical authority, and prior to Appomattox it obviously did not, he could have confronted the civilian authorities with his views of the hopelessness and tragic consequences of fighting on and recommended that the fighting cease. Lee did not do this. Indeed, as late as the winter of 1864–65, as noted by Dowdey, he would not take that responsibility. Had Lee done this, and had the civilian authorities ordered him to fight on, two choices would have then been available to him. He could have fought on and borne history's judgment for having done so, with credit for his effort to avoid the continuation. Or he could have resigned and escaped that judgment.

Readers may form their own opinion as to the time – twenty, fifteen,

ten, or five months before the end – when Lee's personal responsibility
became an imperative. That responsibility was not in fact assumed by
Lee until April 9, 1865. The issue of Lee's personal responsibility
cannot be escaped by romanticizing his continuation of the war. As a
responsible actor in the events of the war, Lee must be fully subject to
history's gaze and must be accountable for his acts.

An apologist for Lee may point out that all wars have gone on too
long, that all wars have invariably been lost long before the losing
side has surrendered or abandoned the war. This is true, but, as regards
the matter considered here, it is beside the point. The point is this: the
Lee literature uniformly expresses admiration for the general's having
carried on the war, despite its devastations, long after the Confederate
cause was hopeless and long after Lee himself knew that it was hopeless. That this was heroic on his part, that it is part of his glory, is Lee
dogma. This dogma is dubious, however, within the context of the
American Civil War, in view of the common nationality and culture of
the North and South, the political circumstances of the sections, Lee's
prewar disapproval of secession, and his prompt postwar application for
amnesty. Taking these factors into account, the harm to Americans,
North and South, should surely be considered in reference to Lee's
status in American history, as should questions concerning the personal
character of his motives for continuing the contest.

It may be easier to grasp the irony and cost of Lee's persistence if one
moves from gross statistics to what happened in microcosm to Southern
soldiers. As has been noted, on March 25, 1865, Lee ordered the
Confederate attack on Fort Stedman, a Federal stronghold in the Petersburg line. After initial success, the assault was beaten back. Federal
reports estimated Confederate casualties to have been between 4,800
and 5,000 men, a count that has also been previously described, and
General Meade reported to General Grant that "permission was
granted the enemy . . . to remove their dead and wounded, under flag of
truce."[53] On April 2, 1865, as the Confederate Petersburg line was at
last pierced, some 400 to 600 men from Wilcox's division and Harris's
brigade were put into Fort Gregg and told to hold it to the last extremity.
They were assaulted by a full division of Federals and ultimately de-

fended themselves with bayonets in hand-to-hand fighting. Finally surrounded, the survivors capitulated, but the Federals also found fifty-five dead and wounded in the fort.[54] In a report reminiscent of Lee's "glory of the soldier's death" document, Freeman cites a source stating that during the Fort Gregg struggle Lee called his staff around him and asked them to witness "a most gallant defense."[55]

Two weeks after Fort Stedman and a week after Fort Gregg, Lee surrendered. On the following day he issued General Order No. 9, revered in history, the farewell to his army that included these words: "Feeling that valor and devotion could accomplish nothing that could compensate for the loss that may have attended the continuance of the contest, I determined to avoid the *useless sacrifice* of those whose past services have endeared them to their countrymen" (emphasis added).[56] And as has been previously stated he then reported to President Davis that he had surrendered because to maintain the battle "one day longer . . . would have been at a great sacrifice of life, and at its end I did not see how a surrender could have been avoided."

The dead and wounded Confederates at Fort Stedman and Fort Gregg, and the Federals killed and wounded there, are symbolic of the problem of the prolongation of the war and General Lee's military accomplishments. As of April 9, 1865, Lee himself believed that further casualties would be a "useless sacrifice," but it was too late for the several thousand who had gone down since he had concluded that the war was futile. Among these, of course, were the 6,266 of his soldiers killed and wounded in the Appomattox campaign itself.

On April 9, 1865, Lee apparently felt that he had fully and finally served his personal sense of duty. He had fulfilled, at last, what Dowdey describes as his personal sense of "duty to do the best he could . . . a sense of the pride of a professional in his craft." He was prepared, at last, again quoting Dowdey, "to assume the responsibility" for introducing a subject "distasteful" to Jefferson Davis. The awful human cost of his persistence had, of course, been paid by countless other people, including his own soldiers.

Giving Lee full credit for good faith and high personal character, the historian must nonetheless – as a practitioner of a discipline regarded as one of the humanities – take into account the human and social consequences of his continuing to lead others in a war that he believed was lost. It is fair to observe that Virginia, reputedly the focus of Lee's primary interest, suffered especially devastating losses of life and property because it was the scene of almost constant warfare. The facts cast serious doubt on the traditional assumption that Lee's persistence was wholly admirable.

CHAPTER SEVEN

Lee after the War

According to Douglas Southall Freeman, "Lee the warrior became Lee the conciliator. Within less than five months [from Appomattox], he was telling Southern men to abandon all opposition, to regard the United States as their country, and to labor for harmony and better understanding. Seldom had a famous man so completely reversed himself in so brief a time, and never more sincerely. In the stormiest of the days that followed he was not to shift a foot." Writing in 1984, Gene Smith reported that Lee expressed no "opinions on the war or the Yankees" during the postwar period. The 1989 *Encyclopedia Americana* carries a similar message: "His last years were spent in working to promote brotherhood and nationalism." That the general was invariably conciliatory, that he was detached from the postwar issues, is another of the widely proclaimed doctrines in the Lee tradition.[1] Lee's place in the American pantheon, his national stature, rests in part on this tradition. It is a tradition worth examining, and an examination of it should begin with some notice of the practical and historical circumstances of Lee's life after the war.

On August 24, 1865, Lee accepted the presidency of Washington

College in Lexington, Virginia, a position he occupied until his death in 1870 at the age of sixty-three. The institution was small and unpromising and, like the South generally, had suffered physically and financially during the war. Although a salary, a residence, and certain additional stipends accompanied the job, it was not a lucrative position. Lee's acceptance of the position and his excellent service to the college and its students, which included curriculum development that was in advance of the times, were wholly praiseworthy.[2]

The years left to Lee in Lexington were, of course, the early years of Reconstruction, a period that has bred its own mythology, a mythology that has only in recent years been reviewed with objectivity. The complicated story of Reconstruction is beyond the scope of this book, but the period must be characterized briefly in order to give context to Lee's postwar activities.

Essentially an extension and outgrowth of the war, the conflicts that marked Reconstruction, like the prewar conflicts and the war itself, centered on sectionalism and race. In regard to sectionalism, the Southern states promptly claimed their prewar status in the Union, including their right to control their domestic institutions. Northerners in the main resisted the Southern claims. This resistance varied in degree and motive, with Northern attitudes that ranged from reform-minded idealism to outright vindictiveness. The postwar version of the race issue had to do with the economic, social, and political status of the former slaves. Slavery had been lost as a means of racial control, but the South remained committed to white supremacy; and, although racism prevailed in the North as well, the cause of civil rights, including suffrage for the blacks, was initially pressed by some Northerners. The race issue, that is, the status of the freedmen, inevitably became involved with the question of the terms on which the states that had seceded were to reestablish their relationship with the Union.

Politically, the Reconstruction era was unusually turgid. Among other complications, both political parties were maneuvering to establish national constituencies. The Republicans' concern for the freedmen was in part idealistic and in part a reflection of the realization that their only natural political allies in the South were these blacks. The Northern Democrats' motives were similarly complex and mixed. Some genuinely wanted to forgive the South and forget the past; others saw the party's national future as dependent on appealing to Southern whites. It was a time of inept and sometimes venal presidents, the Ku Klux Klan and violence, the beginning of Grantism and the Gilded Age, and federal military occupation of the Southern states. And a new set of constitutional issues emerged: the constitutional theory of separation of powers was severely tested, and national restrictions on the powers of the states were proposed in the Thirteenth, Fourteenth, and Fifteenth Amendments.

In short, confronted during Reconstruction with continued sectionalism and racism, the American experiment was not entirely successful, the American system not entirely effective. The system performed as might have been expected under the circumstances. The American people, North and South, had been fighting each other in a cruel and devastating war that was itself the result of a failure of politics. The end of the war changed the forum, techniques, and objectives of the antagonists but did not produce a rational or orderly political process. Such was the rancorous and tumultuous milieu in which Lee passed the last five years of his life.

"Conciliator" fairly describes one aspect of Lee's postwar role. A particularly articulate statement of Lee's conciliatory inclinations appears in a letter dated August 28, 1865, to former governor Letcher of Virginia:

> The questions which for years were in dispute between the State and General Government, and which unhappily were not decided by the dictates of reason, but referred to the decision of war, having been decided against us, it is the part of wisdom to acquiesce in the result, and of candor to recognize the fact.
>
> The interests of the State are therefore the same as those of the United States. Its prosperity will rise or fall with the welfare of the country. The duty of its citizens, then, appears to me too plain to admit of doubt. All should unite in honest efforts to obliterate the effects of war, and to restore the blessings of peace. They should remain, if possible, in the country; promote harmony and good feeling; qualify themselves to vote; and elect to the State and gen-

eral Legislatures wise and patriotic men, who will devote their abilities to the interests of the country, and the healing of all dissensions. I have invariably recommended this course since the cessation of hostilities, and have endeavored to practice it myself.

Several days later he wrote the following to Josiah Tatnall, a former Confederate naval captain:

The war being at an end, the Southern States having laid down their arms, and the questions at issue between them and the Northern States having been decided, I believe it to be the duty of every one to unite in the restoration of the country, and the reestablishment of peace and harmony. . . . It appears to me that the allayment of passion, the dissipation of prejudice, and the restoration of reason, will alone enable the people of the country to acquire a true knowledge and form a correct judgment of the events of the past years.[3]

The same theme was reflected in his letter of acceptance to the trustees of Washington College. "I think it is the duty of every citizen," he wrote, "in the present condition of the country, to do all in his power to aid in the restoration of peace and harmony, and in no way to oppose the policy of the State or General Governments, directed to that object. It is particularly incumbent on those charged with instruction of the young to set them an example of submission to authority."[4]

The Lee reflected in the foregoing communications is, according to Freeman, "the Lee of history."[5] It is surely the Lee of tradition, but whether or not it is also the Lee of history depends on what exactly the tradition purports to say about Lee as conciliator. From the opinions cited in the opening paragraph of this chapter and from Lee's own words, it is clear that the Lee orthodoxy holds that the general advocated the abandonment of all opposition to the United States, insisted that the questions between the sections had been decided and urged acquiescence in the decisions, called for the healing of all dissensions, and refused personally to take part in postwar controversies. How do Lee's actions conform with this traditional picture?

On February 23, 1866, Lee posted a letter to Mrs. Jefferson Davis. Her husband had been captured by Federal cavalry on May 10, 1865, and was then unwisely confined at Fortress Monroe for two years. Indicted for treason, he was released on bail in May 1867, and the indictment was dropped when President Andrew Johnson's General Amnesty Proclamation was issued on December 25, 1868.[6] Lee's letter to Davis's wife included the following lines: "I have felt most keenly the sufferings and imprisonment of your husband. . . . He enjoys the sympathy and respect of all good men; and if, as you state, his trial is now near, the exhibition of the whole truth in his case will, I trust, prove his defense and justification."[7] The expectation that a trial for treason would result in Davis's vindication is significant. Since the facts of any such proceeding would have been undisputed, the case would have turned on the legal question of whether secession was a constitutional right or was revolution. Lee asserted that it was a right.

On October 11, 1867, his St. Louis friend, Gen. E. G. W. Butler, received a letter from Lee stating, "We are obliged to confess that, notwithstanding our boastful assertions to the world for nearly a century, that our government was based on the consent of the people, which we claimed was the only rightful foundation on which any government could stand – it rests upon force as much as any government that ever existed." This, too, would seem to be an assertion of the right of a state to withdraw from the Union with impunity. That this was Lee's view appears from another letter to General Butler. In 1868, Alexander Stephens published his brief for the right of secession, *A Constitutional View of the Late War between the States*. Writing on November 8, 1869, Lee advised Butler, "I have not read the work of Mr. A. H. Stephens, but from what I have seen of it I think it a strong exposition of Southern views on the subject of which it treats and I think the South is indebted to him for his defence of her opinions and acts."[8]

The letters to Butler were not atypical. During the last five years of his life, Lee carried on a vigorous correspondence, and his many letters are marked by the invariable contention that the South's purpose in seceding and in fighting the war had been what he called "constitutional government." The North, according to Lee, had proceeded wrongfully and unconstitutionally.[9]

Additional opinions were voiced in interviews. In the early days of the controversy about black suffrage, in May 1866, Lee was interviewed by the Marquess of Lorne (later the ninth Duke of Argyll). Lee's views, as reported by the marquess, included the following: "The Radical party are likely to do a great deal of harm, for we wish now for good feeling to grow up between North and South, and the President, Mr. Johnson, has been doing much to strengthen the feeling in favour of the Union among us. The relations between the negroes and the whites were friendly formerly, and would remain so if legislation be not passed in favor of the blacks, in a way that will only do them harm." Lee then contended that the North was "raising up feelings of race" and argued that laws in behalf of the blacks would not work to their advantage and would keep alive "bad blood in the South against the North." The South, he stated, should be "left alone"; the contrary course was provocative of Southern hostility. He continued:

> The Southerners took up arms honestly; surely it is to be desired that the goodwill of our people be encouraged, and that there should be no inciting them against the North. To the minds of the Southern men the idea of "Union" was ridiculous when the States that made the Union did not desire it to continue; but the North fought for the Union, and now, if what appears to be the most powerful party among them is to have its own way, they are doing their best to destroy all real union. If they succeed, "Union" can only be a mere name. . . .
>
> Surely if the Union be worth preserving at all, they should try to conciliate the whole nation, and not do all they can against the Southern part of it.[10]

The claim that prewar relations between blacks and whites were "friendly" is surely remarkable. Even the sympathetic English aristocrat might have wondered whether "friendly" was a naive or disingenuous adjective to use in describing chattel slavery. Equally remarkable was the notion that the North risked "raising up feelings of race" in a society in which the whites had for generations enslaved the blacks. In any event, Lee made it plain that the status of the freedmen was not appropriately to be disturbed by legislation in their favor. The Southern states were to be "left alone," their authority unimpaired by the federal government. Any other course meant that the North, at least the Northern majority, was trying to destroy the Union.

In November 1866 Sir John Dalberg Acton, later Lord Acton, ad-

dressed a letter to Lee requesting the general's views on the constitutional issues involved in secession and the larger political outlook in
America.[11] Acton's letter manifested deep sympathy for the Southern
cause:

> Without presuming to decide the purely legal question, on which it
> seems evident to me from Madison's and Hamilton's papers that
> the Fathers of the Constitution were not agreed, I saw in States
> Rights the only availing check upon the absolutism of sovereign
> will, and secession filled me with hope, not as the destruction but as
> the redemption of Democracy. . . . Therefore I deemed that you
> were fighting the battles of our liberty, our progress, and our civili-
> zation.

Acton was, of course, an Englishman. The English constitutional system contained no judicial review of the "sovereign will" to determine
whether acts of the executive or the legislature were beyond the authority of the government, and he was apparently unfamiliar with the fact
that the American system included such a feature. His letter is also curious in that it never mentions slavery, apparently something that did not
cloud his view of "Democracy" or "our progress, and our civilization."

Whether or not Lee had read *The Federalist* or other writings of the
Founding Fathers, before the war he had had a rather strong view of
what they had been about, according to the letter written on January 23,
1861, probably to Custis, that was referred to in Chapter 3. Lee's words
bear repeating:

> Secession is nothing but revolution. The framers of our Constitu-
> tion never exhausted so much labor, wisdom and forbearance in its
> formation, and surrounded it with so many guards and securities, if
> it was intended to be broken by every member of the Confederacy
> at will. It was intended for "perpetual union" so expressed in the
> preamble, and for the establishment of a government, not a com-
> pact, which can only be dissolved by revolution, or the consent of all
> the people in convention assembled. It is idle to talk of secession.
> Anarchy would have been established, and not a government, by
> Washington, Hamilton, Jefferson, Madison, and the other patriots
> of the Revolution.[12]

"Perpetual union," a phrase appearing in the Articles of Confederation, was erroneously attributed by Lee to the Constitution, but his 1861 view was in any event clear.

Lee responded to Acton in a letter dated December 15, 1866 (which was not published until it appeared in a printed collection of Lord Acton's correspondence in 1917). He wrote what was essentially a concurrence with Acton's view:

> While I have considered the preservation of the constitutional power of the General Government to be the foundation of our peace and safety at home and abroad, I yet believe that the maintenance of the rights and authority reserved in the states and to the people, [is] not only essential to the adjustment and balance of the general system, but the safeguard to the continuance of a free government. I consider it as the chief source of stability to our present system, whereas the consolidation of the states into one vast republic, sure to be aggressive abroad and despotic at home, will be the certain precursor of that ruin which has overwhelmed all those that have preceded it.

Concluding his discussion of the secession issue, Lee told Acton:

> But I will not weary you with this unprofitable discussion. Unprofitable because the judgment of reason has been displaced by the arbitrament of war, waged for the purpose as avowed of maintaining the union of the states. If, therefore, the result of the war is to be considered as having decided that the union of the states is inviolable and perpetual under the constitution, it naturally follows that it is as incompetent for the general government to impair its integrity by the exclusion of a state, as for the states to do so by secession; and that the existence and rights of a state by the constitution are as indestructible as the union itself. The legitimate consequence then must be the perfect equality of rights of all the states; the exclusive right of each to regulate its internal affairs under rules established by the constitution, and the right of each state to prescribe for itself the qualification of suffrage. The South has contended only for the supremacy of the constitution, and the just administration of the laws made in pursuance of it. Virginia to the last made great efforts to save the union, and urged harmony and compromise.

Describing efforts to achieve compromise before matters came to a head at Fort Sumter, Lee stated that these efforts would have succeeded "if sustained by the Republican party." Indeed, according to Lee, "The only difficulty in the way of an amicable adjustment was the Republican party. Who then is responsible for the war?" Concluding, he asserted:

> Although the South would have preferred any honorable compromise to the fratricidal war which has taken place, she now accepts in good faith its constitutional results, and receives without reserve the amendment which has already been made to the Constitution for the extinction of slavery. That is an event that has long been sought, though in a different way, and by none has it been more earnestly desired than by citizens of Virginia. In other respects I trust that the constitution may undergo no change, but that it may be handed down to succeeding generations in the form we received it from our forefathers.

It appears that Lee was setting up a straw man, "the consolidation of the states into one vast republic," in the response to Acton. He certainly knew that before secession there had been no movement to eliminate the states. Indeed, the Republicans had even been willing to guarantee slavery in the states where it then existed. Whether slavery was to expand into the territories had been the issue. Nor was there any postwar sentiment to eliminate the states or to consolidate them. The postwar constitutional amendments established only minimum federal standards concerning slavery and the rights of the freedmen. And Lee was standing matters on their head when he insisted that the South had been trying to sustain the supremacy of the Constitution. There is simply no way to construct the proposition that the Constitution of the United States may be sustained by the secession of a group of states and their establishment of a separate nation. Lee's description of the role of the Republican Party is also unrealistic. The Republicans were elected in 1860, pursuant to constitutional procedures, with a commitment to oppose the expansion of slavery. The Southern states rejected this constitutional result and seceded. During the negotiations preceding the attack on Fort Sumter, Senator John J. Crittenden and others proposed compromises that would have insured the opportunity for slavery to expand. The Republicans stood by the commitment on the basis of which they had been elected and opposed these efforts. And the war came. Lee was aware of all these facts, and his contention that the Republicans were responsible for the war was nothing short of outright sectional advocacy. The same unreality marks the assertion of Virginia's long and earnest desire for abolition, an issue discussed in Chapter 2. There was no factual basis for this claim.

Freeman maintains that Lee's "conception of his duty to promote peace and national unity compelled him to put a wall between him and those who might have stirred unhappy memories and would certainly have kept open the old wounds of fratricidal war."[13] This, too, is subject to exception. In August 1868, Lee was asked by Union general William S. Rosecrans, a Democrat, to author a letter to be used in the presidential contest between Grant, the Republican, and Democratic candidate Governor Horatio Seymour of New York. As has been noted earlier, Lee believed before the war that the issue of slavery should be left to the "mild and melting influence of Christianity"; for the sake of white Southerners he undertook political activism. He and other former Confederate leaders, including Confederate vice president Stephens, Gen. P. G. T. Beauregard, and John Letcher, Virginia's wartime governor, signed a public letter to Rosecrans that was widely used in Seymour's behalf in the 1868 canvas.

Drafted by the Virginia lawyer Alexander H. H. Stuart and reviewed and edited by Lee, the Rosecrans letter purported to be a statement of the views of the Southern people concerning their acceptance of the results of the war and their willingness to deal justly with the freedmen, issues at the heart of the debate over Reconstruction policies. Having signed the letter, Lee was active in soliciting the signatures of Confederate leaders who had not initially been available to sign.

After a brief introduction and before brief formal closing remarks, the Rosecrans letter stated:

Whatever opinions may have prevailed in the past with regard to African slavery or the right of a State to secede from the Union, we believe we express the almost unanimous judgment of the Southern people when we declare that they consider these questions were decided by the war, and that it is their intention in good faith to abide by that decision. At the close of the war, the Southern people laid down their arms and sought to resume their former relations to the government of the United States. Through their State conventions, they abolished slavery and annulled their ordinances of secession; and they returned to their peaceful pursuits with a sincere purpose to fulfill all their duties under the Constitution of the United States which they had sworn to support. If their action in these particulars had been met in a spirit of frankness and cordiality, we believe that, ere this, old irritations would have passed away, and the wounds inflicted by the war would have been, in a large measure, healed. As far as we are advised, the people of the South entertain no unfriendly feeling towards the government of the United States, but they complain that their rights under the Constitution are withheld from them in the administration thereof.

The letter then turned to the situation of the freedmen. Denying that there was hostility toward or intent to oppress the blacks, its authors declared:

They have grown up in our midst, and we have been accustomed from childhood to look upon them with kindness. The change in the relations of the two races has brought no change in our feelings towards them. They still constitute an important part of our laboring population. Without their labor, the lands of the South would be comparatively unproductive; without the employment which Southern agriculture affords, they would be destitute of the means of subsistence and become paupers, dependent upon public bounty. Self-interest, if there were no higher motive, would therefore prompt the whites of the South to extend to the negro care and protection.

The important fact that the two races are, under existing circumstances, necessary to each other is gradually becoming apparent to both, and we believe that but for influences exerted to stir up the passions of the negroes, the relations of the two races would soon adjust themselves on a basis of mutual kindness and advantage.

Continuing, the letter attested that the Southern people were "inflexibly opposed to any system of laws that would place the political power of the country in the hands of the negro race" and concluded with a statement of the desires of the Southern people:

They ask a restoration of their rights under the Constitution. They desire relief from oppressive misrule. Above all, they would appeal to their countrymen for the reestablishment, in the Southern States, of that which has been justly regarded as the birth-right of every American, the right of self-government. Establish these on a firm basis, and we can safely promise, on behalf of the Southern people, that they will faithfully obey the Constitution and laws of the United States, treat the negro populations with kindness and humanity and fulfill every duty incumbent on peaceful citizens, loyal to the Constitution of their country.[14]

The Southerners who signed this letter apparently could not see themselves as many Northerners saw them a short three years after Appomattox. The signers presumably did not see any irony in their claim to "frankness and cordiality" and "their rights under the Constitution." The detailed expressions of affection and concern for, as well as dependence on, Southern blacks are of particular interest as they relate to Lee.[15]

Lee's feelings about the freedmen were in fact sharply at odds with the sentiments expressed in the letter to Rosecrans and the statements to Argyll. An illuminating incident occurred in May 1865 when he went to Pampatike, in King William County, to visit his cousin Thomas H. Carter. In discussing farming, Lee advised Carter not to depend for labor on the ninety or so blacks who still lived on the place. The government would, Lee said, provide for them; Carter should employ white people. He then drew a comparison that, like many racist comments since, dealt in stereotypes and completely disregarded cause and effect where race is concerned: "I have always observed that wherever you find the negro, everything is going down around him, and wherever you find the white man, you see everything around him improving."[16]

In the previously noted appearance before the congressional subcommittee concerned with Reconstruction in 1866, Lee's testimony did not suggest humane or kindly feelings toward blacks. Responding to a leading question, he said: "I think it would be better for Virginia if she could get rid of them. That is not a new opinion with me. I have always thought so." Asked then whether Virginia was "absolutely injured and its future impaired by the presence of the black population there," Lee answered, "I think it is."[17]

By 1868, General Lee's antagonism to blacks had also developed political overtones. On March 12, 1868, Lee wrote a long, chatty letter about agriculture to his son Robert, who had taken up farming after the war. In this letter, he wrote, "You will never prosper with the blacks, and it is abhorrent to a reflecting mind to be supporting and cherishing those who are plotting and working for your injury, and all of whose sympathies and associations are antagonistic to yours." As he was wont to do, Lee then resorted to the rhetoric of honor: "I wish them no evil in the world – on the contrary, will do them every good in my power, and know that they are misled by those to whom they have given their confidence." Completing the thought, Lee was careful that his son got the real message: "But our material, social and political interests are naturally with the whites."[18] Since employment and political power were the principal needs of the freedmen – and Lee, along with almost all Southerners and most Northerners, vigorously opposed their having the right to vote – one wonders what his protestation of doing them "every good in [his] power" was supposed to mean. It clearly did not mean providing them with employment, and it did not mean giving them political power.

Shortly after advising his son not to permit freedmen to work for him, Lee exchanged letters with an unidentified person who wished to send money to someone in the South for purposes of the blacks' education and advancement. On December 18, 1868, Lee responded, stating his agreement with the writer that the blacks could "better be attended to by those who are acquainted with their characters and wants than by those who are ignorant of both." The letter concluded: "The colored people in this vicinity are doing very well, are progressing favorably, and, as far as I know, are not in want. There is abundance of work for them, and the whites with whom they are associated retain for them the kindest feelings."[19] The person who received this letter doubtless believed that the general was among these whites with the "kindest feelings." Lee presumably felt comfortable with this inference because, although he opposed either political power or employment for the freedmen, he had told his son that he would "do them every good in [his] power."

In the historical record, Lee's statements and actions after the war present a mixed picture. One thing is clear: Lee was without question opposed to a renewal of military conflict and accepted fully the military loss of the war. He sought for himself, and recommended to others, a resumption of United States citizenship. But beyond this, matters are more murky when one tries to reconcile the difference between Lee's rhetoric and self-validation on the one hand and what he was in fact doing on the other. Rhetorically – which for the Lee traditionalists is enough – he advised Southerners to "abandon all opposition" and dissension and to acquiesce in the decisions that the war had wrought in regard to the issues between the sections. Rhetorically, he insisted that he was not to take part in the postwar controversies. But behind the rhetoric, he believed and asserted, privately and publicly, that secession had been constitutionally correct, that the North was responsible for the war because it opposed the extension of slavery into the territories, that the Southern states and their people should regain their full prewar status immediately and unconditionally, that the Confederate leadership should have immunity, and that the status of the freedmen was the business of the Southern states and not a proper concern of the federal government. In regard to blacks, Lee's public and private assertions were also in conflict. Publicly, he was protective and benign. Everything would be all right if the North did not "stir up" the blacks. Dependent on their labor, the South would, of course, employ them. Privately, he was bitter toward the freedmen and intervened personally to their detriment. In truth, Lee and his fellow Southerners were groping for a new method of white supremacy and exploitation of the blacks. With Northern complicity, the Southern effort was eventually to succeed; the outcome was a hundred years of near-slavery: disenfranchisement, Black Codes, Jim Crow, and suppression.

Some of Lee's communications quoted above – perhaps especially the responses to Argyll and Acton – reveal a posture painfully reminiscent of the prewar Southern position in regard to sectional conflict. If the two sections were to coexist, it would have to be on the South's terms. "Honorable compromise" to the South had meant slavery's protection and expansion as well as its exception from the general provisions of the Constitution, including majority rule and the Bill of Rights. After 1865 slavery as such was gone, and secession had been defeated by force of arms. In postwar terms, for Lee and many Southerners, if the two sections were to coexist, it would have to be on the basis of the Southern states' having unlimited control of their affairs.

The truth is that the tradition of the conciliatory postwar Lee does not hang together. Those who insist on it are caught in obvious contradictions between the dogma of the passive Lee, removed from the postwar issues but quietly urging submission, and the real Lee, who was in fact a Southern partisan and advocate. The orthodoxy regarding Lee's passivity cannot be maintained without disregarding his actual participation in social and political debate, his 1868 presidential campaign letter being a prime example. The orthodoxy is also hard to maintain because Lee apologists themselves seek to enlarge the hagiography. Thus, for example, Marshall W. Fishwick tells us that "instead of stepping into the arena, Lee worked quietly and persistently at his own job as president of his small, independent college." So much for the creed. But Fishwick also wishes to proclaim that Lee was "right" about Southern organizations like the Ku Klux Klan and the Knights of the White Camellia, which Fishwick saw as "racist and terrorist in nature." He writes, therefore, that "against the words implicit and the acts implied by such groups, Robert E. Lee, soldier-turned-citizen, *fought constantly in the closing years of his life*" (emphasis added).[20] In fact, there is no evidence that Lee "fought" against these organizations at all, let alone constantly. Indeed, having publicly declared that "it would be better for Virginia if she could get rid of" her blacks, he clearly shared the racist animosity that lay behind these organizations, whether or not he approved of their tactics. The point is that he either stepped into the public arena or he did not. The traditionalists cannot have it both ways.

Perspective on the real Lee after the war as distinguished from the postwar Lee of tradition can be gained by recalling Lee's attitudes and actions before and during the war. His deep antebellum sectional feelings have been described in Chapter 3. Resentment of the North, a

sense of grievance against the North, was part of his freely acknowledged attitude. Furthermore, as a Southern aristocrat, he tended toward the belief that the Yankees, at least many of them, were a lesser
people. This is reflected in the Reverend John Leyburn's report of his
1869 conversation with Lee. According to Leyburn, Lee then expressed
sadness about the "number of noble young men" killed in the war, but
he insisted that these losses had been "most unequal" between the
sections. The South, he said, had "sacrificed the flower of her land."
The North had sent "many of her valuable young men to the field; but
as in all large cities there is a population *which can well be spared*"
(emphasis added). The North also had recruited "immigrants from
abroad." In describing the Leyburn conversation, Freeman identifies
those who could "well be spared" as coming from "the slums of the
city."[21] In Lee's view, the deaths of immigrants and the poor were
somehow counted in a different way.

During the war, Lee developed a belief in the correctness and necessity of secession despite his prewar opposition to it. His sense of intense
commitment to the Southern cause, once the war began, has already
been described but deserves further attention. Although it was Lee's
wife who actually identified the South's war as "so holy a cause,"[22] this
phrase captures the general's feelings as well. Indeed, he stated that the
cause was "sacred and worthy." These semantics were possible because,
as discussed in *Why the South Lost the Civil War*, Lee and other Southern leaders had exorcised the protection of slavery as the cause of
secession and clothed their crusade in brighter garments. From the
beginning, Lee proposed to fight with fervor: "As long as there is one
horse that can carry his rider and one arm that can wield a sword I
prefer annihilation to submission."[23] Lee's exhortations to his soldiers
were consistent with this sense of the cause. As previously noted, on
September 9, 1861, during the Confederacy's unsuccessful efforts to
hold western Virginia, he spoke to the soldiers in these terms in a special
order: "Keep steadily in view the great principles for which [you] contend. . . . The safety of your homes and the lives of all you hold dear
depend upon your courage and exertions. Let each man resolve to be
victorious, and that the right of self-government, liberty, and peace shall
in him find a defender."[24] His object as a soldier, he wrote, had been
"the defense of those principles of American liberty upon which the

constitutions of the several States were originally founded."[25] As noted in Chapter 5, Lee was intensely bitter toward the North during the war and attributed an almost fiendish malice to the Northern military personnel. In expressing his feelings, he alleged that Federal soldiers would carry off Southern women, mistreat his wife, and rejoice at the grief of a Southern officer whose wife had died.

Finally, in addition to his prewar sectionalism and his wartime zeal and bitterness, Lee's prewar feelings about slavery and race were clearly carried over to the postwar period. Like many Southern leaders, Lee had privately proclaimed slavery as an evil while at the same time declaring it the best relationship that could exist between the races. In any event, slavery was God's problem, not the concern of the people who had inherited it; it should have been shielded from "fiery Controversy." In reference to his views on Reconstruction issues, Lee's prewar belief that the slaves' condition was "a painful discipline . . . necessary for their instruction as a race . . . [to] prepare & lead them to better things" is surely significant. The subjugation of blacks by means of slavery had been terminated by the war, and Lee was bitter toward the freedmen, opposing both political power and employment for them.

In sum, Lee entered and fought the war with sectional partisanship, a Southern aristocrat's feeling about the inferiority of Northern people, a zealous commitment to the Southern cause as truly just, anger over the North's conduct of the war, and a belief in slavery. As might be expected, his defeat and the destruction of his cause in a bloody war exacerbated his sense of commitment to these beliefs. And confident of his own righteousness, he was doubtless influenced in these attitudes, feeling them reinforced, by the fact of his indictment for treason in 1865, even though that proceeding was dismissed early in 1869.[26] The intensity of Lee's postwar anger is plain. It appears in an 1868 letter to his young cousin Annette Carter in the circumstances of the impeachment of President Andrew Johnson. He wrote of "this grand scheme of centralization of power in the hands of one branch of the Govt. to the ruin of all others, and the anihilation [sic] of the Constitution, the liberty of the people and of the country." Continuing, Lee said, "I grieve for posterity, for American principles and American liberty. Our boasted self Govt. is fast becoming the jeer and laughing-stock of the world." And in 1870, the year of his death, he spoke to William Preston Johnston of the "vindictiveness and malignity of the Yankees, of which he had no conception before the war."[27]

Echoes of Lee's anger, allegations of Yankee "vindictiveness and malignity," mark the writing about Lee after the war. The previously noted Joint Congressional Committee on Reconstruction is the focus of some of this writing. Established in December 1865, the committee had as its mandate to inquire into conditions in the South and make legislative recommendations to Congress. As indicated in Chapter 2, Lee was subpoenaed to appear before a subcommittee of the joint committee early in 1866. Not surprisingly, Freeman writes sarcastically about the committee's activities and betrays resentment of Lee's being subpoenaed; Senator Jacob M. Howard of Michigan, chairman of the subcommittee before which Lee appeared, is referred to as the "chief inquisitor" who "returned to the attack" against Lee.

Writing thirty years after Freeman, Fishwick, a professional historian, is even more bitter about the committee and its temerity in calling Lee to testify. His account sees some of the members of the committee as "the most bitter and implacable foes of the South" who sought to "harass former Rebel leaders." Thaddeus Stevens, chairman of the committee but not a member of the subcommittee that questioned Lee, is characterized as "a hungry hawk," who was "vindictive" and "sinister." Senator Howard, Freeman's "chief inquisitor," is identified by Fishwick as "ponderous and pontifical" and is said to have intended to "make Lee lose his temper and shout defiance at the conqueror." The questions of the members of the subcommittee are set forth by Fishwick with barely veiled antagonism. Lee, "the noblest rebel of them all," is described as responding with "restraint" and "consummate skill."[28]

This orthodox treatment of the joint committee and the subcommittee that questioned Lee is suggestive of much that is wrong with traditional writing about Lee. Congressional investigating committees with the power to subpoena were as old as Congress itself.[29] Whatever the faults of congressional inquiries, such inquiries were and are part of the way the American system works. The nation had been through a massive civil war that had left approximately 600,000 soldiers dead and thousands more maimed for life. The economic costs of the war were unprecedented. As related to the millions of slaves, the war had made for revolutionary social and legal change. It is not surprising that, within less than a year from the war's conclusion, Congress would inquire into its consequences and consider legislation in response to them. Nor it is surprising that the principal military leader of the Confederacy would be subpoenaed and questioned. A reasoned reading of the transcript suggests no "attack" on Lee or any mistreatment of the general. Margaret Sanborn, wholly sympathetic to Lee, finds the questions put to Lee "always civil." In short, the Lee traditionalists substitute argument in Lee's behalf for history.

G aines M. Foster has recently characterized the postwar attitudes of "most white southerners":

> Although they continued to champion states' rights and white su-
> premacy, they abandoned forever their vision of an independent
> slaveholders' republic. . . . Southerners realized that they had to
> accept a new order without slavery and had to work within the
> Union. Even though they accepted these developments, they did
> not repudiate their decision to wage war on that Union. Rather,
> throughout the postwar years, they defended their actions in 1861–
> 65 and insisted that the North acknowledge the honor and heroism
> of their cause.[30]

Contrary to the Lee tradition, it appears that after the war the general's attitudes matched those of most of his fellow Southerners in spite of some conciliatory statements. He embraced the conventional claims of the defeated South: states' rights, white supremacy, the correctness of secession and the Southerners' wartime efforts, and an insistence that the North honor their cause. He was, in brief, a mainstream secessionist after the war, the typical Southern partisan one would expect from his environment and experience. Thus, he was human, not the unlikely paragon that the tradition has created.

CHAPTER EIGHT

The Lee Tradition and Civil War History

The facts contradicting the Lee tradition that have been presented in the preceding chapters are not newly discovered. They are not obscure. Indeed, they are set forth in the same biographies that reiterate the tradition; but when the biographers reflect on the character and conduct of General Lee, these facts are exorcised, disregarded, or rationalized. Lee retains his immunity, exempt from the meaning of the facts. He remains, in Stephen Vincent Benét's apt phrase, "The Marble Man."

The distortions of fact that mark the Lee tradition are not unique in Civil War history; on the contrary, they are suggestive of a larger and more widespread problem. Fiction – in the form of misinterpretation or the form of outright misrepresentation – is endemic to the study of the history of the Civil War. A number of these fictions have been identified: that the war was precipitated by abolitionist provocateurs, that the South simply could not have won the war, that the South lost because it was overwhelmed by numbers, that the slaves were faithful to their masters and the South, that slavery was not the central issue in the conflict between North and South, that the South would have abandoned slavery but for Northern agitation, and that the High Tide of the Confederacy came at Gettysburg. And there are others as well. Touching on almost all aspects of the struggle, these fictions have ousted the facts and gained wide currency, so that what is treated as the history of the Civil War is instead a legend, a folk epic told over and over again.

The Lee tradition is typical of the legend, and is, in fact, its personification. The legend is also the context of the Lee tradition. Consideration of the Lee tradition therefore provides a convenient starting point for considering the larger phenomenon of the Civil War as legend.

Fiction and legend do not replace truth by chance. Instead, they are responses to circumstances and needs. What circumstances and needs have dictated the Civil War saga and carried it forward? A synthesis of two essential sources may explain the phenomenon. One of these has a psychological thrust. The other arose out of the postwar necessity of the participants to rationalize the war in social and political terms. Together the psychological and social impulses have created the legend.

Robert Penn Warren has recognized the psychological origins of the Civil War folk epic. He observes: "The Civil War is our only 'felt' history – history lived in the national imagination. This is not to say that the War is always, and by all men, felt in the same way. Quite the contrary. But this fact is an index to the very complexity, depth, and fundamental significance of the event. It is an overwhelming and vital image of human, and national, experience."[1] "Felt" history, history "lived in the . . . imagination," is plainly not objective history. It is subjective history constructed in the psyche, a series of images arising from psychological factors. These factors were the contradictions and traumas that marked the war. Perhaps we can better understand the traditional way in which Civil War history has, until recently, been presented if we are reminded of the contradictions and traumas that are the background of the legend.

The first contradiction involved the Declaration of Independence and slavery. The participants on both sides of the great sectional conflict subscribed to and revered the declaration, while at the same time accepting or tolerating slavery, an egregious contradiction of the document. It is important to acknowledge that both sides were mired in this contradiction: although a majority of the Northern population was opposed to slavery by 1860, they proposed then only to prohibit the extension of slavery, not to abolish it. It must have been difficult for these Northerners to be at ease with themselves when their position would countenance the use of the whip, the breaking up of slave families, and the hunting down of fugitives, so long as these things did not extend into the territories and future states to be created from the territories. In short, the North as well as the South was caught in the conflict between the promise of which all Americans were inordinately proud and the performance of their republic.

The slavery paradox was further complicated by contradictions within the free and slave states. In the North, predominant attitudes about race were not, of themselves, significantly different from those in the South. The free black population in the North was severely discriminated against, socially and in voting, education, and the economic process. In several states, notably those of the Midwest, state constitutions had been drafted to prohibit the migration of free blacks into the states. That most uncommon of men, Lincoln, held common Northern views. Sincerely opposed to slavery, he called it a "monstrous injustice" and said that "if slavery is not wrong, nothing is wrong." But in one of his debates with Stephen Douglas in 1858, he said: "I am not, nor ever have been in favor of bringing about in any way the social and political equality of the white and black races."[2] The antislavery movement in the North therefore struggled with its own interior conflict – a conviction that slavery was wrong, side by side with a crude and virulent racism.

Southern supporters of slavery also had their contradictory feelings about the institution. On the one hand, Southern leaders and theologians proclaimed that slavery was a positive good, for master and slave alike. On the other hand, the Southern leadership class was religiously orthodox, Calvinistic and fundamentalist. The Southerners perceived a discrepancy between the promise of their historic faith and their new faith in slavery. In addition, lascivious connections between masters and female slaves lingered in the system. This fact was not spoken of in the South and was contradicted when alleged, but the presence of numbers of mulattoes could not be denied. In a society that boasted of chivalry, morality, and racial purity, the sexual side of slavery was a disturbing, dirty, and open secret. Finally, the whole Western world was arrayed against the Southern view, as had been many of the Founding Fathers whom the Southern planters respected and sought to emulate. After the war, Porter Alexander wrote that "the trouble was that we were struggling against changes which the advance of the world in railroads & steamboats & telegraphs, in science & knowledge & commerce, &, in short, in civilization, had rendered inevitable."[3]

There is much to suggest that many Southern leaders also recognized in slavery the feature that led Lincoln to comment in his second inaugural address, "It may seem strange that any men should dare to ask a just God's assistance in wringing their bread from the sweat of other men's faces." The mixture of religious tradition, the standards of Western civilization, and the theories of the slavocracy created what Bell I. Wiley calls a widespread "sense of guilt" in the Southern leadership.[4] Calling this "crypto-emancipationism," Warren describes it as "a deep moral, logical, and economic unease" about slavery.[5] Thus, many Southerners had a commitment to the system but simultaneously harbored a sense that it was wrong. The strident claim that slavery was morally good seems not to have stilled the latter feeling. That this tension existed in the South is fairly indicated by the Confederate Constitution. While that document protected the ownership of slaves, it forbade the slave trade – surely an implicit acknowledgment that there was something wrong with slavery.

In short, slavery presented conflicts that by themselves are suggestive of personality disorders, North and South. But there is still more to the story. Appealing to the Southerners in his 1861 inaugural address, Lincoln said: "The mystic chords of memory, stretching from every battle-field, and patriot grave, to every living heart and hearthstone, all over this broad land, will yet swell the chorus of the Union, when again touched, as surely they will be, by the better angels of our nature."[6] His words were in vain, but they were meaningful. The South did have an ancient loyalty to the United States and a culture that it shared, at least in broad terms, with the North; and this was another of the ironic ambiguities of the war. Again to quote Warren, "the nation share[d] deep and significant convictions and [was] not a mere handbasket of factions huddled arbitrarily together by historical happen-so."[7]

The sections shared the same revolutionary experience, the same heroes, the same Founding Fathers; and, despite the South's departures from the Bill of Rights in the effort to protect slavery, they shared, at bottom, a sense of political values. It is true, of course, that the South proclaimed its difference. But, having drafted a constitution expressly protecting slavery, the South proceeded to place George Washington on the seal of the Confederacy and, as described in *Why the South Lost the Civil War*, "simply appropriated as their own the history they shared with the Union and recreated it. . . . Without its own distinctive past upon which to base its nationality, the Confederacy appropriated history and created a mythic past of exiled cavaliers and chivalrous knights that owed more to Sir Walter Scott than to the flesh and blood migrants from the Old World."[8]

This re-creation simply did not work. To expand upon a point mentioned in Chapter 2, Kenneth Stampp has observed:

> Fundamentally [the Confederacy] was not the product of genuine Southern nationalism; indeed, except for the institution of slavery, the South had little to give it a clear national identity. It had no natural frontiers; its white population came from the same stocks as the northern population; its political traditions and religious beliefs were not significantly different from those of the North; it had no history of its own; and the notion of a distinct Southern culture was largely a figment of the romantic imaginations of a handful of intellectuals and proslavery propagandists. . . .
>
> Even after a generation of intense sectional conflict over slavery, the South was still bound to the Union by a heritage of national ideals and traditions.[9]

Consistent with Stampp's analysis, Grady McWhiney contends, "Writers . . . have tended to magnify the differences between the Northerners and Southerners out of all proportion. In 1861 the United States did not contain . . . two civilizations." According to McWhiney, "One of the great myths of American history is that when the Civil War began Southerners were fundamentally different from Northerners."[10] And David M. Potter writes that "the efforts of historians to buttress their claim that the South had a wholly separate culture self-consciously asserting itself as a cultural counterpart of political nationalism, have led, on the whole to paltry results."[11]

The inability of the South to separate itself from the common ground that it shared with the North had predictable results, as the authors of *Why the South Lost the Civil War* point out: "A truly nationalistic movement will not be confused about where its loyalties lie. Yet this was a great source of Confederate confusion. . . . Southerners did indeed suffer a confusion of loyalties."[12] Thus, another contradiction appeared, the conflict between what Stampp has called "the inherent frailty of the cause itself,"[13] on the one hand, and the rhetorical insistence on the grandeur of the cause and the great sacrifices it required, on the other.

As has been suggested, the image of the brothers' war has been overdone, but the common nationalism and culture of the sections did draw the participants into another contradiction. Although fighting against each other with a devastating ferocity, the enlisted men and officers of the two sides tended to trust each other and did not see themselves as enemies in the manner of soldiers in most wars. During the winter of 1862–63, men of the Iron Brigade picketed the north side of the Rappahannock, across the river from their Confederate counterparts. An Iron Brigade officer reported that "there is no hostility and the men sit dozing and staring at each other, and when there are no officers about, they exchange papers and communicate with each other in as friendly a manner as if there was no cause for enmity." A Federal major fined one of his command for "paddling across the Rappahannock on a slab and trading coffee to the rebel pickets for whisky, with which he made half of our men on picket duty drunk."

In another incident involving the Iron Brigade, on December 14, 1862, the day after the battle of Fredericksburg, soldiers of the Second Wisconsin, on picket for their division, arranged a truce with the Confederates opposing them so that the soldiers of both sides could get some rest. During the truce, a Confederate challenged a Sixth Wisconsin soldier to a fist fight on the Bowling Green Road, south of the Rappahannock. Putting aside their weapons, the soldiers gathered around and watched while the combatants fought to what was generally declared a draw. The cheering sections then shook hands all around, traded tobacco and coffee, and agreed that they would not shoot at each other until one army or the other ordered a general advance.[14]

These were not isolated incidents. The diaries and letters of Civil War soldiers are replete with accounts of such events. On one level, there was increasing bitterness as the war was prolonged, but, on another, the soldiers never abandoned their sense of personal comradeship. Indeed, Oliver Wendell Holmes, Jr., suggested that the more intense the combat, the more the soldiers felt for each other. He wrote: "You could not stand up day after day in those indecisive contests . . . without getting at least something of the same brotherhood for the enemy that the north pole of a magnet has for the south."[15]

The soldiers' friendships had their counterparts among the officers who had gone to West Point and had been together in the "old army." West Point classes in the first half of the nineteenth century were relatively small. The academy graduated forty-two men in 1840, including Gens. William T. Sherman and George H. Thomas, who were Union officers, and Gen. Richard S. Ewell, a Confederate corps commander. Twenty-five graduated in the class of 1844, among them Federal general Winfield Scott Hancock and Confederate general Simon Bolivar Buckner. Along with the 1840 graduates already mentioned, well-known officers in attendance at the same time in the 1840s included (for the Union) Gens. John F. Reynolds, Don Carlos Buell, George B. McClellan, Ambrose Burnside, and U. S. Grant and (for the South), Gens. Richard Brooke Garnett, D. H. Hill, Lafayette McLaws, George E. Pickett, Stonewall Jackson, A. P. Hill, and James Longstreet. The class of 1853 included John Bell Hood of the Confederacy and Gens. James B. McPherson and Philip H. Sheridan of the Union.[16] After graduation, these men had in many cases been intimate friends, dependent on each other as companions at isolated and dreary prewar military posts. West Point and career intimacy similarly marked the field officer corps. Such relationships resulted in scenes that were strange in war but which Americans take for granted. When the youthful Confederate general Stephen Dodson Ramseur, West Point 1860, was mortally wounded at Cedar Creek, he was taken to General Sheridan's headquarters. Union generals Wesley Merritt, a West Point classmate, and George Armstrong Custer, class of 1861, sat at his bedside during the night. Ramseur died the following morning.[17]

All things considered, it is not surprising that after the surrender at Appomattox, Grant issued orders to the Federals that there were to be no demonstrations or that the Federal soldiers shared their rations with the hungry rebels. Grant and the Federals were genuinely concerned for these mortal enemies, whom Grant in his memoirs called "their old friends."[18] That Grant's phrase was not simply rhetorical appears from Alexander's description of his experiences immediately after the surrender:

> Of course I met at the Federal headquarters many old army friends & acquaintances & the courtesy, consideration & good will of every one of them was shown in every way possible. Indeed, Gen. Grant's spirit of kindness seemed to imbue his whole army down to the private soldiers & the teamsters one met upon the roads, who would turn out into the mud for any Confederate officer, & salute him with a better grace & courtesy, doubtless, than they sometimes showed to their own officers.[19]

Finally, among the factors from the war that went into the making of its legend, was the awfulness of it all, a trauma that would arrest the attention of any psychologist. James M. McPherson provides a useful snapshot of its scope and intensity: "Night fell on a scene of horror beyond imagining. Nearly 6,000 men lay dead or dying, and another 17,000 wounded groaned in agony or endured in silence. The casualties at Antietam numbered four times the total suffered by American soldiers at the Normandy beaches on June 6, 1944."[20] Robert Penn Warren writes:

> The word *tragedy* is often used loosely. Here we use it at its deepest significance: the image in action of the deepest questions of man's fate and man's attitude toward his fate. For the Civil War is, massively, that. It is the story of a crime of monstrous inhumanity, into which almost innocently men stumbled; of consequences which could not be trammeled up, and of men who tangled themselves more and more vindictively and desperately until the powers of reason were twisted and their very virtues perverted; of a climax drenched with blood but with nobility gleaming ironically, and redeemingly, through the murk; of a conclusion in which, for the participants at least, there is a reconciliation by human recognition.[21]

Again, the contradictions: on the one hand, innocence, nobility, and reconciliation; on the other, inhumanity, perversity, and vindictiveness.

: : : THE LEE TRADITION : : :

The people "stumbled almost innocently" into a coincidence of circumstances that created the "monstrous inhumanity." The period of the 1850s was marked by great advances in weaponry. By the time of the war, the standard weapon was the muzzle loading rifle. The bore was .58 caliber. A veteran soldier could fire three times a minute, in spite of the complicated muzzle loading process. The weapon was highly accurate from 200 to 400 yards and could kill at 1,000 yards.[22] But almost nothing else had kept pace with the progress of weapons. Military tactics were still principally based on the smooth bore musket, which had neither the accuracy nor the range of the rifled gun. The result was that throughout the war massed infantry troops were thrown against formidable defensive positions. This was an effective tactic in the days of the smooth bore musket; but since the defenders had the much improved gun, the assault troops were slaughtered in exaggerated numbers.

Medicine was but a crude science at the time of the war. Bacteriology was unknown. The medical journals of the period identified infection and gangrene as the ordinary second stage of any wound. Amputation, with the surgeon wiping the saw and knife across his apron and proceeding to the next patient, was the standard surgical method for all but superficial wounds to the limbs. Ordinarily, no anesthetic was provided.

Nor were the sciences of nutrition and sanitation more advanced. Of the almost 600,000 men who died in the war, more died of disease, including simple diseases such as dysentery, than died of wounds. Psychology was equally undeveloped; it seems barely to have occurred to anyone that fatigue, continuous combat, and the unavailability of leave could destroy a man as effectively as bullets. And as for the sociology of war, there were no dependents' subsidies for wives and children left at home. The plight of the soldier's family was typically "root hog or die," and the family's suffering aggravated the morale problem of the soldier.

In short, the war itself created precisely those circumstances in which the things that were unknown were essential to know, if terrible deprivation and suffering were to be avoided. So they were not avoided. The plight of the wounded presents perhaps the most graphic picture of the suffering. In his history of the Twenty-fourth Michigan Volunteers, O. B. Curtis of that regiment laconically recorded the fate of some of his comrades. Mason Palmer, he wrote, was wounded at Gettysburg. "Arm amputated. Death hastened by his jumping out of a window in delirium." On the same page, he wrote of Seymour Burns. Wounded in the Wilderness, Burns was "burned up in the woods" when the Wilderness caught fire during that battle.

The diary of a soldier of the Iron Brigade records the following scene after the battle of Antietam, as the soldier lay wounded and unattended:

> It was a painful day to me. All day I sat up and looked upon a scene of suffering. Sergeant Whaley was lying by my side in agony. He was one of my first and kindest friends from the beginning. We tented together from the first. We went on all the hard marches, and finally met a sad fate upon the same tainted field. We had suffered everything together that would make one soldier love another, and now we lay near each other; he was wholly unable to help himself and I was but little better. I had a prospect of soon having the chance to avenge the wound but his was dark forever. We were in a large church but no comforts . . . could be bought, borrowed or stolen.

On the next day, the diarist was moved from the church, but Sergeant Whaley was left behind to die. The diarist told of leaving his friend: "[I left] with scarcely a parting word. I did not like to leave him this way but this was by far the best way to do it. I merely informed him that I was going. He started to rise up in haste but again sank back and wished to know if I wanted my tin cup and I told him no, that I would try to get another."[23]

D. W. Brogan has observed that "there are . . . in the experience of nations, ordeals so novel, so disastrous, physically or morally, so dramatic a destruction of hope, the prelude to some long period of humiliation or despair, that they are watersheds in the nation's history. . . . For the Americans it was the Civil War."[24] The Civil War as a human event was so rife with contradictions and traumas, so confused and painful in its images, that the generations that witnessed it were moved to manufacture a history of the event. They were psychologically impelled to obscure the truth, Warren's "crime of monstrous inhumanity," with tales and traditions that were essentially romantic and more palatable than the facts.

As a consequence, then, of an implicit need to mask the awfulness of their experience, the participants converted their tragedy into a Victorian melodrama, a mawkish romance. This conversion became a dominant aspect of the way in which the history of the Civil War was understood and recorded.

In addition to having psychological impulses to satisfy, the participants needed to deal with the war in a social sense. Brogan has written that "the country that has a 'history,' dramatic, moving, tragic, has to live with it – with the problems it raised but did not solve, with the emotions that it leaves as a damaging legacy, with the defective vision that preoccupation with the heroic, with the disastrous, with the expensive past fosters."[25] The Civil War was the "expensive past" of participants North and South, and to "live with" that past both sides had to account for themselves.

While proclaiming the righteousness of its cause, the South was compelled to accept defeat. It was also required to justify its effort. The defeat, and the deaths and destruction, could not simply be left alone. They had to be rationalized in a social sense. The North had more complicated social rationalizing to do. On the one hand, the North also needed to establish that it had been right, that the war had been worth it. But, insisting that the two sections comprised one nation, the North needed also to reclaim the allegiance of the South. This created an implicit Northern disposition to protect the dignity of the South so as to bind it again to the Union.

There was, to be sure, an initial period of bitterness and a protracted period of maneuvering as the national political parties sought to stake out their Southern constituencies. In the North "bloody shirt" politics were practiced in the interest of Republican political control. Prior to the Hayes-Tilden compromise of 1877, there was even a short-lived Northern effort to act out the Declaration of Independence by guaranteeing civil rights for the freedmen, an effort abrasive to the South and to many in the North. But in the long run, the South's need to dignify its defeat and losses and the North's need to credit the Southern cause for the sake of the Union prevailed. Just as the psychological motive produced a romantic mask for the war's monstrous inhumanity, the participants' need to justify themselves dictated the alteration of critical facts concerning the war.

Because the longstanding disagreement between the sections, and the war itself, had been about slavery and the black race, it is not surprising that the social rationalizations about the conflict were premised on these matters. The South's contribution to the story had two elements: the first concerned the role of slavery; the second involved changing the image of the slave and the freedman.

In regard to slavery, Stampp observes of the Southerners: "They denied that slavery had anything to do with the Confederate cause, thus decontaminating it and turning it into something they could cherish. After Appomattox, Jefferson Davis claimed that slavery 'was in no wise the cause of the conflict,' and Alexander H. Stephens argued that the war 'was not a contest between the advocates or opponents of that Peculiar Institution.' "[26] According to Robert F. Durden, this denial became "a cardinal element of the southern apologia." Durden also points out that "liberty, independence, and especially states' rights were advanced by countless southern spokesmen as the hallowed principles of the Lost Cause."[27] We have seen how Lee embraced this position. It promptly became an almost universal Southern contention.[28]

The new image of the Southern black provided an equally stark reversal. In place of the slaves and freedmen that the Federal soldiers knew, there emerged what William Garrett Piston calls the "happy darky stereotype." Unaware, unknowing, and uncaring, the happy darky eventually came to be universally known through the works of Joel Chandler Harris, Thomas Nelson Page, and other Southern writers.[29]

It is not a coincidence that both of these Southern race myths also served another purpose for the defeated South. According to Gaines M. Foster:

> Southerners, their defense of secession and slavery demonstrated, thought they had acted rightly in the war: neither secession nor slavery had been wrong. Southerners therefore saw no reason to confess any guilt and seemed convinced of their good standing with their maker. And yet the need to consider and reconsider these questions, to defend so ardently the legality of a political right they

admitted had no current relevance and the morality of an institution they accepted as abolished, indicated a persistent disquiet.[30]

This disquiet reflected the South's need for the North to credit its
struggle. Foster states, "Not just political acceptance but northern respect was needed. . . . The North had to acknowledge . . . the honor
of the South, before southerners would be totally at ease within the
Union."[31] By muting, indeed extinguishing, the real issue that had
divided the sections and led them into the war, and by disguising the
real slave and freedman, the Southern leadership enhanced the likelihood of winning the Northern respect that it coveted.

It is hardly surprising that the South discarded the protection of
slavery as the reason for secession. It could not have achieved social
justification for the war on that unseemly ground even among Southerners, who, according to James L. Roark, manifested "a nearly universal desire to escape the ignominy attached to slavery."[32] States' rights,
liberty, and the Constitution were surely more likely shibboleths. Nor is
it surprising that the South was anxious to create the image of the
ignorant and uncaring darky. It replaced a much more complex and
threatening persona: the mistreated, alienated, and angry slave.

This revisionism in regard to the role of slavery and the character of
the slaves could have remained an entirely Southern theme. The revi-
sion could not become part of the Civil War legend without Northern
acceptance, and the North, including its academic historians, did accept the South's rewriting of the record. The North let the South substitute a war for liberty for the war for slavery, and the North ceased to
think of the slaves and freedmen as serious persons. Exported to the
North, the happy darky stereotype was widely embraced, prevailing
well into the twentieth century and pervading the popular imagination
from novels and the press to Walt Disney movies. This Northern contribution to the legend was in part a result of the implicit need to credit the
South's effort. The North had the same problem as the South in extending this credit to a war for slavery. The North, like the South, was
reassured by the new image of the black; it was much easier to disregard
the stereotype than it was to ignore the real freedman. And there was
one more reason why the North was willing to participate in this cre-
ative writing of history. This reason was racism itself.

In spite of widespread Northern opposition to slavery, the North and the South, as has been said, shared an intense racism. Emancipation meant that slavery was no longer available as a means of exercising social control over blacks. The racist North had, all at once, to cope with the idea of free blacks in large numbers who were at least theoretically mobile. Northerners' own fear and dislike of blacks helped persuade them that they surely would not have caused such a fuss about a little thing like the status of these people. The South was right – slavery had not been the issue after all.

Racism not only gave the North a reason to go along with the South's rationalizing of the cause of the war and redefinition of the freedmen but was also perceived as a social need in itself. As has been said, it was a common ground, a shared feeling of the sections. It was, therefore, a force that unified the predominantly white North and predominantly white South. The sections agreed about the blacks. To begin with, slavery was discounted as the issue between the sections; then, except as essentially unknowing or comic bystanders, or as faithful helpmates to "ol' Massa," blacks were virtually read out of the war. That they had fled by the thousands into the Federal lines, had rendered invaluable service as guides to Federal soldiers, had enlisted in large numbers in the Federal army, and had fought and died for the Union were simply omitted from the saga.

In accepting the South's trivializing of slavery as the cause of the war and trivializing of black people in general, the North met the social needs of both sections. It also served its own racist predilections. In Foster's words, "Southerners gloried in northern homage to their conquered banner and in all other signs of northern respect. . . . The North had publicly conceded, as the South had wanted it to since 1865, the honor and nobility of the Confederates' fight. The acknowledgment both sealed reunion and reaffirmed southern honor."[33]

The false treatment of slavery and black people had a profound effect on the making of the Civil War legend because it struck at the core of the truth of the war. And it is hard to exaggerate the profoundly derogatory implications that it had for black people. Removed from their true role as the issue, their actual participation in the struggle ignored, they were historically characterized as irrelevant. Lingering on the sidelines, they were enslaved and brutalized but did not care – a myth that adds appalling insult to grievous injury. The facts notwithstanding, racism became an implicit underpinning of the legendary treatment of the war.[34]

A significant price was paid for disregarding slavery and the real black people. The North deprived itself and the nation as a whole of any high purpose for the war. "The Battle Hymn of the Republic" and the "battle cry of freedom" – always exaggerations – had little relevance to the revised version of the war. The North was left in the position of having, for no apparent reason, acted in such a way within the prewar political process as to provoke secession. A void was substituted for the free-soil movement as the source of conflict between the sections. The discounting of slavery and the blacks also meant that the North had then bloodily defeated secession for the narrow purpose of forcing the Southerners to remain part of a nation against their will.

The fiction of disregarding slavery also meant that cause and effect were unhinged in regard to the war. The void resulting from setting aside slavery did not, of course, remain. The historians came forward. Among them were proponents of an economic interpretation in the early twentieth century. Influenced in part by their own racism, they were able to provide explanations of the nation's ordeal as the result of disputes over tariffs, the control of investment banking, and conflict between industrial and agricultural societies. James G. Randall and his followers, both racist and insensitive to the moral implications of slavery, could later write that the war was "whipped up" by a "blundering generation," North and South. To this Brogan's response is compelling: "To write off, as Randall does, the men who insisted on talking about slavery as mere mischief-makers is to ignore the role of morals and moralists, ideas and ideologues in history." Discarding the real cause of the war has led to an endless string of hypotheses about its origins, most of which are contrived rather than convincing.[35]

From the manufactured claims concerning the role of slavery and the nature of the freedman proceeded other elements of what Foster calls the "codified," "southern interpretation of the war,"[36] all of which were credited by the North and which linger still in the legend. Thus, to quote Piston, "the antebellum period became Edenic, a time before the Fall.

Southern civilization was portrayed as superior, uniquely blessed," a world peopled by "cavalier aristocrats or martyrs," and, of course, by the stereotypical happy darky. In a similar vein, Foster notes that in the codified interpretation "American popular culture sometimes portrayed the South as a land of 'moonlight and magnolias' or a place of grace and gentility." Within a generation of the close of the war, again to quote Piston, "the South, and increasingly the nation as a whole, had developed a romanticized stereotype of the Confederate soldier."[37] Supplementing and reinforcing the melodrama that had been created to mask the harsh tragedy of the war, these elements mark the twentieth century's most popular Civil War story, Margaret Mitchell's *Gone with the Wind*. An orthodox statement of the legend, contributing significantly to its popularity and survival, it explicitly idealized the men and women of the planter class, extolled the superior valor of Southern manhood, imputed gentility to the slaving planter aristocracy, exaggerated the relative material disadvantages of the South's armies, and characterized the Yankees as venal bushwhackers. Consistent with the legend's racist origins, most dramatic was the novel's portrayal of slaves as the simple, happy, and devoted companions of their owners.

The American popular view of the Old South epitomized in *Gone with the Wind* was, and continues to be, significantly flawed. Bertram Wyatt-Brown points out that in the South "honor had always had many faces." The Edenic version of the antebellum South looks away from what he calls the "darker aspects of honor." He writes:

> Individuals and sometimes groups spoke out against popular forms of injustice and honor – duels, summary hangings, mob whippings. These efforts at reform seldom received public acclamation and support. Even historians, whether native to the South or not, have not seen these expressions of public will and private esteem as part of a total cultural pattern. Instead, they have been labeled tragic aberrations, or techniques by which the planter class manipulated lesser, more virtuous folk. Gentility, the nobler, brighter feature of Southern ethics, has been a more congenial topic. Certainly it was the model that Southerners have publicly revered and exalted.[38]

The last three chapters of Wyatt-Brown's *Southern Honor* discuss some of the darker sides of the Southern ethos under the suggestive titles

"Policing Slave Society: Insurrectionary Scares," "Charivari and Lynch Law," and "The Anatomy of a Wife-Killing."

The codified interpretation of the Civil War and its origins also identified the snake in Eden. The abolitionist was cast in this role. The image of the abolitionist, and the North's acceptance of that image, can be seen in a colorful characterization by Charles E. Stowe, the son of Harriet Beecher Stowe. In a speech given in Nashville in 1911, and reported in the *Confederate Veteran*, he accepted the North's shared responsibility for slavery, explaining: "In the minds . . . of pious, church-going, orthodox slaveholders, and many such there were, the abolitionists of the North were looked upon as we to-day regard the bomb-throwing anarchists of Chicago or the most radical wing of the socialist party – as the enemies of society and the enemies of God and his holy Word, the Bible, in which the pious slaveholder of the South found abundant authority for his beloved institution."[39] Stowe was not critical of this Southern perception. He embraced it as fair and suggested that abolitionists had brought on the war. Uniformly stereotyped as extremist, inflexible, and unrealistic, the abolitionist was to become the bête noire of the legend.

The socially correct history of the war extended to a rationalization of the Southern defeat. A set of contradictory theses was codified by the South and adopted by the North. On the one hand, it was established that the South could not have won and, as was inevitable from the beginning, was overwhelmed by numbers. On the other hand, it was asserted that if the South had won at Gettysburg, it would have won the war. The South's loss at Gettysburg was attributed principally to the alleged failure of Gen. James Longstreet on the second day of the battle. The claim that the South would have won the war had it been victorious at Gettysburg and that Longstreet caused the defeat there led to another Southern canon. Foster calls this the "Longstreet-lost-it-at-Gettysburg" theory.[40] As explained by J. William Jones, Lee's early biographer and advocate, the South would have "won Gettysburg, and Independence, but for the failure of *one man*" (emphasis in original).[41] And Jones purported to involve Lee directly in this rationale when he quoted the general as saying: "If I had had Stonewall Jackson at Gettysburg, we should have won a great victory. And I feel confident that a complete success there would have resulted in the establishment of our independence."[42] Longstreet's culpability and the decisiveness of Gettysburg continue to mark Civil War writing – the fact that the war lasted almost two more years, Vicksburg, Missionary Ridge, Atlanta, and Sherman's march notwithstanding.

Piston has described the way in which the military aspect of the war became personified in the saga's orthodoxy. "By the late nineteenth century," he writes, "this view was understood to entail the worship of Lee and the use of Longstreet as scapegoat for Gettysburg and by extension the loss of the war." He also aptly identifies the "Lost Cause themes . . . including the deification of Lee and the vilification of Longstreet." For Lee there was, indeed, "adoration."[43]

Out of these confused caricatures, products of the social needs of the North and South, arose the anomalous result described in *Why the South Lost the Civil War*:

> The death of chattel slavery, along with the surrender of dreams of separate nationhood, allowed the South to claim victory, in partnership with the North, while state rights, white supremacy, and honor proved that the South had not fought in vain. Vanquished only on the field of battle (and over the years they even explained away this defeat), Southerners could claim victory in partnership with the Federals. . . .
>
> If the war was lost over slavery and independence, the peace was waged – and won – for state rights, white supremacy, and honor.[44]

The sections' social rationalizations had profound consequences. In the short run, reunion was facilitated and Southern honor assured. But more than truth was lost in the process. Equal protection of the laws, a promise of the Fourteenth Amendment, and the Fifteenth Amendment's guarantee of suffrage for blacks – both products of the war – were allowed to wither away, unenforced for a hundred years. During Reconstruction, the same racist tradition that distorted the history of the war rationalized the Ku Klux Klan and served to establish the scalawags and carpetbaggers as villains and the freedmen as ignorant and shiftless fools. It therefore became the cornerstone of the history of the postwar period as well as the history of the prewar conflict and the war itself.

In the light of history as one of the humanities, Foster offers this assessment of the Civil War legend:

Rather than looking at the war as a tragic failure and trying to understand it, or even condemn it, Americans, North and South, chose to view it as a glorious time to be celebrated. Most ignored the fact that the nation had failed to resolve a debate over the nature of the Union and to eliminate the contradictions between its equalitarian ideals and the institution of slavery without resort to a bloody civil war. Instead, they celebrated the war's triumphant nationalism and martial glory. Southerners participated in the celebration, even though they had lost the war. Surprisingly, they never questioned whether defeat implied something was wrong with their cause or their society. Their cause had been just and their failure the result only of overwhelming numbers, they concluded. Conceivably, defeat might have impelled them to question the morality of slavery and, in the process, of southern race relations. It might have led southerners to be more skeptical of their nation's sense of innocence and omnipotence. But it did not. Late nineteenth-century southerners gained little wisdom and developed no special perspective from contemplating defeat. Although it served to justify the cause and therefore its veterans, the Confederate celebration did not so much sacralize the memory of the war as it sanitized and trivialized it.[45]

The manufactured "history" of the Civil War that began to take form shortly after the fighting ceased was, then, the result of the combination of the war's actual contradictions and traumas and the postwar social rationalizations of the participants. Both contributed to the fictions that made the legend, producing romance in place of realism and engendering radical distortions of critical facts. The legend has been handed down to historians and the general public. Only recently have unemotional and nonracist eyes sought to look behind it.

Exalted himself, Lee is also a visible sign of the elevation of the Lost Cause. The literature on Lee is symbolic of the South's postwar victory and the folk history of the war. The Lee tradition constitutes the parable of the war, inextricably bound up with the legend and, in a sense, both a cause and an effect of the legend. Douglas Southall Freeman's landmark biography is but one example. Along with carefully researched facts, Freeman and other Lee writers – like Carl Sandburg in his Lincoln biography and in the tradition of Parson Weems's writing about Washington – relate every anecdote, including second- and thirdhand accounts originating long after the fact, that portray their subject as superhuman: Lee rescuing a baby bird under enemy fire, Lee succoring a wounded Federal soldier, Lee carrying a child from a burning building, Lee playing with children during the war, Lee stopping to pray with soldiers in the face of Federal artillery fire, Lee's godlike physical appearance.

Also recounted are other stories that are intended to beguile but, on their face, are improbable or, worse still, suggest doubts about Lee's judgment, his sense of priorities, even his sense of duty. Thus, Marshall W. Fishwick relates that "attending church in Petersburg on February 5 [1865], Lee would not leave, despite word of a Yankee breakthrough, until after he had received Communion"; only then would he ride to the battle line to rally his men. And on another occasion Fishwick writes: "As his beaten army staggered toward Appomattox, one woman, the wife of Dr. Guild, still accompanied the officers. The whole army was collapsing around him, but General Lee insisted on coming early every morning with a cup of coffee for Mrs. Guild, though he himself had none." Turning to Lee's postwar life, Fishwick recounts that "some of the guests in his postwar home left their shoes outside the door at night, thinking a servant would clean them. There was no servant, but the boots were invariably polished – Lee polished them himself."[46]

In the index to volumes 3 and 4 of his biography, under the heading of "Personal Characteristics," Freeman lists a full four columns' worth of Lee's qualities, including the following: abstemiousness, accurate reasoning, alertness, amiability, audacity, boldness, calmness, charm of manner, cheerfulness, courage, courtesy, dignity, diligence, fairness, faith in God, frankness, friendliness, frugality, generosity, gentleness, goodness, good judgment, good looks, grace, heroic character, humility, integrity, intelligence, justice, kindness, magnanimity, mercy, modesty, neatness, patience, poise, politeness, practicality, reasonableness, resourcefulness, self-abnegation, simplicity, sincerity, spirituality, tact, tenderness, thoughtfulness, thrift, and wisdom. When Freeman finds it necessary in the text to recount anything from another commentator that suggests a criticism of Lee, he expressly contradicts the criticism and reprimands the critic for foolishness, bad faith, or malicious motives. On the last page of volume 4, Freeman pictures Lee as an imitation of Christ in a scene in which a young mother brings her baby to him to be blessed.

Christological associations mark other Lee biographies as well. Some of the allusions are muted, as in the case of accounts of Lee's alleged magnanimity – his supposed ability to love his enemies – discussed in Chapter 5. Others are more patent, as in the case of Clifford Dowdey's description of surrender as "the cup that Lee had shrunk from taking."[47]

Other biographies, also removed in time from immediate postwar rationalizations, contain characterizations that would startle a reader not already dulled by the reiteration of the extravagancies of the tradition. A few examples will suffice. In 1925 Sir Frederick Maurice announced that Freeman's noble aristocrat, who in fact disdained black people and Northern immigrants and poor people from the Northern cities, was a "stout democrat."[48] In 1963 Fishwick described him as "Apollo on horseback" and "the general on the beautiful white horse, fighting bravely as did the knights of old." Incongruously, he finds Lee to be both "Saint George slaying Yankee dragons" and St. Francis of Assisi, the latter because "literally everything and everybody loved him."[49] In 1981 Charles Bracelen Flood, presumably impatient with the indirection of others, labeled Lee "a Confederate Santa Claus."[50]

Writing in 1912, Gamaliel Bradford contributed an Orwellian touch when he suggested: "Yet, after all, in fighting for the Confederacy Lee was fighting for slavery, and he must have known perfectly well that if the South triumphed and maintained its independence, slavery would grow and flourish for another generation, if not for another century.... This man, fighting, as he believed, for freedom, for independence, for democracy, *was fighting also to rivet the shackles more firmly on millions of his fellow men*" (emphasis added). Immediately following these words, Bradford set forth this remarkable characterization: "In Lee, no pride, but virtue all; *not liberty for himself alone, but for others, for everyone*" (emphasis added).[51]

And so Lee has been handed down to us not simply as a distinguished American of fine personal character, a representative member of the planter aristocracy that seceded in order to protect slavery, a daring military leader of high skill in combat whose aggressiveness was extremely costly to his army and who persisted in the fight long after he realized it was lost, and a Southerner who held essentially conventional prewar, wartime, and postwar attitudes, but rather as a creature of the Civil War legend. As such, he was antislavery; he seceded out of an inevitable sense of duty (after all, he was a Virginian and had no choice); he was the invincible captain, a military genius; he fought, as he should have, regardless of the consequences, until utterly overwhelmed; he was magnanimous toward the North during the war; and he sought at all times after the war to reconcile the South with the United States and to stand aloof from controversy.

Robert E. Lee is the Odysseus of an American *Odyssey*; but that *Odyssey*, like Homer's, is myth and legend, not history.

Appendix A

Lee's Letter of January 11, 1865,

Concerning the Institution of Slavery

Headquarters Army of Northern Virginia,
January 11, 1865.

Hon. Andrew Hunter,
Richmond, Va.:

Dear Sir:

I have received your letter of the 7th instant, and without confining myself to the order of your interrogatories, will endeavor to answer them by a statement of my views on the subject. I shall be most happy if I can contribute to the solution of a question in which I feel an interest commensurate with my desire for the welfare and happiness of our people.

Considering the relation of master and slave, controlled by humane laws and influenced by Christianity and an enlightened public sentiment, as the best that can exist between the white and black races while intermingled as at present in this country, I would deprecate any sudden disturbance of that relation unless it be necessary to avert a greater calamity to both. I should therefore prefer to rely upon our white population to preserve the ratio between our forces and those of the enemy, which experience has shown to be safe. But in view of the preparations of our enemies, it is our duty to provide for continued war and not for a battle or a campaign, and I fear that we cannot accomplish this without overtaxing the capacity of our white population.

Should the war continue under existing circumstances, the enemy may in course of time penetrate our country and get access to a large part of our negro population. It is his avowed policy to convert the able-bodied men among them into soldiers, and to emancipate all. The success of the Federal arms in the South was followed by a proclamation of President Lincoln for 280,000 men, the effect of which will be to stimulate the Northern States to procure as substitutes for their own people the negroes thus brought within their reach. Many have already been obtained in Virginia, and should the fortune of war expose more of her territory, the enemy would gain a large accession to his strength. His progress will thus add to his numbers, and at the same time destroy slavery in a manner most pernicious to the welfare of our people. Their negroes will be used to hold them in subjection, leaving the remaining force of the enemy free to extend his conquest. Whatever may be the effect of our employing negro troops, it cannot be as mischievous as this. If it end in subverting slavery it will be accomplished by ourselves, and we can devise the means of alleviating the evil consequences to both races. I think, therefore, we must decide whether slavery shall be extinguished by our enemies and the slaves be used against us, or use them ourselves at the risk of the effects which may be produced upon our social institutions. My own opinion is that we should employ them without delay. I believe that with proper regulations they can be made efficient soldiers. They possess the physical qualifications in an eminent degree. Long habits of obedience and subordination, coupled with the moral influence which in our country the white man possesses over the black, furnish an excellent foundation for that discipline which is the best guaranty of military efficiency. Our chief aim should be to secure their fidelity.

There have been formidable armies composed of men having no interest in the cause for which they fought beyond their pay or the hope of plunder. But it is certain that the surest foundation upon which the fidelity of an army can rest, especially in a service which imposes peculiar hardships and privations, is the personal interest of the soldier in the issue of the contest. Such an interest we can give our negroes by giving immediate freedom to all who enlist, and freedom at the end of the war to the families of those who discharge their duties faithfully (whether they survive or not), together with the privilege of residing at the South. To this might be added a bounty for faithful service.

We should not expect slaves to fight for prospective freedom when they can secure it at once by going to the enemy, in whose service they will incur no greater risk than in ours. The reasons that induce me to recommend the employment of negro troops at all render the effect of the measures I have suggested upon slavery immaterial, and in my opinion the best means of securing the efficiency and fidelity of this auxiliary force would be to accompany the measure with a well-digested plan of gradual and general emancipation. As that will be the result of the continuance of the war, and will certainly occur if the enemy succeed, it seems to me most advisable to adopt it at once, and thereby obtain all the benefits that will accrue to our cause.

The employment of negro troops under regulations similar in principle to those above indicated would, in my opinion, greatly increase our military strength and enable us to relieve our white population to some extent. I think we could dispense with the reserve forces except in cases of necessity.

It would disappoint the hopes which our enemies base upon our exhaustion, deprive them in a great measure of the aid they now derive from black troops, and thus throw the burden of the war upon their own people. In addition to the great political advantages that would result to our cause from the adoption of a system of emancipation, it would exercise a salutary influence upon our whole negro population, by rendering more secure the fidelity of those who become soldiers, and diminishing the inducements to the rest to abscond.

I can only say in conclusion that whatever measures are to be adopted should be adopted at once. Every day's delay increases the difficulty. Much time will be required to organize and discipline the men, and action may be deferred until it is too late.

Very respectfully, your obedient servant,

R. E. Lee,
General.

Appendix B

Lee's Letter of February 25, 1868,

Concerning His Resignation and the

Virginia Commission

Lexington, Virginia,
February 25, 1868.

Honourable Reverdy Johnson,
United States Senate, Washington, D.C.

My Dear Sir:

My attention has been called to the official report of the debate in the Senate of the United States, on the 19th instant, in which you did me the kindness to doubt the correctness of the statement made by the Honourable Simon Cameron, in regard to myself. I desire that you may feel certain of my conduct on the occasion referred to, so far as my individual statement can make you. I never intimated to any one that I desired the command of the United States Army; nor did I ever have a conversation with but one gentleman, Mr. Francis Preston Blair, on the subject, which was at his invitation, and, as I understood, at the instance of President Lincoln. After listening to his remarks, I declined the offer he made me, to take command of the army that was to be brought into the field; stating, as candidly and as courteously as I could, that, though opposed to secession and deprecating war, I could take no part in an invasion of the Southern States. I went directly from the interview with Mr. Blair to the office of General Scott; told him of the proposition that had been made to me, and my decision. Upon reflection after returning to my home, I concluded that I ought no longer to retain the commission I held in the United States Army, and on the second morning thereafter I forwarded my resignation to General Scott. At the time, I hoped that peace would have been preserved; that some way would have been found to save the country from the calamities of war; and I then had no other intention than to pass the remainder of my life as a private citizen. Two days afterward, upon the invitation of the Governor of Virginia, I repaired to Richmond; found that the Convention then in session had passed the ordinance withdrawing the State from the Union; and accepted the commission of commander of its forces, which was tendered me.

These are the ample facts of the case, and they shew that Mr. Cameron has been misinformed.

I am with great respect,

Your obedient servant,
R. E. Lee.

Appendix C

An Army Commander's Authority to Surrender

In order to evaluate Lee's conduct after he believed that his army's situation was hopeless it is necessary to have a proper understanding of the authority of a commander to surrender. I have been assisted in this regard by Maj. Thomas J. Romig of the United States Army, who at the time of my research for the present study was an instructor in the International Law Division of the Judge Advocate General's School in Charlottesville, Virginia. A fine lawyer, Major Romig engaged in extensive research on the point and kindly supplied me with the analysis that forms the basis of this appendix, for which I am deeply indebted.

Identifying the Confederacy's position on the authority of an army commander to surrender starts with the fact that in early 1861 the Confederacy adopted the relevant laws of the United States in regard to military affairs. Section 29 of the laws of March 6, 1861, reads, in part:

13. The Rules and Articles of War established by the laws of the United States of America for the government of the army, are

hereby declared to be of force, except that wherever the words "United States" occur, the words "Confederate States" shall be substituted therefor.[1]

In view of this legislation, both North and South began their conflict with the same Rules and Articles of War.

In concept, the issue of an army commander's surrendering falls into two parts: his authority to surrender and the circumstances that permit his exercise of that authority.

The Authority

Given the negative nature of the subject matter, it is perhaps not surprising that the Articles of War did not deal directly with surrender. In spite of the absence of an express provision, however, the articles indirectly addressed the issue and, on analysis, provide an answer to the question of Lee's authority. Articles 50 and 52 of the Articles of War are relevant:

> ART. 50. Any officer or soldier who shall, without urgent necessity, or without the leave of his superior officer, quit his guard, platoon, or division, shall be punished, according to the nature of his offense, by the sentence of a court-martial. . . .
>
> ART. 52. Any officer or soldier who shall misbehave himself before the enemy, run away, or shamefully abandon any fort, post, or guard, which he or they may be commanded to defend, being duly convicted thereof, shall suffer death, or such other punishment as shall be ordered by the sentence of a general court-martial.[2]

Several clues to the answer appear in these provisions. In the first place, Article 50 is expressly conditioned on the absence of "urgent necessity." If "urgent necessity" exists, an offense under Article 50 may not be found. Further, if Articles 50 and 52 are read together and rationalized, when "urgent necessity" exists the acts identified in Article 52 would not have occurred "shamefully," and an Article 52 offense may not be found. The inference is therefore that an army commander is authorized to surrender if the appropriate circumstances exist. In the second place, the forum for determining whether either offense has been committed is a court-martial. It has the power – the jurisdiction – to find the facts and apply Article 50 or Article 52 to those facts.

Because of the key role of the court-martial in regard to the issue, it is appropriate to inquire more precisely into the nature of its power. This is described in Article 69 of the Articles of War, as follows:

> ART. 69. The judge advocate, or some person deputed by him, or by the general or officer commanding the army, department, or garrison, shall prosecute in the name of the Confederate States, and administer to each member of the court, before they proceed upon any trial, the following oath, which shall also be taken by all members of the regimental and garrison courts-martial:
>
> "You, A.B., do swear that you will well and truly try and determine, according to evidence, the matter now before you, between the Confederate States of America and the prisoner to be tried, and that you will duly administer justice, according to the provisions of 'An act establishing rules and articles for the government of the Armies of the Confederate States,' without partiality, favor, or affection; and if any doubt should arise, not explained by said articles, according to your conscience, the best of your understanding, and *the custom of war* in like cases." (Emphasis added.)[3]

The elements of the oath constitute a description of the court-martial's power: in determining whether an Article 50 or Article 52 offense has been committed, the court-martial looks to the definition of offenses described in those articles and, if there is doubt, refers to the "custom of war."

Capt. S. V. Benet, an instructor at West Point during the Civil War, may be consulted regarding the concept of the "custom of war" in court-martial proceedings under Articles 50 and 52. After noting that courts-martial are regulated by the Articles of War and Army Regulations, Benet turns to Article 69 and the custom of war. He writes: "The custom of war is the *lex non scripta*, or common law of the army, and by the 69th article of war is recognized as a guide in administering military justice. It can be considered as authority only so far as to aid in removing any doubt that 'should arise not explained by said articles,' and must be an established custom."[4]

The authority of a commander to surrender has long been recognized as part of the custom of war in the West. It goes as far back as Hugo Grotius's seminal study *De Jure Belli ac Pacis*, published in 1625. According to Grotius:

> It does not fall within the province of the general to conduct negotiations with regard to the causes or the consequences of a war; the terminating of war is, in fact, not a part of the waging of it. Even though the general has been placed in command with absolute power, that must be understood to apply only to the conduct of the war. . . .
>
> Not only generals in command but also officers of lower rank have the power to make a truce, but only with those against whom they are fighting, or whom they are holding in a state of siege. This applies only to themselves and to their troops; for other officers of equal rank are not bound by such a truce.[5]

Addressing the question of whether a military leader's agreement with the enemy binds his government, Grotius concludes that it does because "the one who grants a power grants the means necessary for the exercise of that power."[6] His theory is like that of "implied power" in American constitutional law. The army commander has the implied authority to surrender because of his larger authority, his "absolute power," to conduct the war.

Thus, both the Articles of War, by expressing the "urgent necessity" exception in Article 50, and the custom of war authorize surrender by an army commander.

Exercise of the Authority

Grotius did not address the question of the conditions in which the general could exercise his power to surrender, but there is other authority on that aspect of the issue. On April 24, 1863, the Adjutant General's Office of the United States issued General Orders No. 100, titled "Instructions for the Government of Armies of the United States in the Field."[7] Prepared by Francis Lieber, revised and reviewed by a board of officers, and approved by President Lincoln, these instructions are sometimes called the Lieber Code. They cover a wide range of subjects and are in large part a codification of the then-current "custom of war." For this reason, although an act of the Federal government, the code is useful in regard to the Confederate situation. Section VIII of the code concerns armistice and provides generally that an armistice is subject to ratification by the governments of the contending parties. But Article 129 provides that "in capitulations for the surrender of strong places or fortified camps the commanding officer, *in cases of urgent necessity*, may agree that the troops under his command shall not fight again during the war unless exchanged" (emphasis added).[8] The document that Lee and Grant signed at Appomattox on April 9, 1865, provided that the Confederate officers and men were paroled "not to take up arms against the Government of the United States until properly exchanged."[9]

It appears, therefore, that both the Articles of War themselves and the custom of war identify "urgent necessity" as the circumstance in which the army commander may appropriately exercise his authority to surrender. "Urgent necessity" is the critical issue before the court-martial: if it existed, the exercise of the officer's authority was appropriate; if it did not exist, Article 50 or Article 52 or both have been violated.

Whether or not urgent necessity was present is plainly a question of fact for the court-martial to determine from the evidence. As stated in Chapter 6, Lee's General Order No. 9, dated April 10, 1865, set forth the circumstances of his army at the time of the surrender: it "could accomplish nothing" but the "useless sacrifice" of the men for whom he was responsible. This was the "urgent necessity" that, according to express language of the Articles of War and the custom of war as identified by Lieber, justified Lee's exercise of his authority to surrender. Undoubtedly he was right in surrendering; the facts indeed indicated the urgent necessity of the situation. It remains only to add that at any time prior to his surrender at Appomattox when substantially the same facts obtained, the same urgent necessity existed, and Lee's exercise of his authority would have been equally justified.

Notes

PREFACE

1. Fishwick, *Lee after the War*, p. xii.

CHAPTER ONE

1. Warren, *Legacy of the Civil War*, p. 3.
2. Wilson, "Robert E. Lee," p. 67.
3. Morison, *By Land and by Sea*, pp. 347–48, 353.
4. Downing, "Perfect through Suffering," pp. 194–95.
5. Piston, *Lee's Tarnished Lieutenant*, p. 129.
6. Jones, *Army of Northern Virginia*, p. 122.
7. Wilson, "Robert E. Lee," p. 64; Freeman, *Unpublished Letters of General Robert E. Lee*, p. xxvii.
8. Dowdey, *The Seven Days*, pp. 168–92; Dowdey, *Lee*, p. 275.
9. Piston, *Lee's Tarnished Lieutenant*, p. 183.
10. Connelly, *The Marble Man*, p. 3.
11. Fishwick, "Virginians on Olympus II"; Davis, *Gray Fox*; Fishwick, *Lee after the War*; Dowdey, *Lee*; Sanborn, *Robert E. Lee*; Flood, *Lee – The Last Years*; Smith, *Lee and Grant*; Weidhorn, *Robert E. Lee*; Anderson and Anderson, *The*

Generals. Each of these books – and they will all be referred to later in the text and notes – represents a conventional, orthodox treatment of Lee.

Clifford Dowdey is of Douglas Southall Freeman's Virginia school. Thus, Lee was a military genius and would have prevailed but for Stonewall Jackson's death. An undisguised apologist for the Confederacy, Dowdey believes that slavery had nothing to do with secession and flatly condemns the abolitionists. His book contains an elaborate criticism of the Emancipation Proclamation (pp. 318–21) that includes this statement: "For the ultimate purpose of restoring a union in harmonious concern for the common welfare, it was the single most divisive act since the republic was founded" (p. 318). Dowdey does not state whether he regards secession and the establishment of the Confederacy as divisive, nor does he tell how he ranks these acts in relation to the Emancipation Proclamation. Repeating the Confederate and English criticisms of the proclamation, Dowdey does not understand that its geographical limitations arose from the executive war powers exceptions to the Constitution. He states his resentment of the fact that the proclamation divided the North and South on "spurious moral lines" (p. 319) and contributed to the Northern "illusion that their fight [was] to 'free the slaves'" (p. 319). Dowdey's views of Reconstruction are, of course, the classic views.

12. Freeman, *R. E. Lee*, 1:ix.

13. Ibid., 4:494.

14. Thomas H. Johnson, *Oxford Companion to American History*, p. 468.

CHAPTER TWO

1. Thomas H. Johnson, *Oxford Companion to American History*, p. 468; Faust, *Historical Times Illustrated Encyclopedia of the Civil War*, p. 429.

2. *Encyclopaedia Britannica*, 15th ed., s.v. "Lee, Robert Edward"; Anderson and Anderson, *The Generals*, pp. 9, 150. A recent juvenile biography of Lee states that he "condemned slavery" (Weidhorn, *Robert E. Lee*, p. 23).

3. U.S. Congress, *Report of the Reconstruction Committee*, p. 136; Freeman, *R. E. Lee*, 1:371. Marshall W. Fishwick accepts the orthodox opinion, stating that Lee "condemned slavery" and "had been for gradual emancipation" (*Lee after the War*, pp. 54, 124). In an unusual paring of attitudes about slavery, Clifford Dowdey notes Lincoln's belief in emancipation and states that Lincoln "like Lee . . . believed in emancipation by state action" (*Lee*, p. 320).

4. Freeman, *R. E. Lee*, 1:371, 390.

5. Letter of July 8, 1858 (Mss. 2, W7336C 2), Robert Edward Lee Papers, Virginia Historical Society, Richmond, Va.

6. Freeman, *R. E. Lee*, 1:390. This incident is described by Lee in a letter from Arlington to his son G. W. Custis Lee, dated July 2, 1859, printed in Jones, *Life and Letters of Robert Edward Lee*, p. 102. The incident had a controversial

aftermath. Freeman (*R. E. Lee*, 1:390−92) discusses anonymous letters to the *New York Tribune* and the *New York Times*. The letters alleged that the runaways were flogged when returned to Arlington and that Lee himself applied the whip to the female. In his letter of July 2, 1859, to Custis, Lee acknowledged the accusations and stated, "I shall not reply." Freeman calls the accusations a "libel" and rejects them out of hand. Bertram Wyatt-Brown, in discussing the incident in *Southern Honor* (pp. 371−72), states that Freeman was "perhaps" correct but notes, as Freeman did not, that one of the runaways had given a recorded account of the flogging including the statement that Lee had ordered brine poured into the wounds. In view of this record by one of the runaways, Freeman's statement (p. 390) that there is "no evidence, direct or indirect" of the flogging is simply wrong.

7. Freeman, *R. E. Lee*, 1:371−73. A version of the letter also appears in Jones, *Life and Letters of Robert Edward Lee*, pp. 82−83. Freeman points out (p. 373n) that Jones's version is defective and omits Lee's most severe references to Northern abolitionists. Since Freeman's text is based on his examination of the original letter, then in the Library of Congress, his version is used here.

8. Freeman, *R. E. Lee*, 1:373.

9. Wyatt-Brown, *Southern Honor*, p. 108.

10. Dowdey and Manarin, *Wartime Papers of R. E. Lee*, p. 390.

11. Will of G. W. P. Custis, *Ms. Records of Alexandria County, Virginia*, cited in Freeman, *R. E. Lee*, 1:380n. Freeman describes the will on pp. 380−82.

12. Jones, *Life and Letters of Robert Edward Lee*, p. 102.

13. Dowdey and Manarin, *Wartime Papers of R. E. Lee*, pp. 354, 378.

14. Freeman, *R. E. Lee*, 4:385; see also n. 37 on the same page concerning the recording of the deed of manumission.

15. Coddington, *Gettysburg Campaign*, pp. 159−69; Schildt, *Roads to Gettysburg*, pp. 223−71, 298; Conrad and Alexander, *When War Passed This Way*, pp. 253−54. The 1862 raid into Maryland was accompanied by large-scale depredation by Lee's troops, according to Lee's letter to Jefferson Davis on September 21, 1862. U.S. War Department, *War of the Rebellion, Official Records of the Union and Confederate Armies*, ser. 1, vol. 19, pt. 2, pp. 617−18; hereinafter, the *Official Records* will be abbreviated *OR*, and cited by volume number (and part number, as necessary), followed by page number(s): thus, *OR*, 19 (2):617−18. Unless otherwise indicated, all volumes cited are in series 1. Lee wrote that "stragglers" from his army "wantonly destroy stock and other property." The letter also cited "much unnecessary damage . . . done by the troops both while marching and in camp." These activities Lee characterized as "outrages" and "disgraceful." On September 22, 1862, Lee addressed a strong letter to Longstreet and Jackson on the subject, designed to tighten discipline in respect to such activities. *OR*, 19 (2):618−19.

16. *Franklin Repository*, July 8, 1863; Rev. Philip Schaff, "Gettysburg Week"; Schildt, *Roads to Gettysburg*, pp. 82, 155−56; Conrad and Alexander, *When War*

Passed This Way, pp. 130−49; Woman's Club of Mercersburg, *Old Mercersburg*, pp. 149−60. The *Franklin Repository* report can be found in Moore, *Rebellion Record*, 7:197.

17. *OR*, 51 (2):733; Faust, *Historical Times Illustrated Encyclopedia of the Civil War*, p. 161.

18. James M. McPherson, *Ordeal by Fire*, pp. 450−56.

19. *OR*, ser. 2, 5:795−97, 807−8.

20. *OR*, ser. 2, 5:940.

21. *OR*, ser. 2, 5:128, 696.

22. *OR*, ser. 2, 6:441−42, 647−49, 607−14. It is to be noted that regardless of the issue concerning Federal soldiers who were former slaves, in August 1864 Grant was on record within the Federal government as opposing any exchanges as counterproductive in terms of attrition of Confederate armies, *OR*, ser. 2, 7:606−7, 614−15.

23. *OR*, ser. 2, 6:226, 7:578−79, 687−91.

24. *OR*, ser. 2, 7:906−7.

25. *OR*, ser. 2, 7:909.

26. *OR*, ser. 2, 7:914, 1010−11.

27. U.S. Congress, *Report of the Reconstruction Committee*, p. 135. In Freeman's discussion of Lee's appearance before this subcommittee (*R. E. Lee*, 4:249−56), his highly argumentative treatment of the subcommittee and its examination of Lee is evidence of his own intense bias in favor of Lee and the Confederate cause.

28. William Porcher Miles Papers, Southern Historical Collection, Wilson Library, University of North Carolina, Chapel Hill, cited in Durden, *The Gray and the Black*, pp. 135−37.

29. *OR*, ser. 4, 3:1007−9.

30. *OR*, ser. 4, 3:1012−13. This letter to Hunter is reproduced below as Appendix A. Another letter was sent by Lee on February 18, 1865, to Congressman Ethelbert Barksdale of Mississippi. Also advocating the recruitment of slaves, this letter made no reference to slavery as the best relationship and also omitted any reference to general emancipation. Edward McPherson, *Political History of the United States*, p. 611n.

31. *OR*, ser. 4, 3:1161.

32. Durden, *The Gray and the Black*, pp. 202, 205−6. On March 10, 1865, Lee wrote to Davis urging the prompt enlistment of slaves. Freeman, *Unpublished Letters of General Robert E. Lee*, pp. 373−74.

33. Lee's letter of January 11, 1865, can be compared to Confederate Maj. Gen. Patrick R. Cleburne's letter of January 2, 1864, *OR*, 52 (2):586−92. An Irish immigrant living in Arkansas before the war, Cleburne advocated immediate enlistment of slaves and a "guarantee of freedom within a reasonable time to every slave in the South who shall remain true to the Confederacy in this war." Cleburne acknowledged the existence of widespread miscegenation. His

letter makes it plain that the slave population was pro-North, contrary to one of the Lost Cause fictions, and was therefore a liability to the South. He proposed to convert this liability into an asset by emancipation and the direct military use of blacks. Cleburne's proposal alluded to certain of the more odious aspects of slavery, issues that did not occur to Lee or the indigenous Southern leadership: "We must make free men of them beyond all question, and thus enlist their sympathies also. We can do this more effectually than the North can now do, for we can give the negro not only his freedom, but that of his wife and child, and can secure it to him in his old home. To do this, we must immediately make his marriage and parental relations sacred in the eyes of the law and forbid their sale." Durden's valuable discussion of Cleburne's letter and its suppression by the Confederacy appears in *The Gray and the Black*, pp. 53–67.

Col. William Allan, a faculty member at Washington College and formerly of Gen. Richard S. Ewell's staff, reported a conversation that he had with Lee in Lexington in 1868. According to Allan's memorandum of the conversation, Lee claimed that he "told Mr. Davis often and early in the war that the slaves should be emancipated, that it was the only way to remove a weakness at home and to get sympathy abroad, and to divide our enemies, but Davis would not hear of it" ("Conversations with Gen. R. E. Lee," p. 11, Southern Historical Collection, Wilson Library, University of North Carolina, Chapel Hill). Lee also told William Preston Johnston after the war that in 1861 he "saw the necessity" of a "proclamation of gradual emancipation," but he did not state to Johnston that he had said this to President Davis (Bean, "Memorandum of Conversations between Robert E. Lee and William Preston Johnston," p. 479). There is no evidence corroborating these postwar claims, and the evidence that does exist and is described in this chapter discredits the claims.

34. Freeman, *R. E. Lee*, 3:544; Dowdey, *Lee*, p. 518.

35. Capt. Robert E. Lee, *Recollections and Letters of General Robert E. Lee*, pp. 226–34. Freeman discusses this interview in *R. E. Lee*, 4:237–40.

36. Leyburn, "Interview with Gen. Robert E. Lee," 166–67. Freeman's acknowledgment of his own reliance on Leyburn states: "Doctor Leyburn wrote in 1885, sixteen years after the interview, but as he gave all the circumstances of General Lee's visit with absolute accuracy, there is no reason to doubt his direct quotations" (*R. E. Lee*, 4:401).

37. Avary, *Dixie after the War*, p. 72.

38. Fehrenbacher, *Lincoln in Text and Context*, p. 47.

39. Wyatt-Brown, *Southern Honor*, p. 24; Fehrenbacher, *Lincoln in Text and Context*, p. 69; Brogan, "Fresh Appraisal of the Civil War," p. 187.

40. Stampp, *And the War Came*.

41. Foster, *Ghosts of the Confederacy*, p. 23; Dorris, *Pardon and Amnesty*, p. 137.

42. Fehrenbacher, *Lincoln in Text and Context*, p. 69.

43. Stampp, *Peculiar Institution*, pp. 210–17; Dumond, *Antislavery: The*

Crusade for Freedom, pp. 204−10; Dumond, *Antislavery Origins of the Civil War*, pp. 51−82. See also the discussion of this extralegal Southern response in Stampp, *Imperiled Union*, pp. 235−37.

44. U.S. Bureau of the Census, *Negro Population*, p. 57; Stampp, *Peculiar Institution*, pp. 31−32.

45. Durden, *The Gray and the Black*, pp. 3−7. Durden's text is very useful because it sets forth the relevant portions of the United States and Confederate constitutions side by side.

46. Nevins, *Emergence of Lincoln*, 2:468.

47. Moore, *Rebellion Record*, 1:19, 44−46. Substantial excerpts from this speech can be found in Durden, *The Gray and the Black*, pp. 7−9.

48. Wyatt-Brown, *Southern Honor*, p. 16.

49. Foster, *Ghosts of the Confederacy*, p. 4.

50. Durden, *The Gray and the Black*, p. viii.

51. Ibid., p. 290.

52. Stampp, *Imperiled Union*, pp. 265, 255; Foner, *Reconstruction*, p. xxvii.

53. Brogan, "Fresh Appraisal of the Civil War," p. 185; Beringer et al., *Why the South Lost*, p. 439.

54. Stampp, *Imperiled Union*, pp. 225−30. Stampp carefully analyzes the slavery apologies. The crusade against slavery, he notes, was "not . . . a historical aberration but . . . a logical and predictable development of Western, including American, culture" (p. 225). The Southern manumission movement and anti-slavery activity in the South "virtually ceased, not as a reaction to northern abolitionism but as a result of conditions in the South itself . . . the growing profitability of slavery, the expanding market for surplus slaves in the new areas of the Southwest, the general belief that whites and free blacks could not live together in peace, the harsh state laws designed to suppress antislavery agitation and mob violence" (p. 228). Stampp proposes this plain logic: "The northern movement would never have developed to wage a campaign against a declining institution which Southerners themselves seemed ready to abandon" (p. 230).

CHAPTER THREE

1. Statement of the military service in the United States Army of Colonel Robert E. Lee prepared for the secretary of war, A.G. 201, April 20, 1920, "Selected Military Service Records in the Custody of the National Archives Relating to Robert E. Lee," Record Group 94. This source is hereinafter identified as "Selected Military Service Records," followed by the appropriate record group. See also Freeman, *R. E. Lee*, 1:404−29. Unless otherwise indicated, these sources are the authorities for the discussion of Lee's prewar United States Army activities that follows.

2. Jones, *Life and Letters of Robert Edward Lee*, pp. 115–16.

3. Ibid., p. 118.

4. Richardson, *Messages and Papers of the Presidents*, 5:638.

5. Jones, *Life and Letters of Robert Edward Lee*, pp. 118–19.

6. Anderson, "Texas, before, and on the Eve of the Rebellion," p. 31.

7. Craven, *"To Markie,"* pp. 58–59.

8. Jones, *Personal Reminiscences of Gen. Robert E. Lee*, p. 136.

9. Sanborn, *Robert E. Lee*, 1:314–15.

10. Jones, *Personal Reminiscences of Gen. Robert E. Lee*, pp. 136–37.

11. Freeman, *R. E. Lee*, 1:429.

12. Brig. Gen. Richard W. Johnson, *A Soldier's Reminiscences*, pp. 132–33.

13. Ibid., p. 133.

14. Cosby, "With Gen. R. E. Lee," p. 167.

15. *OR*, 1:503–4.

16. Jones, *Personal Reminiscences of Gen. Robert E. Lee*, pp. 387–88. By a strange coincidence, Lee wrote one of his sons on February 16, 1862, two years to the day from the letter quoted in the text, and stated the same message: "Our country requires now every one to put forth all his ability, regardless of self" (Jones, *Life and Letters of Robert Edward Lee*, p. 160). The message was the same but Lee's "country" had changed.

17. Anderson, "Texas, before, and on the Eve of the Rebellion," p. 32. See also Johnson and Buel, *Battles and Leaders*, 1:36n.

18. Johnson and Buel, *Battles and Leaders*, 1:36n.

19. Anderson, "Texas, before, and on the Eve of the Rebellion," p. 32.

20. Lincoln, *Collected Works*, 4:266.

21. *OR*, ser. 3, 5:691.

22. Keyes, *Fifty Years Observation*, pp. 205–6.

23. *OR*, ser. 4, 1:165–66; Freeman, *R. E. Lee*, 1:434.

24. Letter dated March 30, 1861, from Lee to Col. Lorenzo Thomas, Adjutant General of the United States Army, "Selected Military Service Records," Record Group 94.

25. Letter dated March 15, 1855, from Lee to Col. S. Cooper, Adjutant General of the United States Army, which letter referred to and enclosed the oath, "Selected Military Service Records," Record Group 94.

26. Freeman, *R. E. Lee*, 1:439.

27. Ibid., p. 436; Capt. Robert E. Lee, *Recollections and Letters of General Robert E. Lee*, pp. 27–28. See Appendix B below for the text of Lee's letter of February 25, 1868, to Senator Reverdy Johnson.

28. Freeman, *R. E. Lee*, 1:437.

29. Ibid., p. 473.

30. Ibid., p. 439.

31. Letter dated April 20, 1861, from Lee to Simon Cameron, Secretary of War, "Selected Military Service Records," Record Group 94; Freeman, *R. E.*

Lee, 1:474. The letter of resignation and the letter to General Scott are reproduced in Freeman, *R. E. Lee,* 1:440–42; a facsimile of the letter of resignation appears in Freeman, *R. E. Lee,* immediately following p. 444 in vol. 1.

32. Capt. Robert E. Lee, *Recollections and Letters of General Robert E. Lee,* pp. 25–26, 26–27.

33. Circular to headquarters departments dated April 22, 1861, and cover document showing acceptance of resignation by Simon Cameron, Secretary of War, dated April 25, 1861, "Selected Military Service Records," Record Group 94. See also Freeman, *R. E. Lee,* 1:442 n. 39. A facsimile of the cover document appears in Freeman, *R. E. Lee,* immediately following p. 444 in vol. 1.

34. U.S. War Department, *Regulations for the Army,* p. 4.

35. Freeman, *R. E. Lee,* 1:447; Dowdey and Manarin, *Wartime Papers of R. E. Lee,* p. 5.

36. Freeman, *R. E. Lee,* 1:445–47, 463–64, app. I-3, pp. 637–38. Freeman accurately sets forth the facts of record based on the *Journal of the Virginia Executive Council,* the contemporaneous Robertson-Letcher correspondence in the Virginia State Library and the *Journal of the Virginia Convention of 1861.* The Virginia Executive Council recommendation of Lee's appointment, dated April 21, 1861, can be found in *OR,* 51 (2):21. His confirmation by the Virginia Convention took place on the night of April 22, but the minute of the Virginia Executive Council noting the convention's action is dated April 23, 1861. *OR,* 51 (2):27.

37. *OR,* 51 (2):18, 24.

38. *OR,* ser. 4, 1:242; Alexander H. Stephens, *Constitutional View,* 2:385. See also Freeman, *R. E. Lee,* 1:470–71.

39. *OR,* 2:803–4.

40. *OR,* ser. 4, 1:243–44, 294, 2:827. Confederate War Department form identifying Lee's appointment to brigadier general on May 14, 1861, "Selected Military Service Records," Record Group 109.

41. *OR,* 2:911–12.

42. Dowdey and Manarin, *Wartime Papers of R. E. Lee,* p. 19.

43. Col. William Allan, "Conversations with Gen. R. E. Lee," p. 7, Southern Historical Collection, Wilson Library, University of North Carolina, Chapel Hill.

44. Capt. Robert E. Lee, *Recollections and Letters of General Robert E. Lee,* pp. 27–28.

45. Col. William Allan, "Conversations with Gen. R. E. Lee," p. 6, Southern Historical Collection, Wilson Library, University of North Carolina, Chapel Hill. According to Allan, Lee stated on February 25, 1868, that he had learned "officially" of Virginia's secession from Robertson on Sunday, April 21, 1861.

46. U.S. Congress. *Report of the Reconstruction Committee,* p. 133. Lee's biographers, taking their cue perhaps from Freeman's "Answer He Was Born to Make," go to unusual lengths to avoid analysis of and to dignify Lee's seceding.

A juvenile writer has recently indulged in what may be the ultimate hyperbole, explaining of Lee: "He was a Virginian, and only devotion to God could be more important" (Weidhorn, *Robert E. Lee*, p. 25). Of course Lee never *said* this, and there is no documentation indicating that he believed it. But the statement moots the issue of Lee's military oath and fits neatly with the Lee tradition.

47. *Richmond Dispatch*, March 23, 1861.

48. Kirke [Gilmore], *Down in Tennessee*, p. 278.

49. *Charleston Mercury*, November 19, 1864.

50. Nevins, *Emergence of Lincoln*, 2:291, 324−25, 285.

51. Wolff, "Party and Section," pp. 295−96. See also Russell, "Issues in the Congressional Struggle over the Kansas-Nebraska Bill," p. 188.

52. Freeman, *R. E. Lee*, 1:416.

53. Ibid., p. 439.

54. Nevins, *Ordeal of the Union*, 2:515−54, 543.

55. Ibid., p. 553. After the war, Lee persisted in this view of the Union. In one of his conversations with Col. William Allan in Lexington on March 10, 1868, Lee responded to the criticism of his seceding on the ground that he had been educated at West Point at government expense with the argument that he was sent to West Point by Virginia ("Conversations with Gen. R. E. Lee," p. 10, Southern Historical Collection, Wilson Library, University of North Carolina, Chapel Hill). Jefferson Davis took up this point, and extended it, in defending Lee in a speech given in Richmond on November 3, 1870. Davis said that Lee was "given by Virginia to the service of the United States, he represented her in the Military Academy at West Point. He was not educated by the Federal Government, but by Virginia; for she paid her full share for the support of that institution. . . . Entering the army of the United States, he represented Virginia there also" (Jones, *Personal Reminiscences of Gen. Robert E. Lee*, p. 134).

56. Freeman, *R. E. Lee*, 1:470.

57. Ibid., p. 430.

58. Ibid., p. 447; Jones, *Personal Reminiscences of Gen. Robert E. Lee*, p. 142.

59. Wyatt-Brown, *Southern Honor*, pp. 14−15.

60. *OR*, 27 (3):881−82.

61. *New York Herald*, April 29, 1865.

62. Wyatt-Brown, *Southern Honor*, p. 15.

63. *OR*, 5:192.

64. Jones, *Life and Letters of Robert Edward Lee*, p. 156.

65. Capt. Robert E. Lee, *Recollections and Letters of General Robert E. Lee*, p. 151.

66. Freeman, *R. E. Lee*, 4:303.

67. Capt. Robert E. Lee, *Recollections and Letters of General Robert E. Lee*, p. 233. This statement was made, according to Saunders, in the interview described in Chapter 2 above.

68. Jones, *Personal Reminiscences of Gen. Robert E. Lee*, p. 210.

69. Ibid., p. 218.
70. Ibid., p. 220.
71. "Unpublished Letters of Gen. Lee," *Missouri Republican*, October 3, 1885.
72. Freeman, *R. E. Lee*, 1:404.

CHAPTER FOUR

1. *Encyclopedia Americana*, 1989 ed., s.v. "Lee, Robert Edward"; *Encyclopaedia Britannica*, 15th ed., s.v. "Lee, Robert Edward"; Boatner, *Civil War Dictionary*, p. 476; Fishwick, *Lee after the War*, p. 178; Editors of Time-Life Books, *Lee Takes Command*, p. 8; Weidhorn, *Robert E. Lee*, pp. 50, 106, 76.

The *Americana* alludes to Lee's habit of discretionary orders, one of the well-known issues concerning his leadership. The issue divides the commentators. Louis H. Manarin, a vigorous defender of Lee, says this: "Doubtless Lee's use of discretionary orders led to some confusion, but they were a necessary part of his tactics and strategy: to baffle his opponent by maneuvering to advantage, striking when opportunity presented, always with the objective of destroying the enemy's army or disrupting his campaigns. Weakness required vigilance. Subordinate commanders had to be able to assume the initiative when the opportunity occurred, or execute the correct move as the situation developed. Lee could not be everywhere at the same time. He related to his subordinates, through discretionary orders, his ideas, often outlining necessary moves to counter specific moves by the enemy. A war of movement necessitated the issuance of such discretionary orders" ("Lee in Command," p. 596).

Edward Porter Alexander had quite a different view: "No commander of any army does his whole duty who simply gives orders, however well considered. He should *supervise their execution*, in person or by staff officers, constantly, day & night, so that if the machine balks at any point he may be most promptly informed & may most promptly start it to work" (*Fighting for the Confederacy*, p. 110; emphasis in original). Referring to the second day at Gettysburg and Longstreet's route to the Confederate right, Alexander wrote: "That is just one illustration of how time may be lost in handling troops, and of the need of an abundance of competent staff officers by the generals in command. Scarcely any of our generals had half of what they needed to keep a *constant & close supervision on the execution of important orders*. And that ought always to be done. An army is like a great machine, and in putting it into battle it is not enough for its commander to merely issue the necessary orders. He should have a staff ample to supervise the execution of each step, & to promptly report any difficulty or misunderstanding. There is no telling the value of the hours which were lost by that division that morning" (*Fighting for the Confederacy*, p. 236; emphasis in original).

Manarin seems entirely to overlook the use of staff officers in regard to the supervision of orders. I am persuaded by Alexander, who is critical of Lee's lack of control, and unpersuaded by Manarin's thesis.

2. Prominent critics of Lee's generalship, none of whom has significantly affected the tradition, have appeared in three generations of Civil War writing. They are Lt. Col. George A. Bruce; Maj. Gen. J. F. C. Fuller, the English military historian; and Prof. Thomas L. Connelly.

Bruce's "Strategy of the Civil War" was published in 1913 in *Papers of the Military Historical Society of Massachusetts*. Faulting Lee in a number of specific campaigns, Bruce was especially concerned with Lee's aggressiveness and his unacceptable casualties. His analysis is suggestive of my own thesis. General Fuller wrote *The Generalship of Ulysses S. Grant*, published in 1929. This was followed by *Grant and Lee*, published in the United States in 1933. In both books he examined critically the then-prominent stereotype of Grant, the inept "butcher," and Lee, the great strategist. Like Colonel Bruce, Fuller criticized Lee's addiction to the offensive and the casualties that it entailed.

Thomas L. Connelly, historian of the Confederate Army of Tennessee, is a well-identified modern critic of Lee. He has made several efforts to reevaluate Lee. In 1969, *Civil War History* published his "Robert E. Lee and the Western Confederacy: A Criticism of Lee's Strategic Ability." Although concentrating on Lee's neglect of the war in the West, his lack of understanding of its significance, and his alleged Virginia parochialism, Connelly was also critical of Lee's "penchant for the offensive." Connelly was again heard from in 1973. "The Image and the General: Robert E. Lee in American Historiography" appeared in *Civil War History*. As suggested by its title, this article was less concerned with the pros and cons of Lee's generalship. Remarking that the "sensitivity of Lee partisans to any criticism of the General has enshrouded him in a protective mantel enjoyed by no other Confederate figure," Connelly concentrated on "the process by which his image has developed in American letters since the Civil War." The same year brought still another of Connelly's reevaluations; he and Archer Jones of North Dakota State University published *The Politics of Command*, which returned to and considerably amplified the thesis of the 1969 *Civil War History* article in the context of a thoughtful discussion of the Confederacy's endemic dilemma: in view of limited manpower and resources, how was it to balance their deployment between Virginia and the West?

Connelly's earlier attention to Lee both predicted and culminated in his 1977 book, *The Marble Man: Robert E. Lee and His Image in American Society*. This book had two principal components: an intellectual history of the development of the Lee tradition and a psychological inquiry into the man. In both cases, Lee's aggressiveness and casualties were seen as relevant by Connelly. A recent discussion of Connelly's concerns can be found in Richard M. McMurry's *Two Great Rebel Armies: An Essay in Confederate Military History*.

3. Freeman, *R. E. Lee*, 4:169–70.

4. An interesting discussion of the misplaced offensive tactics of both armies

and an analysis of Lee's casualty percentages can be found in McWhiney and Jamieson, *Attack and Die*. I do not embrace the authors' racial-ethnic theories, but the book is nevertheless useful. Halleck, *Elements of Military Art and Science*, pp. 114, 38; Dupuy, Johnson, and Hayes, *Dictionary of Military Terms*, pp. 214, 209. See also Clausewitz, *On War*, p. 173.

5. *OR*, 46 (2):1205.

6. Wiley, *Road to Appomattox*, p. 77.

7. Donald, *Why the North Won*. This book contains essays by Richard N. Current, T. Harry Williams, Norman A. Graebner, David Donald, and David M. Potter.

8. Beringer et al., *Why the South Lost*, pp. 9, 16.

9. James M. McPherson, *Ordeal by Fire*, p. 184.

10. Fuller, *Generalship of Ulysses S. Grant*, pp. 210, 223.

11. *OR*, 34 (2):610−11, 33:729, 34 (1):11.

12. *OR*, 34 (2):611, 33:828.

13. Fuller, *Generalship of Ulysses S. Grant*, pp. 222−23, 336.

14. Pierce, *Memoir and Letters of Charles Sumner*, 4:114 (letter of January 17, 1863, to Francis Lieber); Lincoln, *Collected Works*, 7:514.

15. Alexander, *Fighting for the Confederacy*, p. 415. Quoting William Swinton, Alexander also writes: "War is sustained quite as much by the moral energy of a people as by its material resources, and the former must be active to bring out and make available the latter. It has not unfrequently occurred that, with abundant resources, a nation has failed in war by the sapping of the animating principle in the minds of its citizens. For armies are things visible and formal, circumscribed by time and space; but the soul of war is a power unseen, bound up with the interests, convictions, passions of men" (p. 416).

16. James M. McPherson, *Ordeal by Fire*, p. 183.

17. Piston, *Lee's Tarnished Lieutenant*, pp. 31−32.

18. Bruce, "Strategy of the Civil War," p. 469.

19. Fuller, *Generalship of Ulysses S. Grant*, p. 376. See also Vandiver, *Rebel Brass*, pp. 16−17.

20. Fuller, *Generalship of Ulysses S. Grant*, p. 365.

21. James M. McPherson, *Battle Cry of Freedom*, p. 338.

22. Fuller, *Generalship of Ulysses S. Grant*, p. 29.

23. Manarin, "Lee in Command," p. 274. It should be noted that Manarin's distinction between offensive and defensive is ambiguous, both with respect to the Confederacy's official policy and Lee's grand strategy. On balance, he seems to conclude that the official policy was defensive but that Lee's was offensive.

24. Weigley, *American Way of War*, pp. 101−2; Thomas, *Confederate Nation*, pp. 104−8; Vandiver, *Their Tattered Flags*, pp. 93−94, 121.

25. Wiley, *The Road to Appomattox*, p. 39; Connelly and Jones, *Politics of Command*.

26. Connelly and Jones, *Politics of Command*, pp. 126, 35.

27. *OR*, 19 (2):590–94; Coddington, *Gettysburg Campaign*, pp. 5–9.

28. Dowdey and Manarin, *Wartime Papers of R. E. Lee*, pp. 532–33.

29. Ibid., p. 816.

30. Ibid., p. 496.

31. *OR*, 27 (3):868–69.

32. *OR*, 51 (2):761.

33. Dowdey and Manarin, *Wartime Papers of R. E. Lee*, p. 469.

34. *OR*, 29 (1):405.

35. Dowdey and Manarin, *Wartime Papers of R. E. Lee*, p. 609.

36. Ibid., p. 631.

37. Ibid., p. 675.

38. Ibid., p. 700.

39. Ibid., p. 747.

40. Ibid., p. 597.

41. Ibid., p. 820.

42. Alexander, *Fighting for the Confederacy*, p. 521.

43. Alexander makes several interesting and relevant observations about the Seven Days. Thus, he writes: "Very few of the reports distinguish between the casualties of the different battles, of which there were four, beside a sharp affair of Magruder's at Savage Station on Sunday the 29th, about which I have never known the particulars except that it was an isolated attack on a strong rear guard by 2½ brigades & it was repulsed, as might have been expected. No *small* force of ours could have hoped for any real success, & all such inadequate attacks were mistakes.

"Of the other four actions, three were assaults by main force right where the enemy wanted us to make them. The first, Ellison's Mill, was an entire failure & very bloody – but fortunately was in a small scale. The second, Cold Harbor or Gaines's Mill, was also a bloody failure at first – being made piecemeal. Finally made in force it was a success. The third, Malvern Hill, was an utter & bloody failure. Ellison's Mill & Malvern Hill could both have been turned, & Gen. D. H. Hill asserts that the enemy's right at Cold Harbor could have [been] better assaulted than the centre or left where our attack was made" (*Fighting for the Confederacy*, p. 120; emphasis in original).

Alexander was especially critical of the Confederates' costly and unsuccessful attack at Malvern Hill: "I don't think any military engineer can read this description of this ground without asking in surprise, & almost in indignation, how on God's earth it happened that our army was put to assault such a position. The whole country was but a gently rolling one with no great natural obstacles anywhere, fairly well cultivated & with farm roads going in every direction. Why was not half our army simply turned to the left & marched by the nearest roads out of the enemy's view & fire to strike his road of retreat, & his long, slow

& cumbersome trains, a few miles below, while the rest in front could threaten & hold his battle array but without attacking it" (*Fighting for the Confederacy*, p. 111).

44. Alexander also discusses the Confederate attacks at Chancellorsville. At the time of Lee's appointment to command the Army of Northern Virginia, Alexander's friend Capt. Joseph C. Ives had told Alexander that Lee was the most audacious man in either army. Alexander writes this about Chancellorsville: "There was still another occasion when I recalled ruefully Ives's prophecy that I would see all the audacity I wanted to see, & felt that it was already overfulfilled: but when, to my intense delight, the enemy crossed the river in retreat during the night, & thus saved us from what would have been probably the bloodiest defeat of the war. It was on the 6th of May 1863 at the end of Chancellorsville. . . . Hooker's entire army, some 90,000 infantry, were in the Wilderness, backed against the Rapidan, & had had nearly three days to fortify a short front, from the river above to the river below. And, in that dense forest of small wood, a timber slashing in front of a line of breastworks could in a few hours make a position absolutely impregnable to assault. But on the afternoon of the 5th Gen. Lee gave orders for a grand assault the next morning by his whole force of about 40,000 infantry, & I was all night getting my artillery in position for it. And how I did thank God when in the morning the enemy were gone!" (*Fighting for the Confederacy*, p. 92).

45. Alexander, *Fighting for the Confederacy*, pp. 92, 506, 507. Lt. Col. Alfred H. Burne comments on Lee's aggressiveness and his sense of casualties as the Federals moved to the west at Petersburg, immediately prior to Five Forks on April 1, 1865, that "in spite of the great loss he had just sustained at Fort Stedman, and the resulting lowering of the morale of the troops, Lee instantly decided on a counter-offensive, *cost what it might*" (*Lee, Grant and Sherman*, p. 186; emphasis added).

46. Manarin, "Lee in Command," pp. v, 260.

47. Connelly and Jones, *Politics of Command*, p. 33.

48. Dowdey and Manarin, *Wartime Papers of R. E. Lee*, pp. 388–89.

49. *OR*, 27 (3):881.

50. Dowdey and Manarin, *Wartime Papers of R. E. Lee*, p. 544.

51. Ibid., pp. 843–44, 847–48.

52. Livermore, *Numbers and Losses*, pp. 86, 140, 88–89, 140, 91, 141; Sears, *Landscape Turned Red*, p. 296; Bigelow, *Campaign of Chancellorsville*, p. 475; Coddington, *Gettysburg Campaign*, p. 536. Dowdey's quote appears in Dowdey and Manarin, *Wartime Papers of R. E. Lee*, p. 426. Freeman is quoted from Freeman, *Unpublished Letters of General Robert E. Lee*, p. xxxvii.

53. *OR*, 19 (1):143; Alexander, *Fighting for the Confederacy*, p. 153.

54. Piston, "Lee's Tarnished Lieutenant," p. 174.

55. *OR*, 19 (2):606, 19 (1):143, 19 (2):617–18, 597, 626–27.

56. *OR*, 19 (2):629–30.

57. Piston, "Lee's Tarnished Lieutenant," p. 176. Manarin, "Lee in Command," pp. 374–75, 378, acknowledges these morale problems.

58. Manarin, "Lee in Command," pp. 413, 578.

59. Freeman, *Lee's Lieutenants*, 3:217.

60. *OR*, 27 (3):1041, 1048, 1052.

61. *OR*, 27 (3):1041, 29 (2):641–42.

62. *OR*, 29 (2):650, 650–51, 692, 768–69.

63. Bruce, "Strategy of the Civil War," p. 467.

64. Connelly and Jones, *Politics of Command*, p. 33.

65. Krick, "Why Lee Went North," p. 11. On May 21, 1863, Lee wrote to General Hood about the need for "proper commanders," suggesting that they were not available (Dowdey and Manarin, *Wartime Papers of R. E. Lee*, p. 490).

66. Heth, "Causes of Lee's Defeat," p. 154; *OR*, 27 (3):868–69, 40 (2):703; Jones, *Personal Reminiscences of Gen. Robert E. Lee*, p. 40.

67. Dowdey and Manarin, *Wartime Papers of R. E. Lee*, p. 744.

68. Freeman, *R. E. Lee*, 4:170.

69. James M. McPherson, *Ordeal by Fire*, pp. 422–23.

70. Dowdey and Manarin, *Wartime Papers of R. E. Lee*, pp. 858, 915.

71. Ibid., p. 411.

72. Ibid., pp. 437–38.

73. *OR*, 27 (3):881. Lee also wrote Davis on this subject on June 25, 1863. See Dowdey and Manarin, *Wartime Papers of R. E. Lee*, p. 530.

74. Bruce, "Strategy of the Civil War," p. 447.

75. Freeman, *R. E. Lee*, 2:301–2; Maurice, *Aide-de-Camp of Lee*, p. 133; Manarin, "Lee in Command," p. 351; Dowdey and Manarin, *Wartime Papers of R. E. Lee*, p. 267.

76. Dowdey and Manarin, *Wartime Papers of R. E. Lee*, p. 287.

77. Freeman, *R. E. Lee*, 2:351.

78. Sears, *Landscape Turned Red*, pp. 66–67.

79. Col. William Allan, "Conversations with Gen. R. E. Lee," p. 3, Southern Historical Collection, Wilson Library, University of North Carolina, Chapel Hill. See also p. 26.

80. Maurice, *Robert E. Lee*, p. 152.

81. Hattaway and Jones, *How the North Won*, pp. 397–98; Maurice, *Robert E. Lee*, p. 189; Krick, "Why Lee Went North," p. 10.

82. Dowdey and Manarin, *Wartime Papers of R. E. Lee*, p. 505; *OR*, 27 (2):305, 308; Hattaway and Jones, *How the North Won*, pp. 319, 414.

83. Maurice, *Aide-de-Camp of Lee*, p. 148.

84. Freeman, *R. E. Lee*, 2:350–51.

85. Brown, "Antietam Tapes."

86. Alexander, *Fighting for the Confederacy*, pp. 149–50, 145.

87. Manarin, "Lee in Command," p. 369. Manarin's defense of Lee at Antietam extends to such statements as "Lee was not dividing his army in the

face of a superior enemy" (p. 383) and "The movements as Lee planned them seemed simple" (p. 388).

88. Maurice, *Aide-de-Camp of Lee*, pp. 190–93.

89. Although concerned with the overland campaign of 1864–65, Andrew A. Humphreys's discussion of the water route alternative illuminates the considerations affecting the choice of routes toward Richmond. Humphreys, *Virginia Campaign*, pp. 6–9.

90. Alexander, *Fighting for the Confederacy*, pp. 233–34, 277–78.

91. Ibid., pp. 145–46.

92. Hattaway and Jones, *How the North Won*, p. 244.

93. Freeman, *R. E. Lee*, 2:499–501; *OR*, 18:906–7.

94. Alexander, *Fighting for the Confederacy*, pp. 92, 258. Alexander states an additional stricture regarding the third day, as follows: "And, as a student of such technical questions, I think that all military engineers, who will study that field, will agree that the point selected for Pickett's attack was very badly chosen – almost as badly chosen as it was possible to be. I have no idea by whom it was done – whether by a general or staff officer, or a consultation of officers. There was a rumor, in our corps, that Ewell & Hill each reported against assault in his front, & so, by a process of exhaustion, it came to Longstreet's" (*Fighting for the Confederacy*, p. 252). On this point, Alexander also refers to "the very great mistake made, in my judgment, in the selection of the point of attack" (p. 278). Related to Lee's control and supervision of his army, Alexander states, "Here again, as when the question of the aggressive or the defensive was up, on the night of the first day, there seems a lack of appreciation of the immense figure which the character of the ground may cut in the results of an aggressive fight. Not only was the selection about as bad as possible, but there does not seem to have been any special thought given to the matter. It seems to have been allowed almost to select itself as if it was a matter of no consequence" (p. 278).

Fitzhugh Lee attempted to rationalize the charge of the third day on the grounds that his uncle intended for additional infantry to participate, at least in support, but that orders to this effect somehow went awry. At one time this was a commonplace defense of Lee's acts, but Lee's later defenders abandoned it, perhaps because, if accepted, it says too much about Lee's lack of control and the fact that he was present as the charge began so that, if the charge was improperly undertaken, he could have done something about it. Fitzhugh Lee's argument, which unintentionally resembles Alexander's "madness" characterization, has an ironic ring today: "A consummate master of war such as Lee would not drive *en masse* a column of fourteen thousand men across an open terrene [*sic*] thirteen or fourteen hundred yards, nearly every foot of it under a concentrated and converging fire of artillery, to attack an army, on fortified heights, of one hundred thousand, less its two days' losses, and give his entering wedge no support! Why, if every man in that assault had been bullet proof, and if the whole of those fourteen thousand splendid troops had arrived unharmed on Cemetery Ridge, what could have been accomplished? Not being able to kill them, there would have been time for the Federals to have seized, tied, and taken them off in wagons, before their supports could have reached them" (*General Lee*, p. 289).

95. Maurice, *Aide-de-Camp of Lee*, pp. 72, 73, 68–69.

96. Weidhorn, *Robert E. Lee*, pp. 105, 120.

97. Burne, *Lee, Grant and Sherman*, pp. 51–52, 65, 67. Burne writes at length about the Federal casualties from the Wilderness to Cold Harbor, noting that "the national will for war was impaired, and a strong move for peace . . . began to make itself felt" (p. 65). He also says about 1864, "Lee was content to stand on the defensive, trusting that the heavy casualties he could inflict . . . would make the Northern people war-weary, and thus bring about the defeat of Lincoln" (p. 67). William Swinton speaks to this point as well, stating that "had not success elsewhere come to brighten the horizon . . . there was at this time great danger of a collapse of the war" (*Campaigns of the Army of the Potomac*, pp. 494–95). My point is that Lee should have undertaken this kind of defensive much earlier in the war.

98. McWhiney, "Robert E. Lee," pp. 66, 67, 68.

99. Vandiver, "Lee during the War," pp. 12, 14, 24, 19, 20–21, 23, 24–25. Freeman's treatment of Lee's decision to remain facing McClellan at Antietam on the day following September 17, 1862, represents the classic traditional reaction to his conduct: Having described the desperate condition of the army and McClellan's superior numbers and uncommitted divisions, rhetorically Freeman asks, "What manner of man was he who would elect after that doubtful battle against vast odds to stand for another day with his back to the river?" (*R. E. Lee*, 2:404). Conditioned by the tradition, including the inevitability of the loss of the Lost Cause, readers are supposed to respond as they would to a quarterback who runs the ball on fourth down and impossible yardage. But Lee was not an athlete or a performer of any kind; he was an army commander responsible for advancing the political cause of his government. The realistic answer to Freeman's question, an answer that I embrace, is that of Gary W. Gallagher: "The answer is that the R. E. Lee of September 18, 1862, was a man who irresponsibly placed at peril his entire army" ("Campaign in Perspective," p. 89).

100. Fuller, *Generalship of Ulysses S. Grant*, pp. 375, 377; Fishwick, *Lee after the War*, p. 96; Dowdey, *Lee*, p. 308.

101. Fuller, *Generalship of Ulysses S. Grant*, p. 381.

102. Maurice, *Robert E. Lee*, pp. 261–62. With respect to Lee's having accomplished the attrition of his army, Bruce makes this observation: "On our side the war was necessarily offensive and, on the other, defensive. For nearly three years these parts were practically reversed. Of the seven great battles

fought in the Eastern zone including the Wilderness, only one was fought by the Army of the Potomac offensively during an offensive campaign, and one, Antietam, to repel an invasion" ("Strategy of the Civil War," p. 468).

103. Bruce, "Strategy of the Civil War," p. 468. Bruce made an interesting comparison between the attitudes of Lee and Gen. Joseph E. Johnston; he perceived the perspective of the latter in these terms: "He came to the sane and correct conclusion that the passion of the Southern people for headlong fighting and great battles with a mortality list of Napoleonic proportions, about equal on each side, and little else to show for them save the deceptive glare of Victory, could have but one ending, – the ultimate defeat of the cause for which they were fought" (p. 440).

104. Freeman, *R. E. Lee*, 4:175, 178.

105. Krick, "Why Lee Went North," p. 11.

106. Alexander, *Fighting for the Confederacy*, p. 265; Editors of Time-Life Books, *Lee Takes Command*, p. 8.

107. Bruce, "Strategy of the Civil War," pp. 468–69. Bruce is quite plain in his statement of the criteria for judging any particular military campaign, and they are the criteria on which this chapter is premised: "Each separate campaign is to be examined and judged successful or unsuccessful in accordance with the aid, and to the extent of the aid, which it contributes towards the final result of the war" (p. 408).

CHAPTER FIVE

1. Bond, *Memories of General Robert E. Lee*, pp. 32–34. Both Douglas Southall Freeman and Charles Bracelen Flood (the latter in his *Lee – The Last Years*) adopt without question or qualification Miss Bond's extensive quotations of Lee based on a conversation that had occurred sixty years previously.

2. Jones, *Personal Reminiscences of Gen. Robert E. Lee*, pp. 186–87, 196; see also p. 295.

3. Bradford, *Lee the American*, p. 45; Maurice, *Robert E. Lee*, p. 16; Dowdey, *Lee*, p. 279; Fishwick, *Lee after the War*, p. 210; Smith, *Lee and Grant*, pp. 229–30. See also Long, *Memoirs of Robert E. Lee*, p. 485; Weidhorn, *Robert E. Lee*, p. 52.

4. Dowdey and Manarin, *Wartime Papers of R. E. Lee*, p. 14.

5. Ibid., p. 18.

6. Ibid., p. 91.

7. *OR*, 6:42–43.

8. Jones, *Personal Reminiscences of Gen. Robert E. Lee*, pp. 385–86.

9. Dowdey and Manarin, *Wartime Papers of R. E. Lee*, p. 98.

10. Ibid., p. 106.

11. Ibid., p. 142.

12. Davis, *Gray Fox*, pp. 107–8; Dowdey and Manarin, *Wartime Papers of R. E. Lee*, p. 224.

13. *OR*, 21:1086, ser. 3, 3:11. Milroy's order threatened death and burning of the homes of suspected guerrillas; see *OR*, ser. 3, 2:944.

14. *OR*, 27 (3):886.

15. Dowdey and Manarin, *Wartime Papers of R. E. Lee*, pp. 559, 646.

16. *OR*, 29 (1):830; Dowdey and Manarin, *Wartime Papers of R. E. Lee*, pp. 829, 678.

17. Lee's communications with Davis and with his subordinate commanders openly report, and complain about, the Confederate soldiers' wanton destruction of property during Lee's raids in the North. See, for example, *OR*, 19 (2):617–19.

CHAPTER SIX

1. Wise, *End of an Era*, p. 429. The Pendleton conversation is reported by Capt. Robert E. Lee, *Recollections and Letters of General Robert E. Lee*, p. 151, and Jones, *Personal Reminiscences of Gen. Robert E. Lee*, p. 297.

2. Freeman, *R. E. Lee*, 4:110 n. 15; Dowdey and Manarin, *Wartime Papers of R. E. Lee*, p. 96; Capt. Robert E. Lee, *Recollections and Letters of General Robert E. Lee*, p. 232.

3. *OR*, 27 (3):881.

4. Freeman, *R. E. Lee*, 3:36.

5. Coddington, *Gettysburg Campaign*, p. 4.

6. *OR*, 24 (2):324–25.

7. Vandiver, *Civil War Diary of General Josiah Gorgas*, p. 55.

8. Ford, *Adams Letters*, 2:60.

9. Alexander, *Fighting for the Confederacy*, pp. 417, 422, 433.

10. Freeman, *R. E. Lee*, 3:499.

11. *OR*, 52 (2):1200, 1228, 1292–93, 52 (3):1144.

12. Freeman, *R. E. Lee*, 1:xi.

13. Alexander, *Fighting for the Confederacy*, p. 433.

14. *OR*, 27 (3):881.

15. Dowdey, *Lee*, p. 502; Alexander, *Fighting for the Confederacy*, p. 502.

16. Freeman, *R. E. Lee*, 4:184–85.

17. Dowdey, *Lee*, p. 503; Vandiver, "Lee during the War," pp. 22–23. See also Fishwick, *Lee after the War*, p. 98.

18. Livermore, *Numbers and Losses*, pp. 111 n. 3, 113, 116, 118, 127, 130.

19. Alexander writes extensively of the "arithmetical process of killing us off little by little" in the Petersburg lines. Alexander, *Fighting for the Confederacy*, p. 470.

20. Taylor, *Four Years with General Lee*, p. 187.

21. Freeman, *R. E. Lee*, 4:19.

22. Dowdey and Manarin, *Wartime Papers of R. E. Lee*, p. 938.

23. Fishwick, *Lee after the War*, pp. 13, 6, 12, 103; Livermore, *Numbers and Losses*, pp. 141, 137.

24. These issues are discussed in Appendix C below.

25. Freeman, *R. E. Lee*, 4:103–10, 121; Long, *Memoirs of Robert E. Lee*, p. 422. Col. C. S. Venable is the authority for Lee's statement about taking the responsibility. Lee was quoted by Venable in an 1870 speech in Richmond. Jones, *Personal Reminiscences of Gen. R. E. Lee*, p. 144.

26. *OR*, 46 (1):1265.

27. Gordon, *Reminiscences of the Civil War*, p. 434. See also Capt. Robert E. Lee, *Recollections and Letters of General Robert E. Lee*, p. 151.

28. Susan P. Lee, *Memoirs of William Nelson Pendleton*, p. 402; Long, *Memoirs of Robert E. Lee*, p. 417; Alexander recounts what Pendleton had told him at the time about the conversation with Lee in *Fighting for the Confederacy*, p. 528.

29. Alexander, *Military Memoirs*, pp. 604–5. Alexander describes the guerrilla warfare conversation in great detail in *Fighting for the Confederacy*, pp. 531–33.

30. Dowdey and Manarin, *Wartime Papers of R. E. Lee*, p. 939.

31. *OR*, 46 (3):1275–76.

32. Freeman, *R. E. Lee*, 4:504.

33. Ibid., pp. 179, 180, 472.

34. Dowdey and Manarin, *Wartime Papers of R. E. Lee*, pp. 897, 898, 935–38. See also Hunter, "Peace Commission," pp. 307–9; Freeman, *R. E. Lee*, 4:3–4. In vol. 4, chap. 1, Freeman traces in detail the communications between Lee and Davis and others during February and March 1865. A discussion of the Hunter meeting and Lee's related conversations with Gen. John B. Gordon regarding peace can be found in Dowdey, *Lee*, pp. 522–27.

The appointment as general-in-chief was dated February 6, 1865 (*OR*, 46 [2]:1205). Clifford Dowdey, a latter-day bitter-end Confederate, says, "Actually, the most practical move Lee could make was to arrange terms to end the suffering of his dwindling band of followers" (*Lee*, p. 520).

In 1890 or 1891, at General Longstreet's request, Gen. William Mahone wrote a letter that purported to describe Mahone's personal observations during the last weeks of the war in Virginia. Mahone described a conversation with General Lee at Appomattox on April 10, 1865, the day following the surrender. He wrote that Lee stated that during the winter of 1864–65 he had advised President Davis to "make terms" and Davis rejected the idea (Mahone, "On the Road to Appomattox," p. 46). Lee was not reluctant after the war to lay claim to earlier acts or opinions that reflected favorably on him. Mahone's account is discredited by the fact that Lee did not himself allege to others that he had so advised Davis and by the absence of other supporting evidence.

35. Foster, *Ghosts of the Confederacy*, p. 35.

36. Beringer et al., *Why the South Lost*, p. 381.

37. Dowdey and Manarin, *Wartime Papers of R. E. Lee*, p. 907; Gordon, *Reminiscences of the Civil War*, p. 389; Taylor, *General Lee – His Campaigns in Virginia*, p. 275.

38. Freeman, *R. E. Lee*, 4:94, 105.

39. Jones, *Personal Reminiscences of Gen. Robert E. Lee*, p. 145; Freeman, *R. E. Lee*, 4:503.

40. Dowdey and Manarin, *Wartime Papers of R. E. Lee*, pp. ix, x. Alexander says this regarding honor and the continuation of the war: "After Richmond fell there was nothing left to fight for but honor, & that would have been the case, probably, at any time in the war, certainly in the last two years" (*Fighting for the Confederacy*, p. 512).

41. Dowdey, *Lee*, p. 517.

42. Freeman, *R. E. Lee*, 4:169–70.

43. James M. McPherson, *Ordeal by Fire*, p. 476.

44. Jones, *Personal Reminiscences of Gen. Robert E. Lee*, p. 145.

45. Taylor, *Four Years with General Lee*, pp. 145–46. Regarding the last several months of the war, Taylor gives a sense of this suffering as it affected Lee's soldiers: "The condition of affairs throughout the South at that period was truly deplorable. Hundreds of letters addressed to soldiers were intercepted and sent to army headquarters, in which mothers, wives and sisters, told of their inability to respond to the appeals of hungry children for bread, or to provide proper care and remedies for the sick; and, in the name of all that was dear, appealed to the men to come home and rescue them from the ills which they suffered and the starvation which threatened them."

46. Beringer et al., *Why the South Lost*, p. 34.

47. Dowdey, *Lee*, pp. 523, 566, 568; letter from Billy to Dear Friends at Home, April 9, 1865, M. Adelaide Smith Collection, Manuscript Section, Suzzallo Library, University of Washington, Seattle, Wash.

48. Edward McPherson, *Political History of the United States*, p. 611n.

49. Dowdey and Manarin, *Wartime Papers of R. E. Lee*, p. 905.

50. *OR*, 46 (3):1339. See also Freeman, *Unpublished Letters of General Robert E. Lee*, pp. 373–74.

51. Dowdey, *Lee*, p. 560.

52. Alexander, *Fighting for the Confederacy*, p. 433. At the same time, Alexander sets forth his own bitter-end views. He remarks that fighting on was required in the interest of "the respect in which a nation & a generation is held" (p. 434).

53. *OR*, 46 (1):155, 156.

54. *OR*, 46 (1):1174; Freeman, *R. E. Lee*, 4:51–52.

55. Freeman, *R. E. Lee*, 4:52n.

56. *OR*, 46 (3):744.

CHAPTER SEVEN

1. Freeman, *R. E. Lee*, 4:219; Smith, *Lee and Grant*, p. 302. This is also the view of Weidhorn, *Robert E. Lee*, p. 128. See also Fishwick, *Lee after the War*.

2. Lee's college presidency is described in detail in Freeman, *R. E. Lee*, vol. 4, beginning with chap. 13.

3. Jones, *Personal Reminiscences of Gen. Robert E. Lee*, pp. 203, 205.

4. Jones, *Life and Letters of Robert Edward Lee*, pp. 408–9.

5. Freeman, *R. E. Lee*, 1:621.

6. Richardson, *Messages and Papers of the Presidents*, 6:708.

7. Jones, *Personal Reminiscences of Gen. Robert E. Lee*, p. 212. The power of the Lost Cause is suggested by the fact that in the American consciousness Davis's imprisonment and the inadequacies of Reconstruction have obscured the genuine glory of the years after the war, namely, the fact that there were no firing squads or gallows and only a brief period of disenfranchisement of the Confederate leadership.

8. "Unpublished Letters of Gen. Lee," *Missouri Republican*, October 3, 1885.

9. Jones, *Personal Reminiscences of Gen. Robert E. Lee*, contains many such letters. For examples, see those of February 10, 1866, p. 248; September 27, 1866, p. 220; March 22, 1869, p. 274; March 26, 1869, p. 275.

10. Duke of Argyll, *Passages from the Past*, 1:165–67.

11. The Acton-Lee correspondence is discussed in Freeman, *R. E. Lee*, 4:302–6, and Acton's letter to Lee is reproduced in app. 4-4 (4:515–17). Lee's answer can be found in Figgis and Laurence, *Correspondence of the First Lord Acton*, pp. 302–5.

12. Jones, *Life and Letters of Robert Edward Lee*, p. 121.

13. Freeman, *R. E. Lee*, 4:496.

14. Ibid., pp. 373–77; *New York Times*, September 5, 1868. See also Robertson, *Alexander Hugh Holmes Stuart*, pp. 260–65.

15. Foster, *Ghosts of the Confederacy*, pp. 21, 140. According to Foster, "The vast majority [of Southerners] remained loyal to old political values and to the principle of white supremacy" (p. 21). This is the substance of the letter to Rosecrans. Referring to the generations after the war, Foster notes that "in the celebration of the war . . . the Confederate tradition came to serve a new and complex function in the society of the New South. Not surprisingly, it supported southern racial and political orthodoxies" (p. 140). The Rosecrans letter seems to be a base document in the Confederate tradition, a statement of racial and political positions that became orthodox.

16. Capt. Robert E. Lee, *Recollections and Letters of General Robert E. Lee*, p. 168. Clifford Dowdey's rationalization of Lee's comments to Carter is a masterpiece of specious argument. They represented the extent of Lee's "breach with the past" according to Dowdey. "Disbelieving in any practice that approximated the use of slave labor," Lee advised his cousin to rid himself of the "colored

working population" (*Lee*, pp. 639–40). In fact, Lee's comment makes plain the racial animus behind his not wanting the former slaves to be employed.

17. U.S. Congress, *Report of the Reconstruction Committee*, p. 136. There are many stories of postwar egalitarian acts by Lee involving individual blacks. One of the most appealing and most frequently reported concerns his having gone forward at St. Paul's Episcopal Church in Richmond to take communion with a black man. The church had segregated seating. The blacks were to come forward to the communion rail only after the whites had completed their communion and returned to their seats. But one black man came forward at the outset of the communion. The other whites "froze," according to the story, and remained in their pews, but Lee went to the chancel rail alone and took communion with the black man. I would note, however, that Lee was committed to the Southern position on all issues. He was a conformist. He was personally hostile to blacks. This story and its counterparts seem highly unlikely. A particularly articulate version of the church story, and its origin in a 1905 account in *Confederate Veteran* 13 (1905): 360, can be found in Flood, *Lee – The Last Years*, pp. 65–66.

18. Capt. Robert E. Lee, *Recollections and Letters of General Robert E. Lee*, p. 306. Captain Lee's book was first published in 1909. It is written in praise of General Lee, Captain Lee's father. Lee's inclusion of his father's racist communications is good evidence of the American racial climate at the time of the book's publication. In *Lee – The Last Years*, Charles Bracelen Flood refers to the same letter that is quoted in the text and quotes portions of it but omits the most telling words: "You will never prosper with the blacks, and it is abhorrent to a reflecting mind to be supporting and cherishing [them]."

19. Jones, *Personal Reminiscences of Gen. Robert E. Lee*, p. 270.

20. Fishwick, *Lee after the War*, pp. 168, 127, 56. Fishwick also states that Lee was "determined not to become embroiled" in political issues after 1865 (pp. 86–87).

21. Freeman, *R. E. Lee*, 4:400; Leyburn, "Interview with Gen. Robert E. Lee," pp. 166–67.

22. Freeman, *R. E. Lee*, 4:198. Freeman quotes a letter dated April 23, 1865, from Mrs. Lee to Mary Meade. The original of the letter is in private hands.

23. Connelly, *The Marble Man*, p. 201.

24. *OR*, 5:192.

25. Jones, *Personal Reminiscences of Gen. Robert E. Lee*, p. 218.

26. Freeman, *R. E. Lee*, 4:202, 381.

27. Flood, *Lee – The Last Years*, p. 186. This letter is identified by Flood as previously unpublished and cited as being from "Letters to Annette Carter." Bean, "Memorandum of Conversations between Robert E. Lee and William Preston Johnston," p. 477. Despite the evidence to the contrary, Fishwick writes that neither "defiance" nor "bitterness" lay behind "Lee's words or deeds" (*Lee after the War*, p. 82).

28. Freeman, *R. E. Lee*, 4:249–56; Fishwick, *Lee after the War*, pp. 109–24; Stampp, *Era of Reconstruction*, pp. 73, 110–11; Sanborn, *Robert E. Lee*, 2:305–6. See also chap. 2, nn. 3 and 27, above.

29. See *John J. McGrain v. Mally S. Daugherty* (1926) 273 U.S. 135. This decision of the United States Supreme Court contains an interesting discussion of the history of congressional investigations. A carryover from the British Parliament to America's colonial legislatures, investigative committees were established by Congress as early as 1792, when one was formed by the House of Representatives. A well-known Senate investigation committee was established in 1859 to inquire into John Brown's raid at Harpers Ferry.

30. Foster, *Ghosts of the Confederacy*, p. 5.

CHAPTER EIGHT

1. Warren, *Legacy of the Civil War*, p. 4.

2. Lincoln, *Collected Works*, 3:145.

3. Alexander, *Fighting for the Confederacy*, p. 503.

4. Wiley, *Road to Appomattox*, p. 102. See also Stampp, *Imperiled Union*, pp. 260–62.

5. Warren, *Legacy of the Civil War*, p. 8.

6. Lincoln, *Collected Works*, 4:271.

7. Warren, *Legacy of the Civil War*, p. 83.

8. Beringer et al., *Why the South Lost*, p. 76.

9. Stampp, *Imperiled Union*, pp. 255–56.

10. McWhiney, *Southerners and Other Americans*, pp. 4, 3.

11. Potter, *The South and the Sectional Conflict*, pp. 68–69.

12. Beringer et al., *Why the South Lost*, p. 78. See also Stampp, *Imperiled Union*, pp. 251–69.

13. Stampp, *Imperiled Union*, p. 255.

14. Nolan, *Iron Brigade*, pp. 191, 185.

15. Oliver Wendell Holmes, Jr., quoted in Warren, *Legacy of the Civil War*, p. 104.

16. *Register of Graduates and Former Cadets of the United States Military Academy*, pp. 188–89, 193, 188–98, 203.

17. Gallagher, *Stephen Dodson Ramseur*, pp. 162–65. Edward Porter Alexander describes another of these haunting incidents. During the Confederate retreat from Richmond to Appomattox, Col. Frank Huger was captured by the Federals and delivered to Gen. George Armstrong Custer. Alexander reports that "Custer & Huger had been great friends & class mates, & Custer made him ride along all day, & sleep with him that night, & treated him very nicely" (*Fighting for the Confederacy*, p. 522).

18. Johnson and Buel, *Battles and Leaders*, 4:743; Grant, *Personal Memoirs*, 2:496, 498.

19. Alexander, *Fighting for the Confederacy*, p. 544.

20. James M. McPherson, *Battle Cry of Freedom*, p. 544.

21. Warren, *Legacy of the Civil War*, p. 102.

22. McWhiney and Jamieson, *Attack and Die*, pp. 3—24. Alexander remarks, "In the Mexican War fought with smooth bore, short range muskets, in fact, the character of the ground cut comparatively little figure. But with the rifled muskets & cannon of this war the affair was very different as was proven both at Malvern Hill, & at Gettysburg" (*Fighting for the Confederacy*, p. 111).

23. Curtis, *History of the Twenty-Fourth Michigan*, p. 375; Nolan, *Iron Brigade*, p. 148.

24. Brogan, "Fresh Appraisal of the Civil War," p. 175.

25. Ibid., p. 174.

26. Stampp, *Imperiled Union*, p. 268.

27. Durden, *The Gray and the Black*, p. 3.

28. Beringer et al., *Why the South Lost*, chaps. 15 and 16.

29. Piston, *Lee's Tarnished Lieutenant*, pp. 157—58.

30. Foster, *Ghosts of the Confederacy*, p. 24.

31. Ibid., p. 66.

32. Roark, *Masters without Slaves*, p. 105.

33. Foster, *Ghosts of the Confederacy*, p. 156.

34. Ibid., p. 194. Commenting on the Confederate celebration of the war, Foster states that it "did reinforce white supremacy. Accounts of good and dutiful slaves and the appearance of faithful blacks at reunions provided models intended to teach the 'new Negro' born since slavery how to behave. And the celebration's symbols of unity could be and were employed in the fight for disenfranchisement and segregation" (p. 194). An excellent response to the racist stereotype can be found in James M. McPherson, *The Negro's Civil War*. See also Cornish, *Sable Arm*.

35. Brogan, "Fresh Appraisal of the Civil War," p. 186; Beale, "What Historians Have Said about the Causes of the Civil War," pp. 55—102; Stampp, *Imperiled Union*, pp. 191—245.

36. Foster, *Ghosts of the Confederacy*, p. 49.

37. Piston, *Lee's Tarnished Lieutenant*, pp. 158, 157; Foster, *Ghosts of the Confederacy*, p. 198.

38. Wyatt-Brown, *Southern Honor*, p. 493.

39. Stowe, "Honest Confession," p. 326.

40. Foster, *Ghosts of the Confederacy*, pp. 57—58.

41. Jones, "Within a Stone's Throw of Independence," p. 111.

42. Jones, *Personal Reminiscences of Gen. Robert E. Lee*, p. 156.

43. Piston, *Lee's Tarnished Lieutenant*, pp. 163, 188.

44. Beringer et al., *Why the South Lost*, pp. 416−17.

45. Foster, *Ghosts of the Confederacy*, p. 196.

46. Fishwick, *Lee after the War*, pp. 97, 103−4, 96.

47. Dowdey, *Lee*, p. 573.

48. Maurice, *Robert E. Lee*, p. 17. Fishwick does not share Maurice's opinion, contending instead that "we cannot call Lee democratic. Nothing in his training or thought favored egalitarianism. [Because Lee was] born, reared and married in a patrician milieu . . . distinctions of place and position were accepted as part of his birthright" (*Lee after the War*, p. 90).

49. Fishwick, *Lee after the War*, pp. 104, 105, 228.

50. Flood, *Lee – The Last Years*, p. 200.

51. Bradford, *Lee the American*, pp. 43−44.

APPENDIX C

1. Act of March 6, 1861, SS 29 Ch 29, reprinted in *Digest of the Military and Naval Laws of the Confederate States*, p. 15.

2. Ibid., p. 255.

3. Ibid., pp. 258−59.

4. Benet, *Treatise on Military Law*, pp. 9−10.

5. Grotius, *Law of War and Peace*, p. 848.

6. Ibid., p. 845.

7. *OR*, ser. 3, 3:148ff. Freidel, *Francis Lieber*, pp. 333−37. See also Hartigan, *Lieber's Code*.

8. *OR*, ser. 3, 3:161.

9. Grant, *Personal Memoirs*, 2:486. A facsimile of the document of surrender appears on p. 486.

Bibliography of Works Cited

MANUSCRIPTS

National Archives, Washington, D.C.
  General Robert E. Lee. "Microfilm of Selected Military Service Records in
    the Custody of the National Archives Relating to Robert E. Lee."
    These selected military service records are parts of:
  Records of the Office of the Chief of Engineers (Record Group 77)
  Records of the Adjutant General's Office (Record Group 94)
  War Department Collection of Confederate Records (Record Group 109)
University of North Carolina, Southern Historical Collection, Wilson Library,
    Chapel Hill, N.C.
  Edward Porter Alexander Papers, no. 7, manuscript vols. 28, 29, 34, 47, 50,
    51, 52
  Col. William Allan. "Conversations with Gen. R. E. Lee."
University of Washington, Manuscripts Section, Suzzallo Library, Seattle,
    Wash.
  Adelaide M. Smith Collection
Virginia Historical Society, Richmond, Va.
  Robert Edward Lee Papers

: : : BIBLIOGRAPHY OF WORKS CITED : : :

GOVERNMENT REPORTS AND PUBLICATIONS

Confederate States. *A Digest of the Military and Naval Laws of the Confederate States.* Columbia, S.C.: Evans and Cogswell, 1864.

John J. McGrain v. Mally S. Daugherty (1926) 273 U.S. 135.

Richardson, J. D., ed. *Compilation of the Messages and Papers of the Presidents, 1789–1897.* 53d Cong., 2d sess., 1907. *House Miscellaneous Document No. 210,* pts. 1–10, 10 vols. Washington, D.C.: Government Printing Office, 1907.

United States. Bureau of the Census. *Negro Population in the United States, 1790–1915.* Washington, D.C.: Government Printing Office, 1918.

United States. Congress. *Report of the Reconstruction Committee.* Reports of the Committees of the House of Representatives. 39th Cong., 1st sess., 1865–66. Part II. Washington, D.C.: Government Printing Office, 1866.

United States. War Department. *Regulations for the Army of the United States.* New York: Harper & Brothers, 1857.

———. *War of the Rebellion: Official Records of the Union and Confederate Armies.* 127 vols. plus index and atlas. Washington, D.C.: Government Printing Office, 1880–1901.

NEWSPAPERS

Charleston [S.C.] Mercury
Franklin Repository (Chambersburg, Pa.)
Missouri Republican (St. Louis, Mo.)
New York Herald
New York Times
Richmond Dispatch

BOOKS, ARTICLES, DISSERTATIONS, AND PAPERS

Alexander, Edward Porter. *Fighting for the Confederacy: The Personal Recollections of General Edward Porter Alexander.* Edited by Gary W. Gallagher. Chapel Hill: University of North Carolina Press, 1989.

———. *The Military Memoirs of a Confederate.* New York: Charles Scribner's Sons, 1907.

Anderson, Charles. "Texas, before, and on the Eve of the Rebellion." Paper presented to the Cincinnati Society of Ex-Army and Navy Officers, Cincinnati, Ohio, June 3, 1884.

Anderson, Nancy Scott, and Dwight Anderson. *The Generals.* New York: Alfred A. Knopf, 1988.

Argyll, Duke of. *Passages from the Past*. 2 vols. New York: Dodd, Mead, 1908.

Avary, Myrta L. *Dixie after the War*. New York: Doubleday, Page, 1906.

Beale, Howard K. "What Historians Have Said about the Causes of the Civil War." In *Theory and Practice in Historical Study: A Report of the Committee on Historiography*. Social Science Research Council Bulletin no. 54. New York: Social Science Research Council, 1946.

Bean, W. G., ed. "Memorandum of Conversations between Robert E. Lee and William Preston Johnston, May 7, 1868, and March 18, 1870." *Virginia Magazine of History and Biography* 73 (October 1965): 474–84.

Benet, S. V. *A Treatise on Military Law and the Practice of Courts-Martial*. 3d ed. New York: D. Van Nostrand, 1863.

Beringer, Richard E., Herman Hattaway, Archer Jones, and William N. Still, Jr. *Why the South Lost the Civil War*. Athens: University of Georgia Press, 1986.

Bigelow, John, Jr. *The Campaign of Chancellorsville*. New Haven: Yale University Press, 1910.

Boatner, Mark Mayo, III. *Civil War Dictionary*. Rev. ed. New York: David McKay, 1988.

Bond, Christiana. *Memories of General Robert E. Lee*. Baltimore: Norman, Remington, 1926.

Bradford, Gamaliel. *Lee the American*. 2d ed. Boston: Houghton Mifflin, 1927.

Brogan, D. W. "A Fresh Appraisal of the Civil War." In *The Open Form*, edited by Alfred Kazin, pp. 173–201. New York: Harcourt, Brace & World, 1965.

Brown, Kent Masterson. "The Antietam Tapes." Video cassette 7. Panel discussion, Antietam seminar, Virginia Country Civil War Society, Harpers Ferry, W.Va., April 19, 1987.

Bruce, Lt. Col. George A. "The Strategy of the Civil War." *Papers of the Military Historical Society of Massachusetts* 13 (1913): 392–483.

Burne, Lt. Col. Alfred H. *Lee, Grant and Sherman*. New York: Charles Scribner's Sons, 1939.

Clausewitz, Carl von. *On War*. Translated by J. J. Graham. Edited by Anatol Rapoport. Baltimore: Penguin Books, 1968.

Coddington, Edwin B. *The Gettysburg Campaign*. New York: Charles Scribner's Sons, 1968. Reprint. Dayton, Ohio: Morningside Bookshop, 1979.

Connelly, Thomas L., "The Image and the General: Robert E. Lee in American Historiography." *Civil War History* 19 (March 1973): 50–64.

———. *The Marble Man: Robert E. Lee and His Image in American Society*. New York: Alfred A. Knopf, 1977.

———. "Robert E. Lee and the Western Confederacy: A Criticism of Lee's Strategic Ability." *Civil War History* 15 (June 1969): 116–32.

: : : BIBLIOGRAPHY OF WORKS CITED : : :

Connelly, Thomas L., and Barbara L. Bellows. *God and General Longstreet.* Baton Rouge: Louisiana State University Press, 1982.

Connelly, Thomas L., and Archer Jones. *The Politics of Command.* Baton Rouge: Louisiana State University Press, 1973.

Conrad, W. P., and Ted Alexander. *When War Passed This Way.* Greencastle, Pa.: A Greencastle Bicentennial Publication in cooperation with the Lilian S. Besore Memorial Library, 1982.

Cornish, Dudley Taylor. *The Sable Arm.* Reprint. Lawrence, Kans.: University Press of Kansas, 1987.

Cosby, George B. "With Gen. R. E. Lee in the Old Army." *Confederate Veteran* 13 (April 1905): 167–68.

Craven, Avery, ed. *"To Markie": The Letters of Robert E. Lee to Martha Custis Lee.* Cambridge: Harvard University Press, 1933.

Curtis, O. B. *History of the Twenty-Fourth Michigan of the Iron Brigade.* Detroit: Winn & Hammond, 1891.

Davis, Burke. *Gray Fox.* New York: Rinehart, 1956.

Donald, David, ed. *Why the North Won the Civil War.* Baton Rouge: Louisiana State University Press, 1960.

Dorris, Jonathan Truman. *Pardon and Amnesty under Lincoln and Johnson: The Restoration of the Confederates to Their Rights and Privileges, 1861–1898.* Chapel Hill: University of North Carolina Press, 1953.

Dowdey, Clifford. *Lee.* Boston: Little, Brown, 1965.

———. *Lee's Last Campaign.* Boston: Little, Brown, 1960.

———. *The Seven Days.* Boston: Little, Brown, 1964.

Dowdey, Clifford, and Louis H. Manarin, eds. *The Wartime Papers of R. E. Lee.* Boston: Little, Brown, 1961.

Downing, Fanny. "Perfect through Suffering." *The Land We Love* 4 (January 1868): 193–205.

Dumond, Dwight Lowell. *Antislavery: The Crusade for Freedom in America.* Ann Arbor: University of Michigan Press, 1961.

———. *Antislavery Origins of the Civil War in the United States.* Ann Arbor: University of Michigan Press, 1939. Reprint. Ann Arbor: University of Michigan Press, 1959.

Dupuy, Trevor N., Curt Johnson, and Grace P. Hayes, comps. *Dictionary of Military Terms.* New York: H. W. Wilson, 1986.

Durden, Robert F. *The Gray and the Black.* Baton Rouge: Louisiana State University Press, 1972.

Editors of Time-Life Books. *Lee Takes Command: From Seven Days to Second Bull Run.* Alexandria, Va.: Time-Life Books, 1984.

Faust, Patricia L., ed. *Historical Times Illustrated Encyclopedia of the Civil War.* New York: Harper & Row, 1986.

Fehrenbacher, Don E. *Lincoln in Text and Context.* Stanford: Stanford University Press, 1987.

Figgis, John Neville, and Robert Vere Lawrence, eds. *Selections from the Correspondence of the First Lord Acton.* London: Longmans, Green, 1917.

Fishwick, Marshall W. *Lee after the War.* New York: Dodd, Mead, 1963.

———. "Virginians on Olympus II, Robert E. Lee: Savior of the Lost Cause." *Virginia Magazine of History and Biography* 58 (April 1950): 163–80.

Flood, Charles Bracelen. *Lee – The Last Years.* Boston: Houghton Mifflin, 1981.

Foner, Eric. *Reconstruction: America's Unfinished Revolution.* New York: Harper & Row, 1988.

Ford, Worthington Chauncey, ed. *A Cycle of Adams Letters, 1861–1865.* 2 vols. Boston: Houghton Mifflin, 1920.

Foster, Gaines M. *Ghosts of the Confederacy.* New York: Oxford University Press, 1987.

Freeman, Douglas Southall. *Lee's Lieutenants.* 3 vols. New York: Charles Scribner's Sons, 1942–44.

———. *R. E. Lee.* 4 vols. New York: Charles Scribner's Sons, 1934–35.

———, ed. *Unpublished Letters of General Robert E. Lee, C.S.A., to Jefferson Davis and the War Department of the Confederate States of America, 1862–65.* Rev. ed., with foreword by Grady McWhiney. New York: G. P. Putnam's Sons, 1957.

Freidel, Frank. *Francis Lieber.* Reprint. Gloucester, Mass.: Peter Smith, 1968.

Fuller, Maj. Gen. J. F. C. *The Generalship of Ulysses S. Grant.* Reprint. Bloomington: Indiana University Press, 1958.

———. *Grant and Lee.* Reprint. Bloomington: Indiana University Press, 1957.

Gallagher, Gary W. "The Campaign in Perspective." In *Antietam: Essays on the 1862 Maryland Campaign,* edited by Gary W. Gallagher, pp. 84–94. Kent, Ohio: Kent State University Press, 1989.

———. *Stephen Dodson Ramseur: Lee's Gallant General.* Chapel Hill: University of North Carolina Press, 1985.

Gordon, John B. *Reminiscences of the Civil War.* New York: Charles Scribner's Sons, 1903.

Grant, U. S. *Personal Memoirs of U. S. Grant.* 2 vols. New York: Charles L. Webster, 1886.

Grotius, Hugo. *The Law of War and Peace.* Translated by Francis W. Kelsey. Indianapolis: Bobbs-Merrill, 1925.

Halleck, H. Wager. *Elements of Military Art and Science.* New York: D. Appleton, 1846.

Hartigan, Richard S. *Lieber's Code and the Law of War.* Chicago: Precedent Publishing, 1983.

Hattaway, Herman, and Archer Jones. *How the North Won.* Urbana: University of Illinois Press, 1983.

: : : BIBLIOGRAPHY OF WORKS CITED : : :

Heth, Henry. "Causes of Lee's Defeat at Gettysburg." *Southern Historical Society Papers* 4 (October 1877): 151–60.

Humphreys, Andrew A. *The Virginia Campaign of '64 and '65*. New York: Charles Scribner's Sons, 1883.

Hunter, R. M. T. "The Peace Commission: Honorable R. M. T. Hunter's Reply to President Davis' Letter." *Southern Historical Society Papers* 4 (October 1877): 303–16.

Johnson, Brig. Gen. Richard W. *A Soldier's Reminiscences in Peace and War*. Philadelphia: J. B. Lippincott, 1886.

Johnson, Robert Underwood, and Clarence Clough Buel, eds. *Battles and Leaders of the Civil War*. 4 vols. New York: Century, 1884–87.

Johnson, Thomas H., ed. *The Oxford Companion to American History*. New York: Oxford University Press, 1966.

Jones, Rev. J. William, D.D. *Army of Northern Virginia Memorial Volume*. Richmond: J. W. Randolph and English, 1880.

———. *Life and Letters of Robert Edward Lee, Soldier and Man*. Reprint. Harrisonburg, Va.: Sprinkle Publications, 1986.

———. *Personal Reminiscences of Gen. Robert E. Lee*. New York: D. Appleton, 1875.

———. "Within a Stone's Throw of Independence at Gettysburg." *Southern Historical Society Papers* 12 (March 1884): 111–12.

Keyes, Erasmus D. *Fifty Years Observation of Men and Events*. New York: Charles Scribner's Sons, 1884.

Kirke, Edmund [James R. Gilmore]. *Down in Tennessee and Back by Way of Richmond*. New York: Carleton, 1864.

Krick, Robert K. "Why Lee Went North." In *Morningside Bookshop Catalogue*, no. 24, pp. 9–16. Dayton, Ohio: Morningside Bookshop, 1988.

Lee, Fitzhugh. *General Lee*. New York: D. Appleton, 1894.

Lee, Capt. Robert E. *Recollections and Letters of General Robert E. Lee*. Reprint. New York: Garden City, 1926.

Lee, Susan P. *Memoirs of William Nelson Pendleton*. Philadelphia: J. B. Lippincott, 1893.

Leyburn, Rev. John. "An Interview with Gen. Robert E. Lee." *Century Illustrated Monthly Magazine* 30 (May 1885): 166–67.

Lincoln, Abraham. *The Collected Works of Abraham Lincoln*. Edited by Roy P. Basler. 8 vols. and index. New Brunswick: Rutgers University Press, 1953–55.

Livermore, Thomas L. *Numbers and Losses in the Civil War in America, 1861–65*. Reprint. Dayton, Ohio: Morningside House, 1986.

Long, A. L. *Memoirs of Robert E. Lee: His Military and Personal History*. New York: J. M. Stoddart, 1886.

McMurry, Richard M. *Two Great Rebel Armies: An Essay in Confederate Military History*. Chapel Hill: University of North Carolina Press, 1989.

McPherson, Edward. *The Political History of the United States of America during the Great Rebellion*. Washington, D.C.: Philp & Solomons, 1865.

McPherson, James M. *Battle Cry of Freedom*. New York: Oxford University Press, 1988.

———. *The Negro's Civil War*. New York: Pantheon Books, 1965.

———. *Ordeal by Fire*. New York: Alfred A. Knopf, 1982.

McWhiney, Grady. "Robert E. Lee: The Man and the Soldier, 1830–1855." In *Confederate History Symposium*, pp. 50–69. Hillsboro, Tex.: Hill Junior College, 1984.

———. *Southerners and Other Americans*. New York: Basic Books, 1973.

McWhiney, Grady, and Perry D. Jamieson. *Attack and Die*. Tuscaloosa: University of Alabama Press, 1982.

Mahone, Maj. Gen. William. "On the Road to Appomattox." *Civil War Times Illustrated* 9 (January 1971): 5–47.

Manarin, Louis H. "Lee in Command: Strategical and Tactical Policies." Ph.D. dissertation, Duke University, 1965.

Maurice, Maj. Gen. Sir Frederick. *Robert E. Lee the Soldier*. Boston: Houghton Mifflin, 1925.

———, ed. *An Aide-de-Camp of Lee: Being the Papers of Colonel Charles Marshall*. Boston: Little, Brown, 1927.

Moore, Frank, gen. ed. *Rebellion Record: A Diary of American Events with Documents, Narratives, Illustrative Incidents, Poetry, Etc.* 11 vols. and supplement. New York: D. Van Nostrand, 1861–68.

Morison, Samuel Eliot. *By Land and by Sea*. New York: Alfred A. Knopf, 1954.

Nevins, Allan. *The Emergence of Lincoln*. 2 vols. New York: Charles Scribner's Sons, 1950.

———. *Ordeal of the Union*. 2 vols. New York: Charles Scribner's Sons, 1947.

Nolan, Alan T. *The Iron Brigade*. New York: Macmillan, 1961.

Pfanz, Harry W. *Gettysburg – The Second Day*. Chapel Hill: University of North Carolina Press, 1987.

Pierce, Edward L. *Memoir and Letters of Charles Sumner*. 4 vols. Boston: Roberts Brothers, 1893.

Piston, William Garrett. *Lee's Tarnished Lieutenant: James Longstreet and His Place in Southern History*. Athens: University of Georgia Press, 1987.

———. "Lee's Tarnished Lieutenant: James Longstreet and His Image in American Society." Ph.D. dissertation, University of South Carolina, 1982.

Potter, David M. *The South and the Sectional Conflict*. Baton Rouge: Louisiana State University Press, 1968.

Register of Graduates and Former Cadets of the United States Military Academy. MacArthur Edition. West Point, N.Y.: West Point Alumni Foundation, 1962.

: : : BIBLIOGRAPHY OF WORKS CITED : : :

Roark, James L. *Masters without Slaves: Southern Planters in the Civil War and Reconstruction*. New York: W. W. Norton, 1977.

Robertson, Alexander F. *Alexander Hugh Holmes Stuart, 1807–1891*. Richmond: William Byrd Press, 1925.

Russell, Robert. "The Issues in the Congressional Struggle over the Kansas-Nebraska Bill, 1854." *Journal of Southern History* 29 (May 1963): 187–210.

Sanborn, Margaret. *Robert E. Lee*. 2 vols. Philadelphia: J. B. Lippincott, 1966–67.

Schaff, Rev. Philip. "The Gettysburg Week." *Scribner's Magazine* 16 (September 1894): 21–30.

Schildt, John W. *Roads to Gettysburg*. Parsons, W.Va.: McClain Printing, 1978.

Sears, Stephen W. *Landscape Turned Red*. New York: Ticknor and Fields, 1983.

Smith, Gene. *Lee and Grant*. New York: McGraw-Hill, 1984.

Stampp, Kenneth M. *And the War Came*. Baton Rouge: Louisiana State University Press, 1950.

———. *The Era of Reconstruction*. New York: Alfred A. Knopf, 1965.

———. *The Imperiled Union*. New York: Oxford University Press, 1980.

———. *The Peculiar Institution*. New York: Alfred A. Knopf, 1963.

Stephens, Alexander H. *A Constitutional View of the War between the States*. 2 vols. Philadelphia: National Publishing, 1868.

Stowe, Charles E. "Honest Confession Good for the Country." *Confederate Veteran* 19 (July 1911): 326–27.

Swinton, William. *Campaigns of the Army of the Potomac*. New York: Charles Scribner's Sons, 1882.

Taylor, Walter H. *Four Years with General Lee*. Reprint. Bloomington: Indiana University Press, 1962.

———. *General Lee – His Campaigns in Virginia, 1861–1865*. Reprint. Dayton, Ohio: Press of the Morningside Bookshop, 1975.

Thomas, Emory M. *The Confederate Nation, 1861–1865*. New York: Harper & Row, 1979.

Vandiver, Frank E., ed. *The Civil War Diary of General Josiah Gorgas*. Tuscaloosa: University of Alabama Press, 1947.

———. "Lee during the War." In *Confederate History Symposium*, pp. 3–25. Hillsboro, Tex.: Hill Junior College, 1984.

———. *Rebel Brass*. Baton Rouge: Louisiana State University Press, 1956.

———. *Their Tattered Flags*. New York: Harper's Magazine Press, 1970.

Warren, Robert Penn. *The Legacy of the Civil War*. New York: Random House, 1961.

Weidhorn, Manfred. *Robert E. Lee*. New York: Atheneum, 1988.

Weigley, Russell F. *The American Way of War*. New York: Macmillan, 1973.

: : : BIBLIOGRAPHY OF WORKS CITED : : :

Wiley, Bell Irwin. *The Road to Appomattox*. Memphis: Memphis State College Press, 1956.

Williams, Kenneth P. *Lincoln Finds a General*. 5 vols. New York: Macmillan, 1950–59.

Wilson, Woodrow. "Robert E. Lee: An Interpretation." In *The Public Papers of Woodrow Wilson*, edited by Ray Stannard Baker and William E. Dodd, 2:64–82. New York: Harper & Brothers, 1925.

Wise, John S. *The End of an Era*. Boston: Houghton Mifflin, 1899.

Wolff, Gerald W. "Party and Section: The Senate and the Kansas-Nebraska Bill." *Civil War History* 18 (December 1972): 293–311.

Woman's Club of Mercersburg. *Old Mercersburg*. Williamsport, Pa.: Grit Publishing Co., 1949.

Wyatt-Brown, Bertram. *Southern Honor: Ethics and Behavior in the Old South*. New York: Oxford University Press, 1983.

Index